THE WORLD'S CLASSICS

MARY
AND
THE WRONGS OF WOMAN

MARY WOLLSTONECRAFT was born in 1759, the grand-daughter of a wealthy Irish manufacturer. Her father spent the fortune he inherited and took to drink, so in 1783 Mary left to keep a school in Newington Green with her sister Eliza. She subsequently became governess to Lord Kingsborough's children, during which time she wrote *Mary, A Fiction* (1788). In it she confronts the problems of sensibility in fiction and life which were sowed in her imagination by her adherence to the philosophy of Rousseau. In France, she met and lived with an American, Gilbert Imlay, by whom she had a daughter, Fanny. His infidelity drove her to return to England and to an attempted suicide. She married William Godwin in 1798, and died a few months later at the birth of her daughter Mary (later to become Shelley's second wife). *The Wrongs of Woman*, a largely autobiographical novel in which she explores the parallels between domestic and political life, private and public morality, was published in 1798.

Her other well-known works include *Vindication of the Rights of Men* (1790) and *A Vindication of the Rights of Women* (1792), in which a general change of heart engendered by the French Revolution occasioned attacks on Rousseau and sensibility.

GARY KELLY is lecturer in English at the University of Alberta, Canada, and author of *The English Jacobin Novel 1780–1805*.

THE WORLD'S CLASSICS

MARY WOLLSTONECRAFT

Mary

AND

The Wrongs of Woman

Edited with an Introduction by

GARY KELLY

Oxford New York

OXFORD UNIVERSITY PRESS

Oxford University Press, Walton Street, Oxford OX2 6DP

Oxford New York Toronto
Delhi Bombay Calcutta Madras Karachi
Petaling Jaya Singapore Hong Kong Tokyo
Nairobi Dar es Salaam Cape Town
Melbourne Auckland

and associated companies in
Berlin Ibadan

Oxford is a trade mark of Oxford University Press

Introduction, Notes, Bibliography, and Chronology
© Oxford University Press, 1976

First published by Oxford University Press 1976
First issued as a World's Classics paperback 1980
Reprinted 1983, 1984, 1987, 1988, 1989

British Library Cataloguing in Publication Data

Wollstonecraft, Mary
Mary, and, The wrongs of woman.
I. Title II. Wollstonecraft, Mary, The wrongs
of woman, or, Maria. III. Kingsley, James
IV. Kelly, Gary

823'.8 PR5841.W8M1 79–41038
ISBN 0–19–281527–X

Printed in Great Britain by
Hazell Watson & Viney Limited
Aylesbury, Bucks

CONTENTS

CONTENTS

INTRODUCTION

MARY WOLLSTONECRAFT's life has always overshadowed her writings. Not only was it romantically short and dramatically ended, but it was also crammed with varied and often melodramatic incident. She was a traveller, a teacher, a family provider, and a defender of the weak; she was a mistress and a mother, before she was a wife; she saw and survived the French Revolution; and she was known and admired by some of the leading politicians, polemicists, publishers, preachers, poets, painters, novelists, and historians of the day.[1] But it was not her varied experience or her vibrant milieu which made her interesting then and of interest now; it was her powerful and original imagination, shaping hard experience and hard-won knowledge into the ardent radical philosophy which lay behind and unified all her work as reviewer, translator, educationist, polemicist, sociologist, historian, and novelist.

She lived and wrote in an age of revolution, when character was destiny, and when principles were invariably traced to personality. A year after her death from childbirth in 1797 the Rev. Richard Polwhele sermonized over the meaning of her life and works in *The Unsex'd Females*, declaring that 'she was given up to her "heart's lusts", and let "to follow her own imaginations", that the fallacy of her doctrines, and the effects of an irreligious conduct, might be manifested to the world', and concluded that 'she died a death that strongly marked the distinction of the sexes, by pointing out the destiny of women, and the diseases to which they are liable', in order that Providence itself might refute her claims for equality for women.[2]

---

[1] Such as Talleyrand, Paine, Richard Price, Joseph Johnson, Wordsworth, Coleridge, Southey, Fuseli, Blake, Godwin, William Roscoe, and Samuel Johnson.

[2] Godwin's mother expressed the same view of her deceased daughter-in-law, in a letter of April 1798 in C. Kegan Paul, *William Godwin: His Friends and Contemporaries* (1876), i. 325.

For the next century and a half Mary Wollstonecraft's life and works were inseparable, held up as a moral to others. She herself thought this should be so, for she was an 'English Jacobin'. This label was accepted by a wide range of English reformers in the 1790s, because, according to John Thelwall, 'it is fixed upon us as a stigma by our enemies'.[1] Like the other English Jacobins, and their French colleagues the Girondins, Mary Wollstonecraft inherited the complex of ideas and values which descended from the eighteenth century empirical tradition, the French and Scottish Enlightenments, and English religious dissent, and which the French Revolution transformed into Romanticism. The essentials of that philosophy were a conviction that experience was the basis of all knowledge, a confidence that environment produced character, a belief that men were innately good and potentially perfectible, and a faith that the truth would make them free.

From these ideas and from their own experience, Mary Wollstonecraft and the English Jacobins fashioned the structure of both their philosophy and their fiction. Their model was Rousseau. The Protestant son of republican Geneva spoke to Dissenters, Revolutionaries, and Enlightenment rationalists alike, but especially to the English Jacobin novelists, who were attempting to renovate fiction with materials drawn from life. His *Confessions* revealed that his philosophical, educational, and political writings arose out of his own peculiar character, background, and experience, and that his novel *La Nouvelle Héloïse* welled from the deepest levels of his personality. Above all, he showed that the creation of fiction could be more than hack-work or genteel recreation, an experience in life that went beyond confession, reparation, or self-justification, to attempt to shape the author's life itself in a perpetual act of creation, a continual quest for self-awareness, a permanent 'revolution'.[2]

[1] Carl Cone, *The English Jacobins* (New York, 1968), p. iii.

[2] See Jean Starobinski, *J.-J. Rousseau, la transparence et l'obstacle* (revised 1971) and Ronald Grimsley, *Jean-Jacques Rousseau, A Study in Self-Awareness* (revised 1969).

Rousseau made it clear that all his acts, his creations, his quests, his 'revolutions',[1] were due to 'sensibility', which he defined as the physical and emotional capacity for feeling, and which he proclaimed as the essential characteristic of man. But if his life and works showed how sensibility could liberate, they also showed how it could limit. This was especially clear to those English Jacobin writers who were women. If Mary Wollstonecraft and her fellow 'hyenas in petticoats' (the phrase came from one of Rousseau's gadflies, Horace Walpole) had an ambivalent attitude to Rousseau, they also had an ambivalent attitude to themselves; if they attributed his false view of the duties and education of women to his excessive sensibility,[2] they also saw the dangers of sensibility in themselves.[3] From Mary Wollstonecraft to Jane Austen, through all shades of political and moral opinion from Mary Hays and Helen Maria Williams, to Charlotte Smith, Mary Robinson, Maria Edgeworth and Hannah More, the women novelists of the Revolutionary and Napoleonic decades had to contend with the problem of sensibility, seen since Rousseau at least as their sex's weakness and their sex's glory.

• Mary Wollstonecraft's first novel confronts the problem of sensibility in fiction and life head on. It was written in the summer of 1787 while she was still an obscure and impoverished governess in the family of an Irish lord, but it reveals an original and self-instructed mind, already rich in thought and feeling, and familiar with the major issues in the art, literature, and philosophy of the day. Both title and preface of *Mary, A Fiction* carefully avoid the word novel, and the preface claims a special status for art in which sensibility mediates between fiction and life: 'Those compositions only have power to delight, and carry us willing captives, where the soul of the author is exhibited, and animates the hidden springs.' Her statement anticipates Romantic narrative art,

---

[1] The term he used to describe the turning points in his life.
[2] *A Vindication of the Rights of Woman*, ed. Carol Poston (New York, 1976), p. 90.
[3] Ibid., p. 33.

for like Coleridge she wished to externalize in 'fictitious history' her inner emotional experience;[1] but the shape of her experience, a conflict between reason and feeling, comes from the age of Sensibility, and gives form to both her novel and her personal letters of this period. Only a few months before she began her novel she wrote to her sister Everina, 'I am now reading Rousseau's Emile, and love his paradoxes. . . . however he rambles into that *chimerical* world in which I have too often wandered. . . . He was a strange inconsistent unhappy clever creature—yet he possessed an uncommon portion of sensibility and penetration.'[2] She obviously identified herself with Rousseau, and like the 'Solitary Walker' she wrote to relieve her 'wounded spirit'. But writing a novel, however autobiographical, forced her to be more objective. She had to arrange her emotional experience—the novel's many lyrical passages, effusions, and fragmentary meditations—into some kind of orderly sequence; she had to provide those passages with appropriate occasions, through plot and incident; and she had to shape her feelings into the character of her heroine and so see herself from a distance.

To help in this task she summoned all the intellectual resources of an ardent auto-didact. For if the matter of the novel is emotional and autobiographical, its form is moral and philosophical, and displays the extent of its author's self-instruction. In a letter of September 1787, after she had finished the novel, she confessed to both autobiography and moral purpose: "Spite of my vexations, I have lately written, a fiction which I intend to give to the world; it is a tale, to illustrate an opinion of mine, that a genius will educate itself. I have drawn from nature.'[3] There is in fact a variety of autobiographical forms in the novel, including confession, fantasy, and self-justification, but all are subdued to its moral

---

[1] Cf. Coleridge's *Biographia Literaria*, ed. J. Shawcross (1907), ii.6.

[2] March 24 and 29, 1787. Printed, with some errors, in William Godwin, *Memoirs of Mary Wollstonecraft*, ed. W. Clark Durant (London and New York, 1927), p. 169.

[3] *Shelley and His Circle*, ed. Kenneth Neill Cameron (Cambridge Mass., 1970), iv.860.

purpose. Using the language of Locke and Hartley, *Mary* attempts to illustrate the philosophy of necessity, as it was later expressed in the English Jacobin doctrine that 'the characters of men originate in their external circumstances.'[1] Such a philosophy demands a form of the fictional pseudo-memoir which is radical in that it traces character back to its roots in early life, and with Rousseau, Mary and her author could say, 'j'ai promis de me peindre tel que je suis et pour me connoitre dans mon âge avancé, il faut m'avoir bien connu dans ma jeunesse.'[2] The religious impulse to self-examination (many of Mary Wollstonecraft's closest friends were Dissenters) accords with the philosophical method of 'necessitarianism'. Mary reconstructs her mental history in an effort to free herself from the past and the 'association of ideas' which produced her excessive sensibility.[3] Gradually she works towards a cure through imagination itself, but imagination channelled and chastened into a rational religion culled from the epistles of St. Paul, the ethics of Adam Smith and Richard Price, the theology of Rousseau's Savoyard Vicar, and the social philosophy of the French Enlightenment.

For if Mary is a prisoner of her sex's sensibility, the causes are shown to be social as well as psychological. Self-examination must take place in a social context because there are no innate ideas or propensities, and the circumstances that form character are mostly social ones. Mary experiences the world as a series of widening social spheres, from family, to friendship, to marriage, to 'polite' society, and finally humanity in general. A keen student of society, Mary notices that some live in selfish luxury, while the majority of mankind wallow in misery and ignorance. Gradually the conflict between sense and sensibility in herself becomes identified with a conflict between self-interest (or 'prudence') and

[1] William Godwin, *Political Justice*, 3rd edition (1798), ed. F. E. L. Priestley (Toronto, 1946), i.24.

[2] Jean-Jacques Rousseau, *Confessions* (Pléiade edition), p. 174.

[3] See John Locke, *Essay Concerning Human Understanding*, bk. ii, ch. 33, and Ernest Lee Tuveson, *The Imagination as a Means of Grace* (1960), p. 36.

benevolence in social relations, until she rejects society altogether. Against a sorrow that is now social as well as personal she administers the Rousseauistic anodyne of 'the smiling face of nature' and the active social utility recommended by her rational religion, but the combination of circumstances and her own morbid sensibility is too great, and she succumbs to 'gloomy egotism' and yearning for death. *Mary* is a radical novel, and it traces the causes of one woman's condition to their roots; but it offers no solutions and apportions no blame. If it attributes Mary's decline to her sensibility, it attributes the sensibility to individual and social causes beyond her control. In the philosophy of necessity there is ultimately no evil, only error; no personal moral responsibility, only cause and effect.[1] For Mary Wollstonecraft, as for Prévost, Rousseau, and a host of female novelists in the late eighteenth century, necessity too easily became fatalism.

The novel itself becomes imprisoned by its author's feminine sensibility. It portrays an individual attempt to escape from the prison of solipsist imagination, and more strongly urges the necessity to do so by throwing the weight of its author's own experiences behind the argument. But tied to its author's life, it can only yield the fruit of experience, and, of necessity Mary would argue, it is a bitter harvest. Many women in late eighteenth-century England took to fiction as imagination's escape from the impossibilities of their moral and social condition, but few admitted the fact that escape was itself a fiction. Mary Wollstonecraft rejected the conventional consolations of the artful happy ending, or the *deus ex machina* in shining armour, but once she had rejected the conventional fields of female endeavour—marriage and the nurturing of others—she too could imagine no alternative in this life. It is revealing that she should keep remembering lines from Young's *Night-Thoughts*, and that even her novel's strange system of punctuation should resemble that of Young's poem;

[1] David Hartley, *Observations on Man* (London, 1749), i.507–8.

for like Young she retreated to an imaginary transformation of present gloom into future glory, and rejected life for the traditional alternatives of the oppressed—religion, death, and the life hereafter.

Another alternative soon burst upon her and an astonished world. A year after *Mary* was published, the hereafter became the here and now, Paradise seemed about to be regained, and imagination was out-done each day as the French Revolution transformed the liberal creed of the eighteenth century into the militant faith of state-reformation. Amongst the chief prophets of this new gospel was Mary Wollstonecraft. Like other women in other revolutions she found her individual fantasies given tangible and universal form by 'the real romanticism of the Revolution',[1] and like Wordsworth and Coleridge, she felt herself to be one of those

> called upon to exercise their skill,
> Not in Utopia,—subterraneous fields,—
> Or some secreted island, Heaven knows where!
> But in the very world which is the world
> Of all of us,—the place in which, in the end,
> We find our happiness, or not at all![2]

Her religion now was reason, and she waged holy war on sensibility and 'romantic' defence of chivalry in her *Vindication of the Rights of Men* (1790),[3] then she denounced Rousseau and the oppression of one half mankind through sensibility, in *A Vindication of the Rights of Woman* (1792). Finally, she analysed the causes of the Revolution itself and declared that 'one great cause of misery in the present imperfect state of society is, that the imagination, continually tantalized, becomes the inflated wen of the mind, draining off the nourishment from the vital parts.'[4] Yearning for a

[1] Alexandra Kollontai, *The Autobiography of a Sexually Emancipated Communist Woman*, trans. Salvator Attanasio (New York, 1971), p. 35.

[2] William Wordsworth, *The Prelude* (1805), x.723–8.

[3] James T. Boulton, *The Language of Politics in the Age of Wilkes and Burke* (1963), pp. 167–76.

[4] Mary Wollstonecraft, *An Historical and Moral View of the Origin and Progress of the French Revolution* (1794), p. 18.

revolution in her own life, she abandoned England and her past altogether, to live in France; and once in Paris she abandoned convention as well, to live with an American, Gilbert Imlay, and bear his child. She had identified her fate completely with the New Millenium.

But she was once more deceived, first by the Revolution, then by romance. The dawn of individual and international liberation soon darkened into a storm of repression, war, and 'the calamitous horrors produced by desperate and enraged factions'.[1] She was herself abandoned, and Imlay left her for commerce and other women, with only her infant daughter to live for, and her divided personality to contend with. She returned to England, revisited scenes of her childhood and youth, travelled through Scandinavia, and in November 1795 attempted suicide. At thirty-six she had exhausted life. But restorative powers had been at work, and she came to realize, once again like Wordsworth and Coleridge, that the real revolution was within.

> Then was the truth received into my heart,
> That, under heaviest sorrow earth can bring,
> Griefs bitterest of ourselves or of our kind,
> If from the affliction somewhere do not grow
> Honour which could not else have been, a faith,
> An elevation and a sanctity,
> If new strength be not given or old retained,
> The blame is ours. . . .[2]

Her journey to the north had restored her to converse with nature and sympathy with man, and in January 1796 she published her romantic and autobiographical *Letters from Sweden*. In the same month she met William Godwin,[3] philosopher and novelist. He read her *Letters*, and later wrote, 'If ever there was a book calculated to make a man in love with

---

[1] Ibid., p. vii.

[2] *The Prelude* (1805), x.423–30.

[3] They had first met long before, in 1791, but the encounter was not a success; see Godwin's *Memoirs of Mary Wollstonecraft*, ed. W. Clark Durant, pp. 62–3.

its author, this appears to me to be the book.'[1] By the summer they were lovers and had embarked on 'that most fruitful experiment'[2] that was to end only with her death in childbirth a year later. But for the moment, and by no coincidence, Mary Wollstonecraft was ready to turn once again to the personal form of the novel.

While she had written her polemical works and survived the Revolution, the English Jacobin novelists—Godwin, Thomas Holcroft, Robert Bage, Elizabeth Inchbald, Mary Hays, and others—had carried the novel into the thick of the political fray. In particular, her friend Mary Hays's *Memoirs of Emma Courtney* (1796) showed how philosophy and politics, feminism and autobiography, could all be transmuted into the form of popular fiction.[3] In the hands of the English Jacobins, the 'English Popular Novel'[4] had become a serious literary kind, and Mary Wollstonecraft could not now but be 'sensible how arduous a task it is to produce a truly excellent novel; and she roused her faculties to grapple with it.'[5] Now she attempted various forms, and rejected them, abandoned her usual manner of rapid but slovenly composition, and wrote and rewrote. When she died a year later she had still completed only a third of her novel, but she had learned that autobiographical fiction could be more objective by paradoxically being more personal. On 4 September 1796 she replied to Godwin's criticisms of her work by declaring, 'I am compelled to think that there is some thing in my writings more valuable, than in the productions of some people on whom you bestow warm eulogiums—I mean more mind—denominate it as you will—more of the observations of my own senses, more of the combinings of my

[1] Ibid., p. 84.
[2] Virginia Woolf, 'Mary Wollstonecraft', in *The Common Reader*, second series.
[3] On *Emma Courtney* see Gina Luria, 'Mary Hays: A Critical Biography', unpub. diss., New York University, 1972, ch. v.
[4] See J. M. S. Tompkins, *The Popular Novel in England, 1770–1800* (1932), ch. viii.
[5] William Godwin, *Memoirs of Mary Wollstonecraft*, ed. W. Clark Durant, p. 111.

own imagination—the effusions of my own feelings and passions. . . .'[1] By extending the range of her 'observations' on the condition of woman, and fusing them with her own 'feelings and passions', she could unite her own experience with that of women everywhere, and still continue to explore all the varieties of autobiographical imagining through allegory and analogy, confession and compensation, fantasy, revenge, and reparation. It was not a classical shapely form, but it was romantically replete.

It was also constructed along the logical if inelegant lines of the typical English Jacobin novel. The militant purpose was outlined in a polemical preface: if like a sentimental or Romantic novelist the author 'rather endeavoured to pourtray passions than manners', like an English Jacobin she also wished to exhibit 'the misery and oppression, peculiar to women, that arise out of the partial laws and customs of society'. Beside the Romantic interest in individual passions is the Enlightenment pursuit of the universal, 'and the history ought rather to be considered, as of woman, than of an individual.' Most interesting of all was the author's desire 'to show the wrongs of different classes of women.' If *Mary* had been a compendium of ideas and attitudes of the age of Sensibility, the new novel was to epitomize the New Philosophy.

For this a new model was needed to replace Rousseau, and Mary Wollstonecraft did not have far to look. Godwin's *Things As They Are; or, The Adventures of Caleb Williams* (1794) had presented a fictive version of his *Enquiry Concerning Political Justice* (1793), and now *The Wrongs of Woman: or, Maria* was to fictionalize the arguments of *A Vindication of the Rights of Woman*. The very title of the novel suggests that it is a revision of *Mary* in the light of *Caleb Williams*, offering an alternative between novel of purpose and variation on the author's name. Godwin's novel provided

---

[1] R. M. Wardle, ed., *Godwin and Mary* (Lawrence Kansas and London, 1967), p. 28. She uses 'mind' in the same way as Johnson, to include both imagination and judgment.

her with a pattern for the *exposé* of legal oppression and 'the modes of domestic and unrecorded despotism',[1] for although she had promised a second volume of the *Vindication* to deal with 'the laws relative to women',[2] the turbulent events of her own life had overtaken her. Now, inspired by Godwin's example, she portrayed a heroine who is literally a prisoner of sex, immured in a madhouse by her husband so that he can control her property, and she traced the maze of legal and domestic oppression of women to the same conclusion reached by the *Vindication*: 'Was not the world a vast prison, and women born slaves?' More important, Godwin showed her how to broaden her fable through form and allusion, and turn the single-centred autobiographical narrative she had written ten years before into a tale of universal human relevance, transcending local and individual destiny. A series of characters, both major and minor, are made to recount their adventures with 'things as they are', until the novel's 'argument' becomes both conclusive and comprehensive. Finally, the main characters are given names with an historical or Biblical resonance, to imply that 'things as they are' have always been that way. Jemima, the downtrodden ex-prostitute whom Maria converts to virtue and benevolence, is named after the first of Job's daughters, promised an equal inheritance with her brothers. Maria herself is as much Mary Wollstonecraft as she is Mary Queen of Scots, prisoner of sex in the age of Reformation, and Marie Roland and Marie Antoinette, victims of a ruined Revolution.[3] In the heroine's fate—and the word now gains force from history and necessitarian philosophy rather than sentimental fiction—is exemplified the accumulated wrongs of woman throughout modern European history.

In addition to examining the social and historical condition

---

[1] William Godwin, *Caleb Williams*, ed. David McCracken (Oxford English Novels, 1970), p. 1.

[2] 'Advertisement' to *A Vindication of the Rights of Woman*.

[3] On M. W. and Marie Roland see Claire Tomalin, *The Life and Death of Mary Wollstonecraft* (1974), pp. 139–41.

of woman, the new novel also extends its predecessor's exploration of the problem of sensibility. Like Mary, Maria is a woman of the middle class, torn between sense and sensibility, and her sufferings have made her so susceptible to 'romantic wishes' that 'she frequently appeared, like a large proportion of her sex, only born to feel.' She too wishes to escape from the real to an ideal world, such as Rousseau's *La Nouvelle Héloïse*, which she had read before, 'but now it seemed to open a new world to her—the only one worth inhabiting'. Maria's experience has made her feel too much, but that of her warder Jemima has made her try to feel nothing, and act on 'prudence' and self-interest alone. Both responses are distortions of character caused by male control of 'things as they are', and if Maria's fate reveals that men control the laws, Jemima's shows that they also control the economic system. Jemima, like Caroline Blood, the sister of Mary Wollstonecraft's beloved friend Fanny, is seduced, abandoned, persecuted by the Poor Laws, and then forced into prostitution by economic necessity. Ironically, she is then more free to mingle in male society; but if she wishes to leave her 'profession' she finds that only the hardest and lowest paid work is reserved for women. Of necessity once again, she enters the employ of the oppressor, until Maria awakens the last vestiges of her precious 'feminine' sympathy and capacity for feeling. At first Jemima feels for Maria as another bereaved mother, then Maria's own liberating passion for Darnford shows Jemima that feeling can be noble, and she resolves to help the lovers escape from their prison. Jemima's 'conversion' reveals both the Biblical promise in her name, and the novel's radical philosophy of revolution through those very qualities which have enslaved women since time began. Feeling, spread by example, is the gentle force that will open mad-house and prison and destroy the moral bastille built by man.

Thus much of the novel was intended as the first of three parts, and it is full of contemporary observations. The allusions to Young and the sentimental reveries of *Mary* are now replaced by references to the Poor Laws, the inadequate hospital system, the corruption of the police, the conditions of woman's work, the effects of the war, the Naval Mutinies, the Treason Trials, the laws of marriage and property, and the hypocrisy of the Evangelical support for the Establishment. But this was the only part of the novel that was completed, and from this point the meaning of the fable is less clear. Part two transforms Darnford from an idealized Imlay to an equally idealized Godwin, and so was probably written in late 1796 or early 1797. The first version of Imlay was George Venables, a romantic hero spun from sheerest female fantasies, but marriage reveals the tyrant inside the knight's shining armour—Mary Wollstonecraft was remembering her blistering attack on Burke's defence of chivalry in her *Vindication of the Rights of Men*. With Darnford Maria discovers the pleasures of a 'rational' passion in which 'esteem seemed to have rivalled love', and love is finally combined with English Jacobin propaganda as Maria defends her lover against proceedings for adultery with the premise, from Godwin's *Political Justice*, that 'definite rules can never apply to indefinite circumstances.' The judge, of course, rejects Maria's 'French principles', for the trial is only a symbol for the Government's legal suppression of English Jacobinism after the Treason Trials of 1794.

The Wrongs of Woman extended the English Jacobins' exploration of the parallels between domestic and political life, private and public morality, but fiction had now caught up with fact, and from this point Mary Wollstonecraft had once again to imagine her own future, as well as that of her heroine. The scattered hints for part three betray a re-emergence of her old fears and despondency, as Maria's relationship with Darnford disintegrates, and she either commits suicide, or attempts it but decides to live for her child. Perhaps revision would have purged this residue of *Mary* and the dark days of 1795. Had she lived, Mary Wollstonecraft, like Wordsworth and Coleridge, might have transcended the conflict of revolution and reaction, overcome personal dejection, and won through to independence and a new resolution of reason and sensibility. *The Wrongs of Woman* might have been the first Romantic novel in England. As it is, the novel resembles its contemporaries, the early drafts of Wordsworth's 'Salisbury Plain' and 'The Ruined Cottage'. But faced with the problem of imagining a solution to the 'wrongs of woman', Mary Wollstonecraft, like Charlotte Smith, Mary Hays, Mary Robinson and the rest of her female contemporaries, could only fall back on the masculine virtue traditionally recommended for women, the resolution of 'fortitude'. In her case such pessimism was more than ironical, it was paradoxical; for in the midst of the greatest happiness she had ever known, her imagination succumbed once again to the errors of sensibility she had devoted her life and her works to correcting.

The conclusion must be that both of these novels are failures. Like their author's life, they are not even complete, since *Mary* shrivels into a hasty and carelessly written ending, and *The Wrongs of Woman* was ended arbitrarily by death, before the new promise of life could be shaped into art. But if Mary Wollstonecraft failed as a novelist, her failure was representative. Unlike most women novelists, she did not depend on fiction as the sole outlet for her inner life. She refused to be driven by social and moral constraints into a life divided between outer decorum and inner emotional extravagance. To a very large degree she succeeded in living a whole life, in thought, and word, and deed. But she had her own constraints, and felt too strongly those endured by others, not to be also addicted to the pleasures of the imagination. She recognized her addiction, and the dangers of failing to reconcile romance with reality: frustrated in turn by religion, romance, and revolution, she was just beginning to turn towards a new resolution in Romanticism when she was frustrated once more, by death. Only in her last year did life provide a hero worthy of her heroines, and only in her last days did life begin to furnish materials for a happy ending.

Moreover, in the age of Revolution between Sensibility and Romanticism, the great works were polemical ones, devoted to public issues but derived from personal experience and conviction. With the exception of William Godwin, none of the English Jacobin novelists were able to transcend their personal commitment to principle for that sustained act of the creative imagination which alone could fuse personal and public issues in the form of art. Mary Wollstonecraft too was a polemicist by personal conviction, and when she tried to unite philosophy and fiction, experience and politics, she too failed to make her fictions more than personal or political documents. And yet the value of these documents is high. Not only did she, like the other English Jacobin novelists, leave a legacy for posterity by bringing a new seriousness to popular fiction; but, like Rousseau and the Romantics, she also left a permanent if imperfect record of the imagination's quest for wholeness in life and art.

ACKNOWLEDGEMENTS

For permission to use the Wollstonecraft and Godwin material in his collection I am indebted to Lord Abinger, and for a wide variety of assistance to the staffs of the Bodleian, British, Pforzheimer, Duke University, and University of New Brunswick libraries. Above all, I wish to thank the University of New Brunswick and the Killam Program of the Canada Council for research grants which enabled me to complete this edition.

NOTE ON THE TEXTS

THE text of *Mary* is that of the first and only edition published by Joseph Johnson in 1788, with four corrections of dropped type and two corrections based on a letter from Mary Wollstonecraft to George Blood (16 May 1788) in the Abinger collection. The absence of proper quotation marks at places in the last pages of the novel indicates some haste in either composition or printing, and has been left uncorrected.

The text of *The Wrongs of Woman* is that published for the first and only time in England in the first two volumes of *Posthumous Works of the Author of A Vindication of the Rights of Woman*, edited by Godwin and published by Joseph Johnson and G. G. and J. Robinson in 1798. Five obvious misprints and two errata have been silently corrected, and four other corrections have been recorded in the Explanatory Notes. The structure of the novel as a series of reported narratives involves careful use of quotation marks, and so the omission of these at places in chapters eight, nine, and thirteen has been corrected to avoid confusion.

SELECT BIBLIOGRAPHY

BIBLIOGRAPHY. A checklist is in the autumn number of the first and subsequent volumes of the *Mary Wollstonecraft Journal*, now *Women and Literature*, edited by Janet Todd, Rutgers University (1972–).

BIOGRAPHY AND CRITICISM. Mary Wollstonecraft's life and works have always been considered to be inseparable. Godwin's *Memoir* was published with her *Posthumous Works* in 1798, and edited, with much additional material, by W. Clark Durant in 1927. Much material relating to her is also found in C. Kegan Paul, *William Godwin, his Friends and Contemporaries* (2 vols., 1876), and there are numerous references in other lives and letters of the period. Her own letters are the best biography, and are available on microfilms of the Abinger Collection (see Duke University *Library Notes*, xxvii, April 1953, 11–17), or published in *Letters from Sweden* (1796), *Posthumous Works*, vols. iii–iv (1798), *Letters to Imlay* (ed. C. Kegan Paul, 1879, and Roger Ingpen, 1908), *The Love-Letters of Mary Hays* (ed. A. F. Wedd, 1925), *Four New Letters of Mary Wollstonecraft and Helen Maria Williams* (ed. Benjamin P. Kurtz and Carrie C. Autrey, 1937), *Godwin and Mary* (ed. R. M. Wardle, 1966), and *Shelley and His Circle*, vols. i–iv (ed. Kenneth Neill Cameron, 1961–70). Contemporary opinions of her (mostly adverse) are printed in Durant, and her life and works were vindicated by Mary Hays in *Annual Necrology, 1797–98* (1800), and by an anonymous writer in *A Defence of the Character and Conduct of the late Mary Wollstonecraft Godwin* (1803). The best nineteenth-century biography is by Elizabeth Robbins Pennell (1885), and the best modern biographies are by Ralph M. Wardle (1951), Eleanor Flexner (1972), Claire Tomalin (1974), and Emily Sunstein (1975).

Mary Wollstonecraft's ideas have been largely ignored in favour of her life, and no biography of her has dealt adequately with the subject. However, Carol Poston's edition of the *Vindication* documents much of her reading and there is some discussion of her thought in Emma Rauschenbusch-Clough, *A Study of Mary Wollstonecraft and the Rights of Woman* (1898); G. R. Stirling Taylor, *Mary Wollstonecraft: A Study in Economics and Romance* (1911); Jacob Bouten, *Mary Wollstonecraft and the Beginnings of Female Emancipation in France and England* (1922); M. S. Storr, *Mary Wollstonecraft et le mouvement féministe dans la littérature anglaise* (1932); and Ida B. O'Malley, *Women in Subjection* (1933). It is interesting to compare Virginia Woolf's appreciation of Mary Wollstonecraft in *The Common Reader*, second series, with the life by her father in the *Dictionary of National Biography*.

Attention to Mary Wollstonecraft's literary achievement has also been subordinated to interest in her life, or else ignored altogether, but there is an excellent analysis of her polemical style in James T. Boulton, *The Language of Politics in the Age of Wilkes and Burke* (1963). Recent studies of interest also include essays by Mitzi Myers in *Studies in Eighteenth-Century Culture*, vols. 6 and 8, and in *The Wordsworth Circle*, 11 (1980), as well as the present editor's essays in *English Studies in Canada*, 5 (1979), and in *Studies on Voltaire and the Eighteenth Century* (1981). Modern feminist investigations of the condition of woman, such as those in *Woman in Sexist Society*, ed. Vivian Gornick and Barbara K. Moran (1971), cast new and interesting light on Mary Wollstonecraft's own prescience, perspicacity, and eloquence.

A CHRONOLOGY OF
MARY WOLLSTONECRAFT

Age

1788   *Original Stories from Real Life* and *Mary, a Fiction*. Translates and adapts Necker's *On the Importance of Religious Opinions*. Meets Fuseli. Contributes reviews to Johnson's *Analytical Review*   29

1789   *The Female Reader* by 'Mr. Cresswick', which includes 'some original pieces'   30

1790   Adapts Mme de Cambon's *Young Grandison*. (November) Burke's *Reflections on the Revolution in France* initiates paper war; her *Vindication of the Rights of Men* one of earliest replies and makes her reputation. Translates and adapts C. G. Salzmann's *Elements of Morality*   31

1791   (November) Meets Godwin for the first time. Her religion becomes increasingly rational   32

1792   (January) *A Vindication of the Rights of Woman*. Her infatuation for Fuseli at its height. Meets Mary Hays. Probably loses her religion altogether.
       (June) Contemplates trip to Paris with Fuseli.
       (8 December) Leaves for France alone. At Paris meets French Girondins and their friends, Helen Maria Williams, Joel Barlow, Thomas Christie, Thomas Cooper, Tom Paine, and Archibald Hamilton Rowan   33

1793   (February) War between France and Britain puts her in danger. (Spring) Meets and begins affair with Gilbert Imlay, former officer in the American Revolutionary Army, land speculator, and author of *A Topographical Description of the Western Territory of North America* (1792) and *The Emigrants*, a novel (1793)   34

1794   (14 May) Daughter Fanny born. (December) *An Historical and Moral View of the French Revolution*   35

1795   (April) Leaves France to join Imlay in London and discovers his infidelity. (May) Attempts suicide but prevented by Imlay, who persuades her to travel to Scandinavia on his business. (October) Arrives back in England and finds Imlay living with his new mistress; attempts suicide by jumping from Putney Bridge (November)   36

1796   (January) Meets Godwin again. (January) *Letters from Sweden* published. (April) Calls on Godwin; they see each other frequently thereafter. (Summer) Begins work on *The Wrongs of Woman*. Accepts Godwin as her lover (August); becomes pregnant (December)   37

1797   (29 March) Marries Godwin. Works on 'Letters on the Management of Children'. (30 August) Daughter Mary born; (10 September) dies of complications resulting from childbirth. (31 December) Godwin begins novel *St. Leon* containing idealized picture of marriage   38

1798   (29 January) Publication of *Posthumous Works* as well as Godwin's *Memoir*

MARY,
A FICTION

———

L'exercice des plus sublimes vertus élève et nourrit le génie.[1]

ROUSSEAU.

Critique of marriage market

Class – no sensitivity

ADVERTISEMENT

In delineating the Heroine of this Fiction, the Author attempts to develop a character different from those generally portrayed. This woman is neither a Clarissa, a Lady G—, nor a* Sophie.[1]—It would be vain to mention the various modifications of these models, as it would to remark, how widely artists wander from nature, when they copy the originals of great masters. They catch the gross parts; but the subtle spirit evaporates; and not having the just ties, affectation disgusts, when grace was expected to charm.

Those compositions only have power to delight, and carry us willing captives, where the soul of the author is exhibited, and animates the hidden springs. Lost in a pleasing enthusiasm, they live in the scenes they represent; and do not measure their steps in a beaten track, solicitous to gather expected flowers, and bind them in a wreath, according to the prescribed rules of art.

These chosen few, wish to speak for themselves, and not to be an echo—even of the sweetest sounds—or the reflector of the most sublime beams. The† paradise they ramble in, must be of their own creating—or the prospect soon grows insipid, and not varied by a vivifying principle, fades and dies.

In an artless tale, without episodes, the mind of a woman, who has thinking powers is displayed. The female organs[2] have been thought too weak for this arduous employment; and experience seems to justify the assertion. Without arguing physically[3] about *possibilities*—in a fiction, such a being may be allowed to exist; whose grandeur is derived from the operations of its own faculties, not subjugated to opinion; but drawn by the individual from the original source.[4]

---

*Rousseau.

†I here give the Reviewers an opportunity of being very witty about the Paradise of Fools, &c.

MARY, A FICTION

CHAPTER ONE

MARY,[1] the heroine of this fiction, was the daughter of Edward, who married Eliza,[2] a gentle, fashionable girl, with a kind of indolence in her temper, which might be termed negative good-nature:[3] her virtues, indeed, were all of that stamp. She carefully attended to the *shews* of things, and her opinions, I should have said prejudices, were such as the generality approved of. She was educated with the expectation of a large fortune, of course became a mere machine: the homage of her attendants[4] made a great part of her puerile amusements, and she never imagined there were any relative duties for her to fulfil: notions of her own consequence, by these means, were interwoven in her mind, and the years of youth spent in acquiring a few superficial accomplishments,[5] without having any taste for them. When she was first introduced into the polite circle, she danced with an officer, whom she faintly wished to be united to; but her father soon after recommending another in a ·more distinguished rank of life, she readily submitted to his will, and promised to love, honour, and obey, (a vicious fool), as in duty bound.[6]

While they resided in London, they lived in the usual fashionable style, and seldom saw each other; nor were they much more sociable when they wooed rural felicity for more than half the year, in a delightful country, where Nature, with lavish hand, had scattered beauties around; for the master, with brute, unconscious gaze, passed them by unobserved, and sought amusement in country sports. He hunted in the morning, and after eating an immoderate dinner, generally fell asleep: this seasonable rest enabled him to digest the cumbrous load; he would then visit some of his pretty tenants; and when he compared their ruddy glow of health with his wife's countenance, which even rouge could not enliven, it is not necessary to say which a *gourmand* would give the preference to. Their vulgar dance of spirits were infinitely more agreeable to his fancy than her sickly, die-away languor. Her voice was but the shadow of a sound, and she had, to complete her delicacy,[1] so relaxed her nerves, that she became a mere nothing.

Many such noughts are there in the female world! yet she had a good opinion of her own merit,—truly, she said long prayers,—and sometimes read her Week's Preparation:[2] she dreaded that horrid place vulgarly called *hell*, the regions below; but whether her's[3] was a mounting spirit, I cannot pretend to determine; or what sort of a planet would have been proper for her, when she left her *material* part in this world, let metaphysicians settle; I have nothing to say to her unclothed spirit.

As she was sometimes obliged to be alone, or only with her French waiting-maid, she sent to the metropolis for all the new publications, and while she was dressing her hair, and she could turn her eyes from the glass, she ran over those most delightful substitutes for bodily dissipation, novels. I say bodily, or the animal soul, for a rational one can find no employment in polite circles. The glare of lights, the studied inelegancies of dress, and the compliments offered up at the shrine of false beauty, are all equally addressed to the senses.

When she could not any longer indulge the caprices of fancy one way, she tried another. The Platonic Marriage, Eliza Warwick,[4] and some other interesting tales were perused with eagerness. Nothing could be more natural than the developement of the passions, nor more striking than the views of the human heart. What delicate struggles! and uncommonly pretty turns of thought! The picture that was found on a bramble-bush, the new sensitive-plant, or tree, which caught the swain by the upper-garment, and presented to his ravished eyes a portrait.—Fatal image!—It planted a thorn in a till then insensible heart, and sent a new kind of a knight-errant into the world. But even this was nothing to the catastrophe, and the circumstance on which it hung, the hornet settling on the sleeping lover's face.[1] What a *heart-rending* accident! She planted, in imitation of those susceptible souls, a rose bush; but there was not a lover to weep in concert with her, when she watered it with her tears.—Alas! Alas!

If my readers would excuse the sportiveness of fancy, and give me credit for genius, I would go on and tell them such tales as would force the sweet tears of sensibility to flow in copious showers down beautiful cheeks, to the discomposure of rouge, &c. &c. Nay, I would make it so interesting, that the fair peruser should beg the hair-dresser to settle the curls himself, and not interrupt her.

She had besides another resource, two most beautiful dogs,[2] who shared her bed, and reclined on cushions near her all the day. These she watched with the most assiduous care, and bestowed on them the warmest caresses. This fondness for animals was not that kind of *attendrissement*[3] which makes a person take pleasure in providing for the subsistence and comfort of a living creature; but it proceeded from vanity, it gave her an opportunity of lisping out the prettiest French expressions of ecstatic fondness, in accents that had never been attuned by tenderness.

She was chaste, according to the vulgar acceptation of the word, that is, she did not make any actual *faux pas*; she feared the world,[4] and was indolent; but then, to make amends for this seeming self-denial, she read all the sentimental novels,[5] dwelt on the love-scenes, and, had she thought while she read, her mind would have been contaminated; as she accompanied the lovers to the lonely arbors, and would walk with them by the clear light of the moon. She wondered her husband did not stay at home. She was jealous—why did he not love her, sit by her side, squeeze her hand, and look unutterable things? Gentle reader, I will tell thee; they neither of them felt what they could not utter. I will not pretend to say that they always annexed an idea to a word; but they had none of those feelings which are not easily analyzed.

CHAPTER TWO

In due time she brought forth a son, a feeble babe; and the following year a daughter. After the mother's throes she felt very few sentiments of maternal tenderness: the children were given to nurses, and she played with her dogs. Want of exercise prevented the least chance of her recovering strength; and two or three milk-fevers brought on a consumption, to which her constitution tended. Her children all died in their infancy,[1] except the two first, and she began to grow fond of the son, as he was remarkably handsome. For years she divided her time between the sofa, and the card-table. She thought not of death, though on the borders of the grave; nor did any of the duties of her station occur to her as necessary. Her children were left in the nursery; and when Mary, the little blushing girl, appeared, she would send the awkward thing away.[2] To own the truth, she was awkward enough, in a house without any play-mates; for her brother had been sent to school,[3] and she scarcely knew how to employ herself; she would ramble about the garden, admire the flowers, and play with the dogs. An old house-keeper told her stories, read to her, and, at last, taught her to read. Her mother talked of enquiring for a governess when her health would permit; and, in the interim desired her own maid to teach her French. As she had learned to read, she perused with avidity every book that came in her way. Neglected in every respect, and left to the operations of her own mind, she considered every thing that came under her inspection, and learned to think. She had heard of a separate state, and that angels sometimes visited this earth. She would sit in a thick wood in the park, and talk to them; make little songs addressed to them, and sing them to tunes of her own composing; and her native wood notes wild[1] were sweet and touching.

Her father always exclaimed against female acquirements, and was glad that his wife's indolence and ill health made her not trouble herself about them. She had besides another reason, she did not wish to have a fine tall girl brought forward into notice as her daughter; she still expected to recover, and figure away in the gay world. Her husband was very tyrannical and passionate; indeed so very easily irritated when inebriated, that Mary was continually in dread lest he should frighten her mother to death;[2] her sickness called forth all Mary's tenderness, and exercised her compassion so continually, that it became more than a match for self-love, and was the governing propensity of her heart through life. She was violent in her temper; but she saw her father's faults, and would weep when obliged to compare his temper with her own.—She did more; artless prayers rose to Heaven for pardon, when she was conscious of having erred; and her contrition was so exceedingly painful, that she watched diligently the first movements of anger and impatience, to save herself this cruel remorse.

Sublime ideas[3] filled her young mind—always connected with devotional sentiments; extemporary effusions of gratitude, and rhapsodies of praise would burst often from her, when she listened to the birds, or pursued the deer. She would gaze on the moon, and ramble through the gloomy path, observing the various shapes the clouds assumed, and listen to the sea that was not far distant. The wandering spirits, which she imagined inhabited every part of nature, were her constant friends and confidants. She began to consider the Great First Cause, formed just notions of his attributes, and, in particular, dwelt on his wisdom and goodness.[4] Could she have loved her father or mother, had they returned her affection, she would not so soon, perhaps, have sought out a new world.

Her sensibility[5] prompted her to search for an object to love; on earth it was not to be found: her mother had often

disappointed her, and the apparent partiality she shewed to
her brother gave her exquisite pain—produced a kind of
habitual melancholy, led her into a fondness for reading tales
of woe, and made her almost realize the fictitious distress.

She had not any notion of death till a little chicken expired
at her feet; and her father had a dog hung in a passion. She
then concluded animals had souls, or they would not have
been subjected to the caprice of man; but what was the soul of
man or beast? In this style year after year rolled on, her
mother still vegetating.

A little girl who attended in the nursery fell sick. Mary paid
her great attention; contrary to her wish, she was sent out of
the house to her mother, a poor woman, whom necessity
obliged to leave her sick child while she earned her daily
bread. The poor wretch, in a fit of delirium stabbed herself,
and Mary saw her dead body, and heard the dismal account;
and so strongly did it impress her imagination, that every
night of her life the bleeding corpse presented itself to her
when she first began to slumber. Tortured by it, she at last
made a vow, that if she was ever mistress of a family she would
herself watch over every part of it. The impression that this
accident made was indelible.

As her mother grew imperceptibly worse and worse, her
father, who did not understand such a lingering complaint,
imagined his wife was only grown still more whimsical, and
that if she could be prevailed on to exert herself, her health
would soon be re-established. In general he treated her with
indifference; but when her illness at all interfered with his
pleasures, he expostulated in the most cruel manner, and
visibly harassed the invalid. Mary would then assiduously try
to turn his attention to something else; and when sent out of
the room, would watch at the door, until the storm was over,
for unless it was, she could not rest. Other causes also
contributed to disturb her repose: her mother's lukewarm
manner of performing her religious duties, filled her with
anguish; and when she observed her father's vices, the
unbidden tears would flow. She was miserable when beggars

were driven from the gate without being relieved; if she could do it unperceived, she would give them her own breakfast, and feel gratified, when, in consequence of it, she was pinched by hunger.

She had once, or twice, told her little secrets to her mother; they were laughed at, and she determined never to do it again. In this manner was she left to reflect on her own feelings; and so strengthened were they by being meditated on, that her character early became singular and permanent. Her understanding was strong and clear, when not clouded by her feelings; but she was too much the creature of impulse, and the slave of compassion.[1]

CHAPTER THREE

NEAR her father's house lived a poor widow, who had been brought up in affluence, but reduced to great distress by the extravagance of her husband; he had destroyed his constitution while he spent his fortune; and dying, left his wife, and five small children, to live on a very scanty pittance. The eldest daughter was for some years educated by a distant relation, a Clergyman. While she was with him a young gentleman, son to a man of property in the neighbourhood, took particular notice of her. It is true, he never talked of love; but then they played and sung in concert; drew landscapes together, and while she worked he read to her, cultivated her taste, and stole imperceptibly her heart. Just at this juncture, when smiling, unanalyzed hope made every prospect bright, and gay expectation danced in her eyes, her benefactor died. She returned to her mother—the companion of her youth forgot her, they took no more sweet counsel together. This disappointment spread a sadness over her countenance, and made it interesting. She grew fond of solitude, and her character appeared similar to Mary's, though her natural disposition was very different.

She was several years older than Mary, yet her refinement, her taste, caught her eye, and she eagerly sought her friendship: before her return she had assisted the family, which was almost reduced to the last ebb; and now she had another motive to actuate her.

As she had often occasion to send messages to Ann,[1] her new friend, mistakes were frequently made; Ann proposed that in future they should be written ones, to obviate this difficulty, and render their intercourse more agreeable. Young people are mostly fond of scribbling; Mary had had very little instruction; but by copying her friend's letters, whose hand she admired, she soon became a proficient; a little practice made her write with tolerable correctness, and her genius gave force to it. In conversation, and in writing, when she felt, she was pathetic, tender and persuasive; and she expressed contempt with such energy, that few could stand the flash of her eyes.

As she grew more intimate with Ann, her manners were softened, and she acquired a degree of equality in her behaviour: yet still her spirits were fluctuating, and her movements rapid. She felt less pain on account of her mother's partiality to her brother, as she hoped now to experience the pleasure of being beloved; but this hope led her into new sorrows, and, as usual, paved the way for disappointment. Ann only felt gratitude; her heart was entirely engrossed by one object, and friendship could not serve as a substitute; memory officiously retraced past scenes, and unavailing wishes made time loiter.

Mary was often hurt by the involuntary indifference which these consequences produced. When her friend was all the world to her, she found she was not as necessary to her happiness; and her delicate mind could not bear to obtrude her affection, or receive love as an alms, the offspring of pity. Very frequently has she ran to her with delight, and not perceiving any thing of the same kind in Ann's countenance, she has shrunk back; and, falling from one extreme into the other, instead of a warm greeting that was just slipping from her tongue, her expressions seemed to be dictated by the most chilling insensibility.

She would then imagine that she looked sickly or unhappy, and then all her tenderness would return like a torrent, and bear away all reflection. In this manner was her sensibility called forth, and exercised, by her mother's illness, her friend's misfortunes, and her own unsettled mind.

CHAPTER FOUR

NEAR to her father's house was a range of mountains; some of them were, literally speaking, cloud-capt, for on them clouds continually rested, and gave grandeur to the prospect; and down many of their sides the little bubbling cascades ran till they swelled a beautiful river. Through the straggling trees and bushes the wind whistled, and on them the birds sung, particularly the robins; they also found shelter in the ivy of an old castle,[1] a haunted one, as the story went; it was situated on the brow of one of the mountains, and commanded a view of the sea. This castle had been inhabited by some of her ancestors; and many tales had the old house-keeper told her of the worthies who had resided there.

When her mother frowned, and her friend looked cool, she would steal to this retirement, where human foot seldom trod—gaze on the sea, observe the grey clouds, or listen to the wind which struggled to free itself from the only thing that impeded its course. When more cheerful, she admired the various dispositions of light and shade, the beautiful tints the gleams of sunshine gave to the distant hills; then she rejoiced in existence, and darted into futurity.

One way home was through the cavity of a rock covered with a thin layer of earth, just sufficient to afford nourishment to a few stunted shrubs and wild plants, which grew on its sides, and nodded over the summit. A clear stream broke out of it, and ran amongst the pieces of rocks fallen into it. Here twilight always reigned—it seemed the Temple of Solitude; yet, paradoxical as the assertion may appear, when the foot sounded on the rock, it terrified the intruder, and inspired a strange feeling, as if the rightful sovereign was dislodged. In this retreat she read Thomson's Seasons, Young's Night-Thoughts, and Paradise Lost.[1]

At a little distance from it were the huts of a few poor fishermen, who supported their numerous children by their precarious labour. In these little huts she frequently rested, and denied herself every childish gratification, in order to relieve the necessities of the inhabitants.[2] Her heart yearned for them, and would dance with joy when she had relieved their wants, or afforded them pleasure.

In these pursuits she learned the luxury of doing good; and the sweet tears of benevolence frequently moistened her eyes, and gave them a sparkle which, exclusive of that, they had not; on the contrary, they were rather fixed, and would never have been observed if her soul had not animated them. They were not at all like those brilliant ones which look like polished diamonds, and dart from every superfice,[3] giving more light to the beholders than they receive themselves.

Her benevolence, indeed, knew no bounds; the distress of others carried her out of herself; and she rested not till she had relieved or comforted them. The warmth of her compassion often made her so diligent, that many things occurred to her, which might have escaped a less interested observer.

In like manner, she entered with such spirit into whatever she read, and the emotions thereby raised were so strong, that it soon became a part of her mind.

Enthusiastic[4] sentiments of devotion at this period actuated her; her Creator was almost apparent to her senses in his works; but they were mostly the grand or solemn features of Nature which she delighted to contemplate. She would stand and behold the waves rolling, and think of the voice that could still the tumultuous deep.

These propensities gave the colour to her mind, before the passions began to exercise their tyrannic sway, and particularly pointed out those which the soil would have a tendency to nurse.

Years after, when wandering through the same scenes, her imagination has strayed back, to trace the first placid sentiments they inspired, and she would earnestly desire to regain the same peaceful tranquillity.

Many nights she sat up, if I may be allowed the expression, *conversing*[1] with the Author of Nature, making verses, and singing hymns of her own composing. She considered also, and tried to discern what end her various faculties were destined to pursue; and had a glimpse of a truth, which afterwards more fully unfolded itself.

She thought that only an infinite being could fill the human soul, and that when other objects were followed as a means of happiness, the delusion led to misery, the consequence of disappointment. Under the influence of ardent affections, how often has she forgot this conviction, and as often returned to it again, when it struck her with redoubled force. Often did she taste unmixed delight; her joys, her ecstacies arose from genius.[2] *her natural disposition*

She was now fifteen, and she wished to receive the holy sacrament; and perusing the scriptures, and discussing some points of doctrine which puzzled her, she would sit up half the night, her favourite time for employing her mind; she too plainly perceived that she saw through a glass darkly;[3] and that the bounds set to stop our intellectual researches, is one of the trials of a probationary state.

But her affections were roused by the display of divine mercy; and she eagerly desired to commemorate the dying love of her great benefactor. The night before the important day, when she was to take on herself her baptismal vow, she could not go to bed; the sun broke in on her meditations, and found her not exhausted by her watching.

The orient pearls were strewed around—she hailed the morn, and sung with wild delight, Glory to God on high, good will towards men. She was indeed so much affected when she joined in the prayer for her eternal preservation, that she could hardly conceal her violent emotions; and the recollection never failed to wake her dormant piety when earthly passions made it grow languid.

These various movements of her mind were not commented on, nor were the luxuriant shoots restrained by culture. The servants and the poor adored her.

In order to be enabled to gratify herself in the highest degree, she practised the most rigid œconomy, and had such power over her appetites and whims, that without any great effort she conquered them so entirely, that when her understanding or affections had an object, she almost forgot she had a body which required nourishment.

This habit of thinking, this kind of absorption, gave strength to the passions.

We will now enter on the more active field of life.

CHAPTER FIVE

A FEW months after Mary was turned of seventeen, her brother was attacked by a violent fever, and died before his father could reach the school.

She was now an heiress,[1] and her mother began to think her of consequence, and did not call her *the child*. Proper masters were sent for; she was taught to dance,[2] and an extraordinary master procured to perfect her in that most necessary of all accomplishments.

A part of the estate she was to inherit had been litigated, and the heir of the person who still carried on a Chancery suit,[3] was only two years younger than our heroine. The fathers, spite of the dispute, frequently met, and, in order to settle it amicably, they one day, over a bottle, determined to quash it by a marriage, and, by uniting the two estates, to preclude all farther enquiries into the merits of their different claims.

While this important matter was settling, Mary was

otherwise employed. Ann's mother's resources were failing; and the ghastly phantom, poverty, made hasty strides to catch them in his clutches. Ann had not fortitude enough to brave such accumulated misery; besides, the canker-worm was lodged in her heart, and preyed on her health. She denied herself every little comfort; things that would be no sacrifice when a person is well, are absolutely necessary to alleviate bodily pain, and support the animal functions.

There were many elegant amusements, that she had acquired a relish for, which might have taken her mind off from its most destructive bent; but these her indigence would not allow her to enjoy: forced then, by way of relaxation, to play the tunes her lover admired, and handle the pencil he taught her to hold, no wonder his image floated on her imagination, and that taste invigorated love.

Poverty, and all its inelegant attendants, were in her mother's abode; and she, though a good sort of a woman, was not calculated to banish, by her trivial, uninteresting chat, the delirium in which her daughter was lost.

This ill-fated love[1] had given a bewitching softness to her manners, a delicacy so truly feminine, that a man of any feeling could not behold her without wishing to chase her sorrows away. She was timid and irresolute, and rather fond of dissipation; grief only had power to make her reflect.

In every thing it was not the great, but the beautiful, or the pretty, that caught her attention. And in composition, the polish of style, and harmony of numbers, interested her much more than the flights of genius, or abstracted speculations.[2]

She often wondered at the books Mary chose, who, though she had a lively imagination, would frequently study authors whose works were addressed to the understanding. This liking taught her to arrange her thoughts, and argue with herself, even when under the influence of the most violent passions.

Ann's misfortunes and ill health were strong ties to bind Mary to her; she wished so continually to have a home to receive her in, that it drove every other desire out of her mind;

and, dwelling on the tender schemes which compassion and friendship dictated, she longed most ardently to put them in practice.

Fondly as she loved her friend, she did not forget her mother, whose decline was so imperceptible, that they were not aware of her approaching dissolution. The physician, however, observing the most alarming symptoms; her husband was apprised of her immediate danger; and then first mentioned to her his designs with respect to his daughter.

She approved of them; Mary was sent for; she was not at home; she had rambled to visit Ann, and found her in an hysteric fit. The landlord of her little farm had sent his agent for the rent, which had long been due to him; and he threatened to seize the stock that still remained, and turn them out, if they did not very shortly discharge the arrears.

As this man made a private fortune by harassing the tenants of the person to whom he was deputy, little was to be expected from his forbearance.

All this was told to Mary—and the mother added, she had many other creditors who would, in all probability, take the alarm, and snatch from them all that had been saved out of the wreck. 'I could bear all,' she cried; 'but what will become of my children? Of this child,' pointing to the fainting Ann, 'whose constitution is already undermined by care and grief—where will she go?'—Mary's heart ceased to beat while she asked the question—She attempted to speak; but the inarticulate sounds died away. Before she had recovered herself, her father called himself to enquire for her; and desired her instantly to accompany him home.

Engrossed by the scene of misery she had been witness to, she walked silently by his side, when he roused her out of her reverie by telling her that in all likelihood her mother had not many hours to live; and before she could return him any answer, informed her that they had both determined to marry her to Charles, his friend's son; he added, the ceremony was to be performed directly, that her mother might be witness of it; for such a desire she had expressed with childish eagerness.

Overwhelmed by this intelligence, Mary rolled her eyes about, then, with a vacant stare, fixed them on her father's face; but they were no longer a sense; they conveyed no ideas to the brain.[1] As she drew near the house, her wonted presence of mind returned: after this suspension of thought, a thousand darted into her mind,—her dying mother,—her friend's miserable situation,—and an extreme horror at taking—at being forced to take, such a hasty step; but she did not feel the disgust, the reluctance, which arises from a prior attachment.

She loved Ann better than any one in the world—to snatch her from the very jaws of destruction—she would have encountered a lion. To have this friend constantly with her; to make her mind easy with respect to her family, would it not be superlative bliss?

Full of these thoughts she entered her mother's chamber, but they then fled at the sight of a dying parent. She went to her, took her hand; it feebly pressed her's. 'My child,' said the languid mother: the words reached her heart; she had seldom heard them pronounced with accents denoting affection; 'My child, I have not always treated you with kindness—God forgive me! do you?'—Mary's tears strayed in a disregarded stream; on her bosom the big drops fell, but did not relieve the fluttering tenant. 'I forgive you!' said she, in a tone of astonishment.

The clergyman came in to read the service for the sick, and afterwards the marriage ceremony was performed. Mary stood like a statue of Despair,[2] and pronounced the awful vow without thinking of it; and then ran to support her mother, who expired the same night in her arms.

Her husband set off for the continent the same day,[3] with a tutor, to finish his studies at one of the foreign universities.

Ann was sent for to console her, not on account of the departure of her new relation, a boy she seldom took any notice of, but to reconcile her to her fate; besides, it was necessary she should have a female companion, and there was not any maiden aunt in the family, or cousin[4] of the same class.

CHAPTER SIX

MARY was allowed to pay the rent which gave her so much uneasiness, and she exerted every nerve to prevail on her father effectually to succour the family; but the utmost she could obtain was a small sum very inadequate to the purpose, to enable the poor woman to carry into execution a little scheme of industry near the metropolis.

Her intention of leaving that part of the country, had much more weight with him, than Mary's arguments, drawn from motives of philanthropy and friendship; this was a language he did not understand, expressive of occult qualities he never thought of, as they could not be seen or felt.

After the departure of her mother, Ann still continued to languish, though she had a nurse who was entirely engrossed by the desire of amusing her. Had her health been re-established, the time would have passed in a tranquil, improving manner.

During the year of mourning they lived in retirement; music, drawing, and reading, filled up the time; and Mary's taste and judgment were both improved by contracting a habit of observation, and permitting the simple beauties of Nature to occupy her thoughts.

She had a wonderful quickness in discerning distinctions and combining ideas, that at the first glance did not appear to be similar. But these various pursuits did not banish all her cares, or carry off all her constitutional black bile.[1] Before she enjoyed Ann's society, she imagined it would have made her completely happy: she was disappointed, and yet knew not what to complain of.

As her friend could not accompany her in her walks, and wished to be alone, for a very obvious reason, she would return to her old haunts, retrace her anticipated pleasures—and wonder how they changed their colour in possession, and proved so futile.

She had not yet found the companion she looked for. Ann and she were not congenial minds, nor did she contribute to her comfort in the degree she expected. She shielded her from poverty; but this was only a negative blessing; when under the pressure it was very grievous, and still more so were the apprehensions; but when exempt from them, she was not contented.

Such is human nature, its laws were not to be inverted to gratify our heroine, and stop the progress of her understanding, happiness only flourished in paradise—we cannot taste and live.

Another year passed away with increasing apprehensions. Ann had a hectic cough, and many unfavourable prognostics: Mary then forgot every thing but the fear of losing her, and even imagined that her recovery would have made her happy.

Her anxiety led her to study physic,[1] and for some time she only read books of that cast; and this knowledge, literally speaking, ended in vanity and vexation of spirit, as it enabled her to foresee what she could not prevent.

As her mind expanded, her marriage appeared a dreadful misfortune; she was sometimes reminded of the heavy yoke, and bitter was the recollection.

In one thing there seemed to be a sympathy between them, for she wrote formal answers to his as formal letters. An extreme dislike took root in her mind; the sound of his name made her turn sick; but she forgot all, listening to Ann's cough, and supporting her languid frame. She would then catch her to her bosom with convulsive eagerness, as if to save her from sinking into an opening grave.

CHAPTER SEVEN

I T was the will of Providence that Mary should experience almost every species of sorrow. Her father was thrown from his horse, when his blood was in a very inflammatory state, and as the bruises were very dangerous, his recovery was not expected by the physical tribe.[1]

Terrified of seeing him so near death, and yet so ill prepared for it, his daughter sat by his bed, oppressed by the keenest anguish, which her piety increased.

Her grief had nothing selfish in it; he was not a friend or protector; but he was her father, an unhappy wretch, going into eternity, depraved and thoughtless. Could a life of sensuality be a preparation for a peaceful death? Thus meditating, she passed the still midnight hour by his bedside.

The nurse fell asleep, nor did a violent thunder storm interrupt her repose, though it made the night appear still more terrific to Mary. Her father's unequal breathing alarmed her, when she heard a long drawn breath, she feared it was his last, and watching for another, a dreadful peal of thunder struck her ears. Considering the separation of the soul and body, this night seemed sadly solemn, and the hours long.

Death is indeed a king of terrors when he attacks the vicious man! The compassionate heart finds not any comfort; but dreads an eternal separation. No transporting greetings are anticipated, when the survivors also shall have finished their course; but all is black!—the grave may truly be said to receive the departed—this is the sting of death!

Night after night Mary watched, and this excessive fatigue impaired her own health, but had a worse effect on Ann; though she constantly went to bed, she could not rest; a number of uneasy thoughts obtruded themselves; and apprehensions about Mary, whom she loved as well as her exhausted heart could love, harassed her mind. After a sleepless, feverish night she had a violent fit of coughing, and burst a blood-vessel. The physician, who was in the house, was sent for, and when he left the patient, Mary, with an authoritative voice, insisted on knowing his real opinion. Reluctantly he gave it, that her friend was in a critical state; and if she passed the approaching winter in England, he imagined she would die in the spring; a season fatal to consumptive disorders. The spring!—Her husband was then expected.——Gracious Heaven, could she bear all this.

In a few days her father breathed his last. The horrid sensations his death occasioned were too poignant to be durable: and Ann's danger, and her own situation, made Mary deliberate what mode of conduct she should pursue. She feared this event might hasten the return of her husband, and prevent her putting into execution a plan she had determined on. It was to accompany Ann to a more salubrious climate.

Favorable to health

CHAPTER EIGHT

I MENTIONED before, that Mary had never had any particular attachment, to give rise to the disgust that daily gained ground. Her friendship for Ann occupied her heart, and resembled a passion. She had had, indeed, several transient likings;[1] but they did not amount to love. The society of men of genius delighted her, and improved her faculties. With beings of this class she did not often meet; it is a rare genus; her first favourites were men past the meridian of life, and of a philosophic turn.[2]

Determined on going to the South of France, or Lisbon; she wrote to the man she had promised to obey. The physicians had said change of air was necessary for her as well as her friend. She mentioned this, and added, 'Her comfort, almost her existence, depended on the recovery of the invalid she wished to attend; and that should she neglect to follow the medical advice she had received, she should never forgive herself, or those who endeavoured to prevent her.' Full of her design, she wrote with more than usual freedom; and this letter was like most of her others, a transcript of her heart.

'This dear friend,' she exclaimed, 'I love for her agreeable qualities, and substantial virtues. Continual attention to her health, and the tender office of a nurse, have created an affection very like a maternal one—I am her only support, she leans on me—could I forsake the forsaken, and break the bruised reed—No—I would die first! I must—I will go.'

She would have added, 'you would very much oblige me by consenting;' but her heart revolted—and irresolutely she wrote something about wishing him happy.—'Do I not wish all the world well?' she cried, as she subscribed her name—It was blotted, the letter sealed in a hurry, and sent out of her sight; and she began to prepare for her journey.

By the return of the post she received an answer; it contained some commonplace remarks on her romantic[1] friendship, as he termed it; 'But as the physicians advised change of air, he had no objection.'

CHAPTER NINE

THERE was nothing now to retard their journey; and Mary chose Lisbon rather than France, on account of its being further removed from the only person she wished not to see.

They set off accordingly for Falmouth, in their way to that city. The journey was of use to Ann, and Mary's spirits were raised by her recovered looks—She had been in despair—now she gave way to hope, and was intoxicated with it. On ship-board Ann always remained in the cabin; the sight of the water terrified her: on the contrary, Mary, after she was gone to bed, or when she fell asleep in the day, went on deck, conversed with the sailors, and surveyed the boundless expanse before her with delight. One instant she would regard the ocean, the next the beings who braved its fury. Their insensibility and want of fear, she could not name courage; their thoughtless mirth was quite of an animal kind, and their feelings as impetuous and uncertain as the element they plowed.

They had only been a week at sea when they hailed the rock of Lisbon, and the next morning anchored at the castle. After the customary visits, they were permitted to go on shore, about three miles from the city; and while one of the crew,

who understood the language, went to procure them one of
the ugly carriages peculiar to the country, they waited in the
Irish convent, which is situated close to the Tagus.

Some of the people offered to conduct them into the
church, where there was a fine organ playing; Mary followed
them, but Ann preferred staying with a nun she had entered
into conversation with.

One of the nuns, who had a sweet voice, was singing; Mary
was struck with awe; her heart joined in the devotion; and
tears of gratitude and tenderness flowed from her eyes. My
Father, I thank thee! burst from her—words were inadequate
to express her feelings. Silently, she surveyed the lofty dome;
heard unaccustomed sounds; and saw faces, strange ones, that
she could not yet greet with fraternal love.

In an unknown land, she considered that the Being she
adored inhabited eternity, was ever present in unnumbered
worlds. [1](When she had not any one she loved near her, she
was particularly sensible of the presence of her Almighty
Friend.)

The arrival of the carriage put a stop to her speculations; it
was to conduct them to an hotel, fitted up for the reception of
invalids. Unfortunately, before they could reach it there was a
violent shower of rain; and as the wind was very high, it beat
against the leather curtains, which they drew along the front
of the vehicle, to shelter themselves from it; but it availed not,
some of the rain forced its way, and Ann felt the effects of it,
for she caught cold, spite of Mary's precautions.

As is the custom, the rest of the invalids, or lodgers, sent to
enquire after their health; and as soon as Ann left her
chamber, in which her complaints seldom confined her the
whole day, they came in person to pay their compliments.
Three fashionable females, and two gentlemen; the one a
brother of the eldest of the young ladies, and the other an
invalid, who came, like themselves, for the benefit of the air.
They entered into conversation immediately.

People who meet in a strange country, and are all together
in a house, soon get acquainted, without the formalities which

attend visiting in separate houses, where they are surrounded by domestic friends. Ann was particularly delighted at meeting with agreeable society; a little hectic fever generally made her low-spirited in the morning, and lively in the evening, when she wished for company. Mary, who only thought of her, determined to cultivate their acquaintance, as she knew, that if her mind could be diverted, her body might gain strength.

They were all musical, and proposed having little concerts. One of the gentlemen played on the violin, and the other on the german-flute.[1] The instruments were brought in, with all the eagerness that attends putting a new scheme in execution.

Mary had not said much, for she was diffident; she seldom joined in general conversations; though her quickness of penetration enabled her soon to enter into the characters of those she conversed with; and her sensibility made her desirous of pleasing every human creature. Besides, if her mind was not occupied by any particular sorrow, or study, she caught reflected pleasure, and was glad to see others happy, though their mirth did not interest her.

This day she was continually thinking of Ann's recovery, and encouraging the cheerful hopes, which though they dissipated the spirits that had been condensed by melancholy, yet made her wish to be silent. The music, more than the conversation, disturbed her reflections; but not at first. The gentleman who played on the german-flute, was a handsome, well-bred, sensible man; and his observations, if not original, were pertinent.

The other, who had not said much, began to touch the violin,[2] and played a little Scotch ballad; he brought such a thrilling sound out of the instrument, that Mary started, and looking at him with more attention than she had done before, and saw, in a face rather ugly, strong lines of genius.[3] His manners were awkward, that kind of awkwardness which is often found in literary men: he seemed a thinker, and delivered his opinions in elegant expressions, and musical tones of voice.

When the concert was over, they all retired to their apartments. Mary always slept with Ann, as she was subject to terrifying dreams; and frequently in the night was obliged to be supported, to avoid suffocation. They chatted about their new acquaintance in their own apartment, and, with respect to the gentlemen, differed in opinion.

CHAPTER TEN

EVERY day almost they saw their new acquaintance; and civility produced intimacy. Mary sometimes left her friend with them; while she indulged herself in viewing new modes of life, and searching out the causes which produced them. She had a metaphysical turn, which inclined her to reflect on every object that passed by her; and her mind was not like a mirror, which receives every floating image, but does not retain them: she had not any prejudices, for every opinion was examined before it was adopted.

The Roman Catholic ceremonies attracted her attention, and gave rise to conversations when they all met; and one of the gentlemen continually introduced deistical notions, when he ridiculed the pageantry they all were surprised at observing. Mary thought of both the subjects, the Romish tenets, and the deistical doubts; and though not a sceptic, thought it right to examine the evidence on which her faith was built. She read Butler's Analogy,[1] and some other authors: and these researches made her a christian from conviction, and she learned charity, particularly with respect to sectaries; saw that apparently good and solid arguments might take their rise from different points of view; and she rejoiced to find that those she should not concur with had some reason on their side.[2]

When I mentioned the three ladies, I said they were fashionable women; and it was all the praise, as a faithful historian, I could bestow on them; the only thing in which they were consistent. I forgot to mention that they were all of one family, a mother, her daughter, and niece. The daughter was sent by her physician, to avoid a northerly winter; the mother, her niece, and nephew, accompanied her.

They were people of rank;[1] but unfortunately, though of an ancient family, the title had descended to a very remote branch—a branch they took care to be intimate with; and servilely copied the Countess's airs. Their minds were shackled with a set of notions concerning propriety, the fitness of things for the world's eye, trammels which always hamper weak people. What will the world say? was the first thing that was thought of, when they intended doing any thing they had not done before. Or what would the Countess do on such an occasion? And when this question was answered, the right or wrong was discovered without the trouble of their having any idea of the matter in their own heads. This same Countess was a fine planet, and the satellites observed a most harmonic dance around her.

After this account it is scarcely necessary to add, that their minds had received very little cultivation. They were taught French, Italian, and Spanish; English was their vulgar tongue. And what did they learn? Hamlet will tell you—words—words. But let me not forget that they squalled Italian songs in the true *gusto*.[2] Without having any seeds sown in their understanding, or the affections of the heart set to work, they were brought out of their nursery, or the place they were secluded in, to prevent their faces being common: like blazing stars, to captivate Lords.

They were pretty, and hurrying from one party of pleasure to another, occasioned the disorder which required change of air. The mother, if we except her being near twenty years

older, was just the same creature; and these additional years
only served to make her more tenaciously adhere to her habits
of folly, and decide with stupid gravity, some trivial points of
ceremony, as a matter of the last importance; of which she was
a competent judge, from having lived in the fashionable world
so long: that world to which the ignorant look up as we do to
the sun.

It appears to me that every creature has some notion—or
rather relish, of the sublime. Riches, and the consequent state,
are the sublime of weak minds:—These images fill, nay, are
too big for their narrow souls.

One afternoon, which they had engaged to spend together,
Ann was so ill, that Mary was obliged to send an apology for
not attending the tea-table. The apology brought them on the
carpet; and the mother, with a look of solemn importance,
turned to the sick man, whose name was Henry, and said;
'Though people of the first fashion are frequently at places of
this kind, intimate with they know not who; yet I do not
choose that my daughter, whose family is so respectable,
should be intimate with any one she would blush to know
elsewhere. It is only on that account, for I never suffer her to
be with any one but in my company,' added she, sitting more
erect; and a smile of self-complacency dressed her
countenance.

'I have enquired concerning these strangers, and find that
the one who has the most dignity in her manners, is really a
woman of fortune.' 'Lord, mamma, how ill she dresses:'
mamma went on; 'She is a romantic creature, you must not
copy her, miss; yet she is an heiress of the large fortune in
————shire, of which you may remember to have heard the
Countess speak the night you had on the dancing-dress that
was so much admired; but she is married.'

She then told them the whole story as she heard it from her
maid, who picked it out of Mary's servant. 'She is a foolish
creature, and this friend that she pays as much attention to as
if she was a lady of quality, is a beggar.' 'Well, how strange!'
cried the girls.

'She is, however, a charming creature,' said her nephew. Henry sighed, and strode across the room once or twice; then took up his violin, and played the air which first struck Mary; he had often heard her praise it.

The music was uncommonly melodious, 'And came stealing on the senses like the sweet south.'[1] The well-known sounds reached Mary as she sat by her friend—she listened without knowing that she did—and shed tears almost without being conscious of it. Ann soon fell asleep, as she had taken an opiate. Mary, then brooding over her fears, began to imagine she had deceived herself—Ann was still very ill; hope had beguiled many heavy hours; yet she was displeased with herself for admitting this welcome guest.—And she worked up her mind to such a degree of anxiety, that she determined, once more, to seek medical aid.

No sooner did she determine, than she ran down with a discomposed look, to enquire of the ladies who she should send for. When she entered the room she could not articulate her fears—it appeared like pronouncing Ann's sentence of death; her faultering tongue dropped some broken words, and she remained silent. The ladies wondered that a person of her sense should be so little mistress of herself; and began to administer some common-place comfort, as, that it was our duty to submit to the will of Heaven, and the like trite consolations, which Mary did not answer; but waving her hand, with an air of impatience, she exclaimed, 'I cannot live without her!—I have no other friend; if I lose her, what a desart will the world be to me.' 'No other friend,' re-echoed they, 'have you not a husband?'

Mary shrunk back, and was alternately pale and red. A delicate sense of propriety prevented her replying; and recalled her bewildered reason.—Assuming, in consequence of her recollection, a more composed manner, she made the intended enquiry, and left the room. Henry's eyes followed her while the females very freely animadverted on her strange behaviour.

CHAPTER TWELVE

THE physician was sent for; his prescription afforded Ann a little temporary relief; and they again joined the circle. Unfortunately, the weather happened to be constantly wet for more than a week, and confined them to the house. Ann then found the ladies not so agreeable; when they sat whole hours together, the thread-bare topics were exhausted; and, but for cards or music, the long evenings would have been yawned away in listless indolence.

The bad weather had had as ill an effect on Henry as on Ann. He was frequently very thoughtful, or rather melancholy; this melancholy would of itself have attracted Mary's notice, if she had not found his conversation so infinitely superior to the rest of the group. When she conversed with him, all the faculties of her soul unfolded themselves; genius animated her expressive countenance; and the most graceful, unaffected gestures gave energy to her discourse.

They frequently discussed very important subjects, while the rest were singing or playing cards, nor were they observed for doing so, as Henry, whom they all were pleased with, in the way of gallantry shewed them all more attention than her. Besides, as there was nothing alluring in her dress[1] or manner, they never dreamt of her being preferred to them.

Henry was a man of learning; he had also studied mankind, and knew many of the intricacies of the human heart, from having felt the infirmities of his own. His taste was just, as it had a standard—Nature, which he observed with a critical eye. Mary could not help thinking that in his company her mind expanded, as he always went below the surface. She increased her stock of ideas, and her taste was improved.

He was also a pious man; his rational religious sentiments received warmth from his sensibility; and, except on very particular occasions, kept it in proper bounds; these sentiments had likewise formed his temper; he was gentle, and easily to be intreated. The ridiculous ceremonies they were every day witness to, led them into what are termed grave subjects, and made him explain his opinions, which, at other times, he was neither ashamed of, nor unnecessarily brought forward to notice.

CHAPTER THIRTEEN

WHEN the weather began to clear up, Mary sometimes rode out alone, purposely to view the ruins that still remained of the earthquake:[1] or she would ride to the banks of the Tagus, to feast her eyes with the sight of that magnificent river. At other times she would visit the churches, as she was particularly fond of seeing historical paintings.

One of these visits gave rise to the subject, and the whole party descanted on it; but as the ladies could not handle it well, they soon adverted to portraits;[2] and talked of the attitudes and characters in which they should wish to be drawn. Mary did not fix on one—when Henry, with more apparent warmth than usual, said, 'I would give the world for your picture, with the expression I have seen in your face, when you have been supporting your friend.'

This delicate compliment did not gratify her vanity, but it reached her heart. She then recollected that she had once sat for her picture—for whom was it designed? For a boy! Her cheeks flushed with indignation, so strongly did she feel an emotion of contempt at having been thrown away—given in with an estate.

As Mary again gave way to hope, her mind was more disengaged; and her thoughts were employed about the objects around her.

She visited several convents, and found that solitude only eradicates some passions, to give strength to others; the most baneful ones. She saw that religion does not consist in ceremonies; and that many prayers may fall from the lips without purifying the heart.[1]

They who imagine they can be religious without governing their tempers, or exercising benevolence in its most extensive sense, must certainly allow, that their religious duties are only practised from selfish principles; how then can they be called good?[2] The pattern of all goodness went about *doing* good. Wrapped up in themselves, the nuns only thought of inferior gratifications. And a number of intrigues were carried on to accelerate certain points on which their hearts were fixed:

Such as obtaining offices of trust or authority; or avoiding those that were servile or laborious. In short, when they could be neither wives nor mothers, they aimed at being superiors, and became the most selfish creatures in the world: the passions that were curbed gave strength to the appetites, or to those mean passions which only tend to provide for the gratification of them. Was this seclusion from the world? or did they conquer its vanities or avoid its vexations?

In these abodes the unhappy individual, who, in the first paroxysm of grief, flies to them for refuge, finds too late she took a wrong step. The same warmth which determined her will make her repent; and sorrow, the rust of the mind, will never have a chance of being rubbed off by sensible conversation, or new-born affections of the heart.

She will find that those affections that have once been called forth and strengthened by exercise, are only smothered, not killed, by disappointment; and that in one form or other discontent will corrode the heart, and produce those maladies of the imagination, for which there is no specific.

The community at large Mary disliked; but pitied many of them whose private distresses she was informed of; and to pity and relieve were the same things with her.

The exercise of her various virtues gave vigor to her genius,[3] and dignity to her mind; she was sometimes inconsiderate, and violent; but never mean or cunning.

CHAPTER FOURTEEN

THE Portuguese are certainly the most uncivilized nation in Europe. Dr. Johnson would have said, 'They have the least mind.'[1] And can such serve their Creator in spirit and in truth? No, the gross ritual of Romish ceremonies is all they can comprehend: they can do penance, but not conquer their revenge, or lust. Religion, or love, has never humanized their hearts; they want the vital part; the mere body worships. Taste is unknown; Gothic finery, and unnatural decorations, which they term ornaments, are conspicuous in their churches and dress. Reverence for mental excellence is only to be found in a polished nation.

Could the contemplation of such a people gratify Mary's heart? No: she turned disgusted from the prospects—turned to a man of refinement. Henry had been some time ill and low-spirited; Mary would have been attentive to any one in that situation; but to him she was particularly so; she thought herself bound in gratitude, on account of his constant endeavours to amuse Ann, and prevent her dwelling on the dreary prospect before her, which sometimes she could not help anticipating with a kind of quiet despair.

She found some excuse for going more frequently into the room they all met in; nay, she avowed her desire to amuse him: offered to read to him, and tried to draw him into amusing conversations; and when she was full of these little schemes, she looked at him with a degree of tenderness that she was not conscious of. This divided attention was of use to her, and prevented her continually thinking of Ann, whose fluctuating disorder often gave rise to false hopes.

A trifling thing occurred now which occasioned Mary some uneasiness. Her maid, a well-looking girl, had captivated the clerk of a neighbouring compting-house. As the match was an advantageous one, Mary could not raise any objection to it, though at this juncture it was very disagreeable to her to have a stranger about her person. However, the girl consented to delay the marriage, as she had some affection for her mistress; and, besides, looked forward to Ann's death as a time of harvest.

Henry's illness was not alarming, it was rather pleasing, as it gave Mary an excuse to herself for shewing him how much she was interested about him; and giving little artless proofs of affection, which the purity of her heart made her never wish to restrain.

The only visible return he made was not obvious to common observers. He would sometimes fix his eyes on her, and take them off with a sigh that was coughed away; or when he was leisurely walking into the room, and did not expect to see her, he would quicken his steps, and come up to her with eagerness to ask some trivial question. In the same style, he would try to detain her when he had nothing to say—or said nothing.

Ann did not take notice of either his or Mary's behaviour, nor did she suspect that he was a favourite, on any other account than his appearing neither well nor happy. She had often seen that when a person was unfortunate, Mary's pity[1] might easily be mistaken for love, and, indeed, it was a temporary sensation of that kind. Such it was—why it was so, let others define, I cannot argue against instincts. As reason is cultivated in man, they are supposed to grow weaker, and this may have given rise to the assertion, 'That as judgment improves, genius evaporates.'[2]

CHAPTER FIFTEEN

ONE morning they set out to visit the aqueduct; though the day was very fine when they left home, a very heavy shower fell before they reached it; they lengthened their ride, the clouds dispersed, and the sun came from behind them uncommonly bright.

Mary would fain have persuaded Ann not to have left the carriage; but she was in spirits, and obviated all her objections, and insisted on walking, tho' the ground was damp. But her strength was not equal to her spirits; she was soon obliged to return to the carriage so much fatigued, that she fainted, and remained insensible a long time.

Henry would have supported her; but Mary would not permit him; her recollection was instantaneous, and she feared sitting on the damp ground might do him a material injury: she was on that account positive, though the company did not guess the cause of her being so. As to herself, she did not fear bodily pain; and, when her mind was agitated, she could endure the greatest fatigue without appearing sensible of it.

When Ann recovered, they returned slowly home; she was carried to bed, and the next morning Mary thought she observed a visible change for the worse. The physician was sent for, who pronounced her to be in the most imminent danger.

All Mary's former fears now returned like a torrent, and carried every other care away; she even added to her present anguish by upbraiding herself for her late tranquillity—it haunted her in the form of a crime.

The disorder made the most rapid advances—there was no hope!—Bereft of it, Mary again was tranquil; but it was a very different kind of tranquillity. She stood to brave the approaching storm, conscious she only could be overwhelmed by it.

She did not think of Henry, or if her thoughts glanced towards him, it was only to find fault with herself for suffering a thought to have strayed from Ann.—Ann!—this dear friend was soon torn from her—she died suddenly as Mary was assisting her to walk across the room.—The first string was severed from her heart—and this 'slow, sudden-death'[1] disturbed her reasoning faculties; she seemed stunned by it; unable to reflect, or even to feel her misery.

The body was stolen out of the house the second night,[2] and

Mary refused to see her former companions. She desired her maid to conclude her marriage, and request her intended husband to inform her when the first merchantman was to leave the port, and she determined not to stay in that hated place any longer than was absolutely necessary.

She then sent to request the ladies to visit her; she wished to avoid a parade of grief—her sorrows were her own, and appeared to her not to admit of increase or softening. She was right; the sight of them did not affect her, or turn the stream of her sullen sorrow; the black wave rolled along in the same course; it was equal to her where she cast her eyes; all was impenetrable gloom.

CHAPTER SIXTEEN

SOON after the ladies left her, she received a message from Henry, requesting, as she saw company, to be permitted to visit her: she consented, and he entered immediately, with an unassured pace. She ran eagerly up to him—saw the tear trembling in his eye, and his countenance softened by the tenderest compassion; the hand which pressed hers seemed that of a fellow-creature. She burst into tears; and, unable to restrain them, she hid her face with both her hands: these tears relieved her, (she had before had a difficulty in breathing,) and she sat down by him more composed than she had appeared since Ann's death; but her conversation was incoherent.

She called herself 'a poor disconsolate creature!'—'Mine is a selfish grief,' she exclaimed—'Yet, Heaven is my witness, I do not wish her back now she has reached those peaceful mansions, where the weary rest. Her pure spirit is happy; but what a wretch am I!'

Henry forgot his cautious reserve. 'Would you allow me to call you friend?' said he in a hesitating voice. 'I feel, dear girl, the tenderest interest in whatever concerns thee.' His eyes spoke the rest. They were both silent a few moments; then Henry resumed the conversation. 'I have also been acquainted with grief! I mourn the loss of a woman who was not worthy of my regard. Let me give thee some account of the man who now solicits thy friendship; and who, from motives of the purest benevolence, wishes to give comfort to thy wounded heart.

'I have myself,' said he, mournfully, 'shaken hands with happiness, and am dead to the world; I wait patiently for my dissolution; but, for thee, Mary, there may be many bright days in store.'

'Impossible,' replied she, in a peevish tone, as if he had insulted her by the supposition; her feelings were so much in unison with his, that she was in love with misery.

He smiled at her impatience, and went on. 'My father died before I knew him, and my mother was so attached to my eldest brother, that she took very little pains to fit me for the profession to which I was destined: and, may I tell thee, I left my family, and, in many different stations, rambled about the world; saw mankind in every rank of life; and, in order to be independent, exerted those talents Nature has given me: these exertions improved my understanding; and the miseries I was witness to, gave a keener edge to my. sensibility. My constitution is naturally weak; and, perhaps, two or three lingering disorders in my youth, first gave me a habit of reflecting, and enabled me to obtain some dominion over my passions. At least,' added he, stifling a sigh, 'over the violent ones, though I fear, refinement and reflection only renders the tender ones more tyrannic.

'I have told you already I have been in love, and disappointed—the object is now no more; let her faults sleep with her! Yet this passion has pervaded my whole soul, and mixed itself with all my affections and pursuits.—I am not peacefully indifferent; yet it is only to my violin I tell the sorrows I now confide with thee. The object I loved forfeited my esteem; yet, true to the sentiment, my fancy has too frequently delighted to form a creature that I could love, that could convey to my soul sensations which the gross part of mankind have not any conception of.'

He stopped, as Mary seemed lost in thought; but as she was still in a listening attitude, continued his little narrative. 'I kept up an irregular correspondence with my mother; my brother's extravagance and ingratitude had almost broken her heart, and made her feel something like a pang of remorse, on account of her behaviour to me. I hastened to comfort her—and was a comfort to her.

'My declining health prevented my taking orders, as I had intended; but I with warmth entered into literary pursuits; perhaps my heart, not having an object, made me embrace the substitute with more eagerness. But, do not imagine I have always been a die-away swain. No: I have frequented the cheerful haunts of men, and wit!—enchanting wit! has made many moments fly free from care. I am too fond of the elegant arts; and woman—lovely woman! thou hast charmed me, though, perhaps, it would not be easy to find one to whom my reason would allow me to be constant.

'I have now only to tell you, that my mother insisted on my spending this winter in a warmer climate; and I fixed on Lisbon, as I had before visited the Continent.' He then looked Mary full in the face; and, with the most insinuating accents, asked 'if he might hope for her friendship? If she would rely on him as if he was her father; and that the tenderest father could not more anxiously interest himself in the fate of a darling child, than he did in her's.'

Such a crowd of thoughts all at once rushed into Mary's mind, that she in vain attempted to express the sentiments which were most predominant. Her heart longed to receive a new guest; there was a void in it: accustomed to have some one to love, she was alone, and comfortless, if not engrossed by a particular affection.

Henry saw her distress, and not to increase it, left the room. He had exerted himself to turn her thoughts into a new channel, and had succeeded; she thought of him till she began to chide herself for defrauding the dead, and, determining to grieve for Ann, she dwelt on Henry's misfortunes and ill health; and the interest he took in her fate was a balm to her sick mind. She did not reason on the subject; but she felt he was attached to her: lost in this delirium, she never asked herself what kind of an affection she had for him, or what it tended to; nor did she know that love and friendship are very distinct; she thought with rapture, that there was one person in the world who had an affection for her, and that person she admired—had a friendship for.

He had called her his dear girl; the words might have fallen from him by accident; but they did not fall to the ground. My child! His child, what an association of ideas![1] If I had had a father, such a father!—She could not dwell on the thoughts, the wishes which obtruded themselves. Her mind was unhinged, and passion unperceived filled her whole soul. Lost, in waking dreams, she considered and reconsidered Henry's account of himself; till she actually thought she would tell Ann—a bitter recollection then roused her out of her reverie; and aloud she begged forgiveness of her.

By these kind of conflicts the day was lengthened; and when she went to bed, the night passed away in feverish slumbers; though they did not refresh her, she was spared the labour of thinking, of restraining her imagination; it sported uncontrouled; but took its colour from her waking train of thoughts. One instant she was supporting her dying mother; then Ann was breathing her last, and Henry was comforting her.

The unwelcome light visited her languid eyes; yet, I must tell the truth, she thought she should see Henry, and this hope set her spirits in motion: but they were quickly depressed by her maid, who came to tell her that she had heard of a vessel on board of which she could be accommodated, and that there was to be another female passenger on board, a vulgar[2] one; but perhaps she would be more useful on that account—Mary did not want a companion.

As she had given orders for her passage to be engaged in the first vessel that sailed, she could not now retract; and must prepare for the lonely voyage, as the Captain intended taking advantage of the first fair wind. She had too much strength of mind to waver in her determination; but to determine wrung her very heart, opened all her old wounds, and made them bleed afresh. What was she to do? where go? Could she set a seal to a hasty vow, and tell a deliberate lie; promise to love one man, when the image of another was ever present to her—her soul revolted. 'I might gain the applause of the world by such mock heroism; but should I not forfeit my own? forfeit thine, my father!'

There is a solemnity in the shortest ejaculation, which, for a while, stills the tumult of passion. Mary's mind had been thrown off its poise; her devotion had been, perhaps, more fervent for some time past; but less regular. She forgot that happiness was not to be found on earth, and built a terrestrial paradise liable to be destroyed by the first serious thought: when she reasoned she became inexpressibly sad, to render life bearable she gave way to fancy—this was madness.

In a few days she must again go to sea; the weather was very tempestuous—what of that, the tempest¹ in her soul rendered every other trifling—it was not the contending elements, but *herself* she feared!

CHAPTER SEVENTEEN

IN order to gain strength to support the expected interview, she went out in a carriage. The day was fine; but all nature was to her a universal blank; she could neither enjoy it, nor weep that she could not. She passed by the ruins of an old monastery on a very high hill; she got out to walk amongst the ruins; the wind blew violently, she did not avoid its fury, on the contrary, wildly bid it blow on, and seemed glad to contend with it, or rather walk against it. Exhausted, she returned to the carriage, was soon at home, and in the old room.

Henry started at the sight of her altered appearance; the day before her complexion had been of the most pallid hue; but now her cheeks were flushed, and her eyes enlivened with a false vivacity, an unusual fire. He was not well, his illness was apparent in his countenance, and he owned he had not closed his eyes all night; this roused her dormant tenderness, she forgot they were so soon to part—engrossed by the present happiness of seeing, of hearing him.

Once or twice she essayed to tell him that she was, in a few days, to depart; but she could not; she was irresolute; it will do to-morrow; should the wind change they could not sail in such a hurry; thus she thought, and insensibly grew more calm. The ladies prevailed on her to spend the evening with them; but she retired very early to rest, and sat on the side of her bed several hours, then threw herself on it, and waited for the dreaded to-morrow.

CHAPTER EIGHTEEN

THE ladies heard that her servant was to be married that day, and that she was to sail in the vessel which was then clearing out at the Custom-house. Henry heard, but did not make any remarks; and Mary called up all her fortitude to support her, and enable her to hide from the females her internal struggles. She durst not encounter Henry's glances when she found he had been informed of her intention; and, trying to draw a veil over her wretched state of mind, she talked incessantly, she knew not what; flashes of wit burst from her, and when she began to laugh she could not stop herself.

Henry smiled at some of her sallies, and looked at her with such benignity and compassion, that he recalled her scattered thoughts; and, the ladies going to dress for dinner, they were left alone; and remained silent a few moments: after the noisy conversation it appeared solemn. Henry began. 'You are going, Mary, and going by yourself; your mind is not in a state to be left to its own operations—yet I cannot, dissuade you; if I attempted to do it, I should ill deserve the title I wish to merit. I only think of your happiness; could I obey the strongest impulse of my heart, I should accompany thee to England; but such a step might endanger your future peace.'

Mary, then, with all the frankness which marked her character, explained her situation to him, and mentioned her fatal tie with such disgust that he trembled for her. 'I cannot see him; he is not the man formed for me to love!' Her delicacy[1] did not restrain her, for her dislike to her husband had taken root in her mind long before she knew Henry. Did she not fix on Lisbon rather than France on purpose to avoid him? and if Ann had been in tolerable health she would have flown with her to some remote corner to have escaped from him.

'I intend,' said Henry, 'to follow you in the next packet; where shall I hear of your health?' 'Oh! let me hear of thine,' replied Mary. 'I am well, very well; but thou art very ill—thy health is in the most precarious state.' She then mentioned her intention of going to Ann's relations. 'I am her representative, I have duties to fulfil for her: during my voyage I shall have time enough for reflection; though I think I have already determined.'

'Be not too hasty, my child,' interrupted Henry; 'far be it from me to persuade thee to do violence to thy feelings—but consider that all thy future life may probably take its colour from thy present mode of conduct. Our affections as well as our sentiments are fluctuating; you will not perhaps always either think or feel as you do at present: the object you now shun may appear in a different light.' He paused. 'In advising thee in this style, I have only thy good at heart, Mary.'

She only answered to expostulate. 'My affections are involuntary—yet they can only be fixed by reflection, and when they are they make quite a part of my soul, are interwoven in it, animate my actions, and form my taste: certain qualities are calculated to call forth my sympathies, and make me all I am capable of being. The governing

affection gives its stamp to the rest—because I am capable of
loving one, I have that kind of charity to all my fellow-
creatures which is not easily provoked. Milton has asserted,
That earthly love is the scale by which to heavenly we may
ascend.'[1]

She went on with eagerness. 'My opinions on some subjects
are not wavering; my pursuit through life has ever been the
same: in solitude were my sentiments formed; they are
indelible, and nothing can efface them but death—No, death
itself cannot efface them, or my soul must be created afresh,
and not improved. Yet a little while am I parted from my
Ann—I could not exist without the hope of seeing her again—I
could not bear to think that time could wear away an affection
that was founded on what is not liable to perish; you might as
well attempt to persuade me that my soul is matter, and that
its feelings arose from certain modifications of it.'[2]

'Dear enthusiastic creature,' whispered Henry, 'how you
steal into my soul.' She still continued. 'The same turn of
mind which leads me to adore the Author of all
Perfection—which leads me to conclude that he only can fill
my soul; forces me to admire the faint image—the shadows of
his attributes here below; and my imagination gives still
bolder strokes to them. I know I am in some degree under the
influence of a delusion—but does not this strong delusion
prove that I myself "am *of subtiler essence than the trodden
clod:*"[3] these flights of the imagination point to futurity; I
cannot banish them. Every cause in nature produces an effect;
and am I an exception to the general rule? have I desires
implanted in me only to make me miserable? will they never
be gratified? shall I never be happy? My feelings do not
accord with the notion of solitary happiness. In a state of bliss,
it will be the society of beings we can love, without the alloy
that earthly infirmities mix with our best affections, that will
constitute great part of our happiness.

'With these notions can I conform to the maxims of worldly
wisdom? can I listen to the cold dictates of worldly
prudence,[4] and bid my tumultuous passions cease to vex me,

be still, find content in grovelling pursuits, and the admiration of the misjudging crowd, when it is only one I wish to please—one who could be all the world to me. Argue not with me, I am bound by human ties; but did my spirit ever promise to love, or could I consider when forced to bind myself—to take a vow, that at the awful day of judgment I must give an account of. My conscience does not smite me, and that Being who is greater than the internal monitor, may approve of what the world condemns; sensible that in Him I live, could I brave His presence, or hope in solitude to find peace, if I acted contrary to conviction, that the world might approve of my conduct—what could the world give to compensate for my own esteem? it is ever hostile and armed against the feeling heart!

'Riches and honours await me, and the cold moralist might desire me to sit down and enjoy them—I cannot conquer my feelings, and till I do, what are these baubles to me? you may tell me I follow a fleeting good, an *ignis fatuus*; but this chase, these struggles prepare me for eternity—when I no longer see through a glass darkly I shall not reason about, but *feel* in what happiness consists.'[1]

Henry had not attempted to interrupt her; he saw she was determined, and that these sentiments were not the effusion of the moment, but well digested ones, the result of strong affections, a high sense of honour, and respect for the source of all virtue and truth. He was startled, if not entirely convinced by her arguments; indeed her voice, her gestures were all persuasive.

Some one now entered the room; he looked an answer to her long harangue; it was fortunate for him, or he might have been led to say what in a cooler moment he had determined to conceal; but were words necessary to reveal it? He wished not to influence her conduct—vain precaution; she knew she was beloved; and could she forget that such a man loved her, or rest satisfied with any inferior gratification. When passion first enters the heart, it is only a return of affection that is sought after, and every other remembrance and wish is blotted out.

CHAPTER NINETEEN

Two days passed away without any particular conversation; Henry, trying to be indifferent, or to appear so, was more assiduous than ever. The conflict was too violent for his present state of health; the spirit was willing, but the body suffered; he lost his appetite, and looked wretchedly; his spirits were calmly low—the world seemed to fade away—what was that world to him that Mary did not inhabit; she lived not for him.

He was mistaken; his affection was her only support; without this dear prop she had sunk into the grave of her lost—long-loved friend;——his attention snatched her from despair. Inscrutable are the ways of Heaven!

The third day Mary was desired to prepare herself; for if the wind continued in the same point, they should set sail the next evening. She tried to prepare her mind, and her efforts were not useless; she appeared less agitated than could have been expected, and talked of her voyage with composure. On great occasions she was generally calm and collected, her resolution would brace her unstrung nerves; but after the victory she had no triumph; she would sink into a state of moping melancholy, and feel ten-fold misery when the heroic enthusiasm was over.

The morning of the day fixed on for her departure she was alone with Henry only a few moments, and an awkward kind of formality made them slip away without their having said much to each other. Henry was afraid to discover his passion, or give any other name to his regard but friendship; yet his anxious solicitude for her welfare was ever breaking out—while she as artlessly expressed again and again, her fears with respect to his declining health.

'We shall soon meet,' said he, with a faint smile; Mary smiled too; she caught the sickly beam; it was still fainter by being reflected, and not knowing what she wished to do, started up and left the room. When she was alone she regretted she had left him so precipitately. 'The few precious moments I have thus thrown away may never return,' she thought—the reflection led to misery.

She waited for, nay, almost wished for the summons to depart. She could not avoid spending the intermediate time with the ladies and Henry; and the trivial conversations she was obliged to bear a part in harassed her more than can be well conceived.

The summons came, and the whole party attended her to the vessel. For a while the remembrance of Ann banished her regret at parting with Henry, though his pale figure pressed on her sight; it may seem a paradox, but he was more present to her when she sailed; her tears then were all his own.

'My poor Ann!' thought Mary, 'along this road we came, and near this spot you called me your guardian angel—and now I leave thee here! ah! no, I do not—thy spirit is not confined to its mouldering tenement! Tell me, thou soul of her I love, tell me, ah! whither art thou fled?' Ann occupied her until they reached the ship.

The anchor was weighed. Nothing can be more irksome than waiting to say farewell. As the day was serene, they accompanied her a little way, and then got into the boat; Henry was the last; he pressed her hand, it had not any life in it; she leaned over the side of the ship without looking at the boat, till it was so far distant, that she could not see the countenances of those that were in it: a mist spread itself over her sight—she longed to exchange one look—tried to recollect the last;—the universe contained no being but Henry!—The grief of parting with him had swept all others clean away. Her eyes followed the keel of the boat, and when she could no longer perceive its traces: she looked round on the wide waste of waters, thought of the precious moments which had been stolen from the waste of murdered time.

She then descended into the cabin, regardless of the surrounding beauties of nature, and throwing herself on her bed in the little hole which was called the state-room—she

Romantic love has taken away her love of Nature

wished to forget her existence. On this bed she remained two days, listening to the dashing waves, unable to close her eyes. A small taper made the darkness visible;[1] and the third night, by its glimmering light, she wrote the following fragment.

'Poor solitary wretch that I am; here alone do I listen to the whistling winds and dashing waves;—on no human support can I rest—when not lost to hope I found pleasure in the society of those rough beings; but now they appear not like my fellow creatures; no social ties draw me to them. How long, how dreary has this day been; yet I scarcely wish it over—for what will to-morrow bring—to-morrow, and to-morrow[2] will only be marked with unvaried characters of wretchedness.—Yet surely, I am not alone!'

Her moistened eyes were lifted up to heaven; a crowd of thoughts darted into her mind, and pressing her hand against her forehead, as if to bear the intellectual weight, she tried, but tried in vain, to arrange them. 'Father of Mercies, compose this troubled spirit: do I indeed wish it to be composed—to forget my Henry?' the *my*, the pen was directly drawn across in an agony.

CHAPTER TWENTY

THE mate of the ship, who heard her stir, came to offer her some refreshment; and she, who formerly received every offer of kindness or civility with pleasure, now shrunk away disgusted: peevishly she desired him not to disturb her; but the words were hardly articulated when her heart smote her, she called him back, and requested something to drink. After drinking it, fatigued by her mental exertions, she fell into a death-like slumber, which lasted some hours; but did not refresh her, on the contrary, she awoke languid and stupid.

The wind still continued contrary; a week, a dismal week, had she struggled with her sorrows; and the struggle brought on a slow fever, which sometimes gave her false spirits.

The winds then became very tempestuous, the Great Deep was troubled, and all the passengers appalled. Mary then left her bed, and went on deck, to survey the contending elements: the scene accorded with the present state of her soul; she thought in a few hours I may go home; the prisoner may be released. The vessel rose on a wave and descended into a yawning gulph—Not slower did her mounting soul return to earth, for—Ah! her treasure and her heart was there. The squalls rattled amongst the sails, which were quickly taken down; the wind would then die away, and the wild undirected waves rushed on every side with a tremendous roar. In a little vessel in the midst of such a storm she was not dismayed; she felt herself independent.

Just then one of the crew perceived a signal of distress;[1] by the help of a glass he could plainly discover a small vessel dismasted, drifted about, for the rudder had been broken by the violence of the storm. Mary's thoughts were now all engrossed by the crew on the brink of destruction. They bore down to the wreck; they reached it, and hailed the trembling wretches: at the sound of the friendly greeting, loud cries of tumultuous joy were mixed with the roaring of the waves, and with ecstatic transport they leaped on the shattered deck, launched their boat in a moment, and committed themselves to the mercy of the sea. Stowed between two casks, and leaning on a sail, she watched the boat, and when a wave intercepted it from her view—she ceased to breathe, or rather held her breath until it rose again.

At last the boat arrived safe along-side the ship, and Mary caught the poor trembling wretches as they stumbled into it, and joined them in thanking that gracious Being, who though He had not thought fit to still the raging of the sea, had afforded them unexpected succour.

Amongst the wretched crew was one poor woman, who fainted when she was hauled on board: Mary undressed her, and when she had recovered, and soothed her, left her to enjoy the rest she required to recruit her strength, which fear had quite exhausted. She returned again to view the angry deep;

and when she gazed on its perturbed state, she thought of the
Being who rode on the wings of the wind, and stilled the noise
of the sea; and the madness of the people[1]—He only could
speak peace to her troubled spirit! she grew more calm; the
late transaction had gratified her benevolence, and stole her
out of herself.

One of the sailors, happening to say to another, 'that he
believed the world was going to be at an end;' this observation
led her into a new train of thoughts: some of Handel's sublime
compositions occurred to her, and she sung them to the grand
accompaniment. The Lord God Omnipotent reigned, and
would reign for ever, and ever![2]—Why then did she fear the
sorrows that were passing away, when she knew that He
would bind up the broken-hearted, and receive those who
came out of great tribulation. She retired to her cabin; and
wrote in the little book that was now her only confident. It was
after midnight.

'At this solemn hour, the great day of judgment fills my
thoughts; the day of retribution, when the secrets of all hearts
will be revealed; when all worldly distinctions will fade away,[3]
and be no more seen. I have not words to express the sublime
images which the bare contemplation of this awful day raises
in my mind. Then, indeed, the Lord Omnipotent will reign,
and He will wipe the tearful eye, and support the trembling
heart—yet a little while He hideth his face, and the dun shades
of sorrow, and the thick clouds of folly separate us from our
God; but when the glad dawn of an eternal day breaks, we
shall know even as we are known. Here we walk by faith, and
not by sight; and we have this alternative, either to enjoy the
pleasures of life, which are but for a season, or look forward to
the prize of our high calling, and with fortitude, and that
wisdom which is from above, endeavour to bear the warfare of
life. We know that many run the race; but he that striveth
obtaineth the crown of victory. Our race is an arduous one!
How many are betrayed by traitors lodged in their own
breasts, who wear the garb of Virtue, and are so near akin; we
sigh to think they should ever lead into folly, and slide

imperceptibly into vice. Surely any thing like happiness is madness! Shall probationers of an hour presume to pluck the fruit of immortality, before they have conquered death? it is guarded, when the great day, to which I allude, arrives, the way will again be opened. Ye dear delusions, gay deceits, farewell! and yet I cannot banish ye for ever; still does my panting soul push forward, and live in futurity, in the deep shades o'er which darkness hangs.—I try to pierce the gloom, and find a resting-place, where my thirst of knowledge will be gratified, and my ardent affections find an object to fix them. Every thing material must change; happiness and this fluctuating principle is not compatible. Eternity, immateriality, and happiness,—what are ye? How shall I grasp the mighty and fleeting conceptions ye create?'

After writing, serenely she delivered her soul into the hands of the Father of Spirits; and slept in peace.

CHAPTER TWENTY-ONE

MARY rose early, refreshed by the seasonable rest, and went to visit the poor woman, whom she found quite recovered: and, on enquiry, heard that she had lately buried her husband, a common sailor; and that her only surviving child had been washed over-board the day before. Full of her own danger, she scarcely thought of her child till that was over; and then she gave way to boisterous emotions.

Mary endeavoured to calm her at first, by sympathizing with her; and she tried to point out the only solid source of comfort; but in doing this she encountered many difficulties; she found her grossly ignorant, yet she did not despair: and as the poor creature could not receive comfort from the operations of her own mind, she laboured to beguile the hours which grief made heavy, by adapting her conversation to her capacity.

There are many minds that only receive impressions

through the medium of the senses: to them did Mary address herself; she made her some presents, and promised to assist her when they should arrive in England. This employment roused her out of her late stupor, and again set the faculties of her soul in motion; made the understanding contend with the imagination, and the heart throbbed not so irregularly during the contention. How short-lived was the calm! when the English coast was descried, her sorrows returned with redoubled vigor.—She was to visit and comfort the mother of her lost friend—And where then should she take up her residence? These thoughts suspended the exertions of her understanding; abstracted reflections gave way to alarming apprehensions; and tenderness undermined fortitude.

CHAPTER TWENTY-TWO

IN England then landed the forlorn wanderer. She looked round for some few moments—her affections were not attracted to any particular part of the Island. She knew none of the inhabitants of the vast city to which she was going: the mass of buildings appeared to her a huge body without an informing soul. As she passed through the streets in an hackney-coach, disgust and horror alternately filled her mind. She met some women drunk; and the manners of those who attacked the sailors, made her shrink into herself, and exclaim, are these my fellow creatures.

Detained by a number of carts near the water-side, for she came up the river in the vessel, not having reason to hasten on shore, she saw vulgarity, dirt, and vice—her soul sickened; this was the first time such complicated misery obtruded itself on her sight.[1]—Forgetting her own griefs, she gave the world a much indebted tear; mourned for a world in ruins. She then perceived, that great part of her comfort must arise from viewing the smiling face of nature, and be reflected from the view of innocent enjoyments: she was fond of seeing animals play, and could not bear to see her own species sink below them.

In a little dwelling in one of the villages near London, lived the mother of Ann; two of her children still remained with her; but they did not resemble Ann. To her house Mary directed the coach, and told the unfortunate mother of her loss. The poor woman, oppressed by it, and her many other cares, after an inundation of tears, began to enumerate all her past misfortunes, and present cares. The heavy tale lasted until midnight, and the impression it made on Mary's mind was so strong, that it banished sleep till towards morning; when tired nature sought forgetfulness, and the soul ceased to ruminate about many things.

She sent for the poor woman they took up at sea, provided her a lodging, and relieved her present necessities. A few days were spent in a kind of listless way; then the mother of Ann began to enquire when she thought of returning home. She had hitherto treated her with the greatest respect, and concealed her wonder at Mary's choosing a remote room in the house near the garden, and ordering some alterations to be made, as if she intended living in it.

Mary did not choose to explain herself; had Ann lived, it is probable she would never have loved Henry so fondly; but if she had, she could not have talked of her passion to any human creature. She deliberated, and at last informed the family, that she had a reason for not living with her husband, which must some time remain a secret—they stared—Not live with him! how will you live then? This was a question she could not answer; she had only about eighty pounds remaining, of the money she took with her to Lisbon; when it was exhausted where could she get more? I will work, she cried, do any thing rather than be a slave.

CHAPTER TWENTY-THREE

UNHAPPY, she wandered about the village, and relieved the poor; it was the only employment that eased her aching heart; she became more intimate with misery—the misery that rises from poverty and the want of education. She was in the vicinity of a great city; the vicious poor in and about it must ever grieve a benevolent contemplative mind.

One evening a man who stood weeping in a little lane, near the house she resided in, caught her eye. She accosted him; in a confused manner, he informed her, that his wife was dying, and his children crying for the bread he could not earn. Mary desired to be conducted to his habitation; it was not very distant, and was the upper room in an old mansion-house, which had been once the abode of luxury.[1] Some tattered shreds of rich hangings still remained, covered with cobwebs and filth; round the ceiling, through which the rain drop'd, was a beautiful cornice mouldering; and a spacious gallery was rendered dark by the broken windows being blocked up; through the apertures the wind forced its way in hollow sounds, and reverberated along the former scene of festivity.

It was crowded with inhabitants: some were scolding, others swearing, or singing indecent songs. What a sight for Mary! Her blood ran cold; yet she had sufficient resolution to mount to the top of the house. On the floor, in one corner of a very small room, lay an emaciated figure of a woman; a window over her head scarcely admitted any light, for the broken panes were stuffed with dirty rags. Near her were five children, all young, and covered with dirt; their sallow cheeks, and languid eyes, exhibited none of the charms of childhood. Some were fighting, and others crying for food; their yells were mixed with their mother's groans, and the wind which rushed through the passage. Mary was petrified; but soon assuming more courage, approached the bed, and, regardless of the surrounding nastiness, knelt down by the poor wretch, and breathed the most poisonous air; for the unfortunate creature was dying of a putrid fever, the consequence of dirt and want.

Their state did not require much explanation. Mary sent the husband for a poor neighbour, whom she hired to nurse the woman, and take care of the children; and then went herself to buy them some necessaries at a shop not far distant. Her knowledge of physic had enabled her to prescribe for the woman; and she left the house, with a mixture of horror and satisfaction.

She visited them every day, and procured them every comfort; contrary to her expectation, the woman began to recover; cleanliness and wholesome food had a wonderful effect; and Mary saw her rising as it were from the grave. Not aware of the danger she ran into, she did not think of it till she perceived she had caught the fever. It made such an alarming progress, that she was prevailed on to send for a physician; but the disorder was so violent, that for some days it baffled his skill; and Mary felt not her danger, as she was delirious. After the crisis, the symptoms were more favourable, and she slowly recovered, without regaining much strength or spirits; indeed they were intolerably low: she wanted a tender nurse.

For some time she had observed, that she was not treated with the same respect as formerly; her favors were forgotten when no more were expected. This ingratitude hurt her, as did a similar instance in the woman who came out of the ship. Mary had hitherto supported her; as her finances were growing low, she hinted to her, that she ought to try to earn her own subsistence: the woman in return loaded her with abuse.

Two months were elapsed; she had not seen, or heard from Henry. He was sick—nay, perhaps had forgotten her; all the world was dreary, and all the people ungrateful.

She sunk into apathy, and endeavouring to rouse herself out of it, she wrote in her book another fragment:

'Surely life is a dream, a frightful one! and after those rude, disjointed images are fled, will light ever break in? Shall I ever feel joy? Do all suffer like me; or am I framed so as to be particularly susceptible of misery? It is true, I have experienced the most rapturous emotions—short-lived delight!—ethereal beam, which only serves to shew my present misery—yet lie still, my throbbing heart, or burst; and my brain—why dost thou whirl about at such a terrifying rate? why do thoughts so rapidly rush into my mind, and yet when they disappear leave such deep traces? I could almost wish for the madman's happiness, and in a strong imagination lose a sense of woe.[1]

Oh! reason, thou boasted guide, why desert me, like the world, when I most need thy assistance! Canst thou not calm this internal tumult, and drive away the death-like sadness which presses so sorely on me,—a sadness surely very nearly allied to despair. I am now the prey of apathy—I could wish for the former storms! a ray of hope sometimes illumined my path; I had a pursuit; but now *it visits not my haunts forlorn.*[2] Too well have I loved my fellow creatures! I have been wounded by ingratitude; from every one it has something of the serpent's tooth.

'When overwhelmed by sorrow, I have met unkindness; I looked for some one to have pity on me; but found none!—The healing balm of sympathy is denied; I weep, a solitary wretch, and the hot tears scald my cheeks. I have not the medicine of life, the dear chimera I have so often chased, a friend. Shade of my loved Ann! dost thou ever visit thy poor Mary? Refined spirit, thou wouldst weep, could angels weep, to see her struggling with passions she cannot subdue; and feelings which corrode her small portion of comfort!'

She could not write any more; she wished herself far distant from all human society; a thick gloom spread itself over her mind: but did not make her forget the very beings she wished to fly from. She sent for the poor woman she found in the garret; gave her money to clothe herself and children, and buy some furniture for a little hut, in a large garden, the master of which agreed to employ her husband, who had been bred a gardener. Mary promised to visit the family, and see their new abode when she was able to go out.

CHAPTER TWENTY-FOUR

MARY still continued weak and low, though it was spring,[1] and all nature began to look gay; with more than usual brightness the sun shone, and a little robin which she had cherished during the winter sung one of his best songs. The family were particularly civil this fine morning, and tried to prevail on her to walk out. Any thing like kindness melted her; she consented.

Softer emotions banished her melancholy, and she directed her steps to the habitation she had rendered comfortable.

Emerging out of a dreary chamber, all nature looked cheerful; when she had last walked out, snow covered the ground, and bleak winds pierced her through and through: now the hedges were green, the blossoms adorned the trees, and the birds sung. She reached the dwelling, without being much exhausted; and while she rested there, observed the children sporting on the grass, with improved complexions. The mother with tears thanked her deliverer, and pointed out her comforts. Mary's tears flowed not only from sympathy, but a complication of feelings and recollections; the affections which bound her to her fellow creatures began again to play, and reanimated nature. She observed the change in herself, tried to account for it, and wrote with her pencil a rhapsody on sensibility.[2]

'Sensibility is the most exquisite feeling of which the human soul is susceptible: when it pervades us, we feel happy; and could it last unmixed, we might form some conjecture of the bliss of those paradisiacal days, when the obedient passions were under the dominion of reason, and the impulses of the heart did not need correction.

'It is this quickness, this delicacy of feeling, which enables us to relish the sublime touches of the poet, and the painter; it is this, which expands the soul, gives an enthusiastic greatness, mixed with tenderness, when we view the

magnificent objects of nature; or hear of a good action. The
same effect we experience in the spring, when we hail the
returning sun, and the consequent renovation of nature; when
the flowers unfold themselves, and exhale their sweets, and
the voice of music is heard in the land. Softened by
tenderness; the soul is disposed to be virtuous. Is any sensual
gratification to be compared to that of feeling the eyes
moistened after having comforted the unfortunate?

'Sensibility is indeed the foundation of all our happiness;
but these raptures are unknown to the depraved sensualist,
who is only moved by what strikes his gross senses; the
delicate embellishments of nature escape his notice; as do the
gentle and interesting affections.—But it is only to be felt; it
escapes discussion.'

She then returned home, and partook of the family meal,
which was rendered more cheerful by the presence of a man,
past the meridian of life, of polished manners, and dazzling
wit. He endeavoured to draw Mary out, and succeeded; she
entered into conversation, and some of her artless flights of
genius struck him with surprise; he found she had a capacious
mind, and that her reason was as profound as her imagination
was lively. She glanced from earth to heaven, and caught the
light of truth. Her expressive countenance shewed what
passed in her mind, and her tongue was ever the faithful
interpreter of her heart; duplicity never threw a shade over
her words or actions. Mary found him a man of learning;
and the exercise of her understanding would frequently make
her forget her griefs, when nothing else could, except
benevolence.

This man had known the mistress of the house in her
youth; good nature induced him to visit her; but when he saw
Mary he had another inducement. Her appearance, and above
all, her genius, and cultivation of mind, roused his curiosity;
but her dignified manners had such an effect on him, he was
obliged to suppress it. He knew men, as well as books; his
conversation was entertaining and improving. In Mary's
company he doubted whether heaven was peopled with spirits

masculine; and almost forgot that he had called the sex 'the pretty play things that render life tolerable.'

He had been the slave of beauty, the captive of sense; love he ne'er had felt; the mind never rivetted the chain, nor had the purity of it made the body appear lovely in his eyes. He was humane, despised meanness; but was vain of his abilities, and by no means a useful member of society. He talked often of the beauty of virtue; but not having any solid foundation to build the practice on, he was only a shining, or rather a sparkling character: and though his fortune enabled him to hunt down pleasure, he was discontented.

Mary observed his character, and wrote down a train of reflections, which these observations led her to make; these reflections received a tinge from her mind; the present state of it, was that kind of painful quietness which arises from reason clouded by disgust; she had not yet learned to be resigned; vague hopes agitated her.

'There are some subjects that are so enveloped in clouds, as you dissipate one, another overspreads it. Of this kind are our reasonings concerning happiness, till we are obliged to cry out with the Apostle,[1] *That it hath not entered into the heart of man to conceive in what it could consist*, or how satiety could be prevented. Man seems formed for action, though the passions are seldom properly managed; they are either so languid as not to serve as a spur, or else so violent, as to overleap all bounds.

'Every individual has its own peculiar trials; and anguish, in one shape or other, visits every heart. Sensibility produces flights of virtue; and not curbed by reason, is on the brink of vice talking, and even thinking of virtue.

'Christianity can only[2] afford just principles to govern the wayward feelings and impulses of the heart: every good disposition runs wild, if not transplanted into this soil; but how hard is it to keep the heart diligently, though convinced that the issues of life depend on it.

'It is very difficult to discipline the mind of a thinker, or reconcile him to the weakness, the inconsistency of his understanding; and a still more laborious task for him to conquer his passions, and learn to seek content, instead of happiness. Good dispositions, and virtuous propensities, without the light of the Gospel, produce eccentric characters: comet-like, they are always in extremes; while revelation resembles the laws of attraction, and produces uniformity; but too often is the attraction feeble; and the light so obscured by passion, as to force the bewildered soul to fly into void space, and wander in confusion.'

CHAPTER TWENTY-FIVE

A FEW mornings after, as Mary was sitting ruminating, harassed by perplexing thoughts, and fears, a letter was delivered to her: the servant waited for an answer. Her heart palpitated; it was from Henry; she held it some time in her hand, then tore it open; it was not a long one; and only contained an account of a relapse, which prevented his sailing in the first packet, as he had intended. Some tender enquiries were added, concerning her health, and state of mind; but they were expressed in rather a formal style: it vexed her, and the more so, as it stopped the current of affection, which the account of his arrival and illness had made flow to her heart—it ceased to beat for a moment—she read the passage over again; but could not tell what she was hurt by—only that it did not answer the expectations of her affection. She wrote a laconic, incoherent note in return, allowing him to call on her the next day—he had requested permission at the conclusion of his letter.

Her mind was then painfully active; she could not read or walk; she tried to fly from herself, to forget the long hours that were yet to run before to-morrow could arrive: she knew not what time he would come; certainly in the morning, she concluded; the morning then was anxiously wished for; and every wish produced a sigh, that arose from expectation on the stretch, damped by fear and vain regret.

To beguile the tedious time, Henry's favorite tunes were sung; the books they read together turned over; and the short epistle read at least a hundred times.—Any one who who had seen her, would have supposed that she was trying to decypher Chinese characters.

After a sleepless night, she hailed the tardy day, watched the rising sun, and then listened for every footstep, and started if she heard the street door opened. At last he came, and she who had been counting the hours, and doubting whether the earth moved, would gladly have escaped the approaching interview.

With an unequal, irresolute pace, she went to meet him; but when she beheld his emaciated countenance, all the tenderness, which the formality of his letter had damped, returned, and a mournful presentiment stilled the internal conflict. She caught his hand, and looking wistfully at him, exclaimed, 'Indeed, you are not well!'

'I am very far from well; but it matters not,' added he with a smile of resignation; 'my native air may work wonders, and besides, my mother is a tender nurse, and I shall sometimes see thee.'

Mary felt for the first time in her life, envy; she wished involuntarily, that all the comfort he received should be from her. She enquired about the symptoms of his disorder; and heard that he had been very ill; she hastily drove away the fears, that former dear bought experience suggested: and again and again did she repeat, that she was sure he would soon recover. She would then look in his face, to see if he assented, and ask more questions to the same purport. She tried to avoid speaking of herself, and Henry left her, with a promise of visiting her the next day.

Her mind was now engrossed by one fear—yet she would not allow herself to think that she feared an event she could not name. She still saw his pale face; the sound of his voice still vibrated on her ears; she tried to retain it; she listened, looked round, wept, and prayed.

Henry had enlightened the desolate scene: was this charm

of life to fade away, and, like the baseless fabric of a vision, leave not a wreck behind? These thoughts disturbed her reason, she shook her head, as if to drive them out of it; a weight, a heavy one, was on her heart; all was not well there.

Out of this reverie she was soon woke to keener anguish, by the arrival of a letter from her husband; it came to Lisbon after her departure: Henry had forwarded it to her, but did not choose to deliver it himself, for a very obvious reason; it might have produced a conversation he wished for some time to avoid; and his precaution took its rise almost equally from benevolence and love.

She could not muster up sufficient resolution to break the seal: her fears were not prophetic, for the contents gave her comfort. He informed her that he intended prolonging his tour, as he was now his own master, and wished to remain some time on the continent, and in particular to visit Italy without any restraint: but his reasons for it appeared childish; it was not to cultivate his taste, or tread on classic ground, where poets and philosophers caught their lore; but to join in the masquerades, and such burlesque amusements.

These instances of folly relieved Mary, in some degree reconciled her to herself, added fuel to the devouring flame—and silenced something like a pang, which reason and conscience made her feel, when she reflected, that it is the office of Religion to reconcile us to the seemingly hard dispensations of providence; and that no inclination, however strong, should oblige us to desert the post assigned us, or force us to forget that virtue should be an active principle; and that the most desirable station, is the one that exercises our faculties, refines our affections, and enables us to be useful.

One reflection continually wounded her repose; she feared not poverty; her wants were few; but in giving up a fortune, she gave up the power of comforting the miserable, and making the sad heart sing for joy.

Heaven had endowed her with uncommon humanity, to render her one of His benevolent agents, a messenger of peace; and should she attend to her own inclinations?[1]

These suggestions, though they could not subdue a violent passion, increased her misery. One moment she was a heroine, half determined to bear whatever fate should inflict; the next, her mind would recoil—and tenderness possessed her whole soul. Some instances of Henry's affection, his worth and genius, were remembered: and the earth was only a vale of tears, because he was not to sojourn with her.

CHAPTER TWENTY-SIX

HENRY came the next day, and once or twice in the course of the following week; but still Mary kept up some little formality, a certain consciousness restrained her; and Henry did not enter on the subject which he found she wished to avoid. In the course of conversation, however, she mentioned to him, that she earnestly desired to obtain a place in one of the public offices for Ann's brother, as the family were again in a declining way.

Henry attended, made a few enquiries, and dropped the subject; but the following week, she heard him enter with unusual haste; it was to inform her, that he had made interest with a person of some consequence, whom he had once obliged in a very disagreeable exigency, in a foreign country; and that he had procured a place for her friend, which would infallibly lead to something better, if he behaved with propriety. Mary could not speak to thank him; emotions of gratitude and love suffused her face; her blood eloquently spoke. She delighted to receive benefits through the medium of her fellow creatures; but to receive them from Henry was exquisite pleasure.

As the summer advanced, Henry grew worse; the closeness of the air, in the metropolis, affected his breath; and his mother insisted on his fixing on some place in the country, where she would accompany him. He could not think of going far off, but chose a little village[1] on the banks of the Thames, near Mary's dwelling: he then introduced her to his mother.

They frequently went down the river in a boat; Henry would take his violin, and Mary would sometimes sing, or read, to them. She pleased his mother; she inchanted him. It was an advantage to Mary that friendship first possessed her heart; it opened it to all the softer sentiments of humanity:—and when this first affection was torn away, a similar one sprung up, with a still tenderer sentiment added to it.

The last evening they were on the water, the clouds grew suddenly black, and broke in violent showers, which interrupted the solemn stillness that had prevailed previous to it. The thunder roared; and the oars plying quickly, in order to reach the shore, occasioned a not unpleasing sound. Mary drew still nearer Henry; she wished to have sought with him a watry grave; to have escaped the horror of surviving him.—She spoke not, but Henry saw the workings of her mind—he felt them; threw his arm round her waist—and they enjoyed the luxury of wretchedness.—As they touched the shore, Mary perceived that Henry was wet; with eager anxiety she cried, What shall I do!—this day will kill thee, and I shall not die with thee!

This accident[1] put a stop to their pleasurable excursions; it had injured him, and brought on the spitting of blood he was subject to—perhaps it was not the cold that he caught, that occasioned it. In vain did Mary try to shut her eyes; her fate pursued her! Henry every day grew worse and worse.

CHAPTER TWENTY-SEVEN

OPPRESSED by her forboding fears, her sore mind was hurt by new instances of ingratitude: disgusted with the family, whose misfortunes had often disturbed her repose, and lost in anticipated sorrow, she rambled she knew not where; when turning down a shady walk, she discovered her feet had taken the path they delighted to tread. She saw Henry sitting in his garden alone; he quickly opened the garden-gate, and she sat down by him.

'I did not,' said he, 'expect to see thee this evening, my dearest Mary; but I was thinking of thee. Heaven has endowed thee with an uncommon portion of fortitude, to support one of the most affectionate hearts in the world. This is not a time for disguise; I know I am dear to thee—and my affection for thee is twisted with every fibre of my heart.—I loved thee ever since I have been acquainted with thine: thou art the being my fancy has delighted to form; but which I imagined existed only there! In a little while the shades of death will encompass me—ill-fated love perhaps added strength to my disease, and smoothed the rugged path. Try, my love, to fulfil thy destined course—try to add to thy other virtues patience. I could have wished, for thy sake, that we could have died together—or that I could live to shield thee from the assaults of an unfeeling world! Could I but offer thee an asylum in these arms—a faithful bosom, in which thou couldst repose all thy griefs—He pressed her to it, and she returned the pressure—he felt her throbbing heart. A mournful silence ensued! when he resumed the conversation. 'I wished to prepare thee for the blow—too surely do I feel that it will not be long delayed! The passion I have nursed is so pure, that death cannot extinguish it—or tear away the impression thy virtues have made on my soul. I would fain comfort thee—'

'Talk not of comfort,' interrupted Mary, 'it will be in heaven with thee and Ann—while I shall remain on earth the veriest wretch!'—She grasped his hand.

'There we shall meet, my love, my Mary, in our Father's'—His voice faultered; he could not finish the sentence; he was almost suffocated—they both wept, their tears relieved them; they walked slowly to the garden-gate (Mary would not go into the house); they could not say farewel when they reached it—and Mary hurried down the lane, to spare Henry the pain of witnessing her emotions.

When she lost sight of the house she sat down on the ground, till it grew late, thinking of all that had passed. Full of these thoughts, she crept along, regardless of the descending rain; when lifting up her eyes to heaven, and then turning them wildly on the prospects around, without marking them; she only felt that the scene accorded with her present state of mind. It was the last glimmering of twilight, with a full moon, over which clouds continually flitted. Where am I wandering, God of Mercy! she thought; she alluded to the wanderings of her mind. In what a labyrinth am I lost! What miseries have I already encountered—and what a number lie still before me.

Her thoughts flew rapidly to something. I could be happy listening to him, soothing his cares.—Would he not smile upon me—call me his own Mary? I am not his—said she with fierceness—I am a wretch! and she heaved a sigh that almost broke her heart, while the big tears rolled down her burning cheeks; but still her exercised mind, accustomed to think, began to observe its operation, though the barrier of reason was almost carried away, and all the faculties not restrained by her, were running into confusion. Wherefore am I made thus? Vain are my efforts—I cannot live without loving—and love leads to madness.—Yet I will not weep; and her eyes were now fixed by despair, dry and motionless; and then quickly whirled about with a look of distraction.

She looked for hope; but found none—all was troubled waters.—No where could she find rest. I have already paced to and fro in the earth; it is not my abiding place—may I not too go home! Ah! no. Is this complying with my Henry's request, could a spirit thus disengaged expect to associate with his? Tears of tenderness strayed down her relaxed countenance, and her softened heart heaved more regularly. She felt the rain, and turned to her solitary home.

Fatigued by the tumultuous emotions she had endured, when she entered the house she ran to her own room, sunk on the bed, and exhausted nature soon closed her eyes; but active fancy was still awake, and a thousand fearful dreams interrupted her slumbers.

Feverish and languid, she opened her eyes, and saw the unwelcome sun dart his rays through a window, the curtains of which she had forgotten to draw. The dew hung on the adjacent trees, and added to the lustre; the little robin began his song, and distant birds joined. She looked; her countenance was still vacant—her sensibility was absorbed by one object.

Did I ever admire the rising sun, she slightly thought, turning from the window, and shutting her eyes: she recalled to view the last night's scene. His faltering voice, lingering step, and the look of tender woe, were all graven on her heart; as were the words 'Could these arms shield thee from sorrow—afford thee an asylum from an unfeeling world.' The pressure to his bosom was not forgot. For a moment she was happy; but in a long-drawn sigh every delightful sensation evaporated. Soon—yes, very soon, will the grave again receive all I love! and the remnant of my days—she could not proceed—Were there then days to come after that?

CHAPTER TWENTY-EIGHT

JUST as she was going to quit her room, to visit Henry, his mother called on her.

'My son is worse to-day,' said she. 'I come to request you to spend not only this day, but a week or two with me.—Why should I conceal any thing from you? Last night my child made his mother his confident, and, in the anguish of his heart, requested me to be thy friend—when I shall be childless. I will not attempt to describe what I felt when he talked thus to me. If I am to lose the support of my age, and be again a widow—may I call her Child whom my Henry wishes me to adopt?'

This new instance of Henry's disinterested affection, Mary felt most forcibly; and striving to restrain the complicated emotions, and sooth the wretched mother, she almost fainted: when the unhappy parent forced tears from her, by saying, 'I deserve this blow; my partial fondness made me neglect him, when most he wanted a mother's care; this neglect, perhaps, first injured his constitution: righteous Heaven has made my crime its own punishment; and now I am indeed a mother, I shall lose my child—my only child!'

When they were a little more composed they hastened to the invalide; but during the short ride, the mother related several instances of Henry's goodness of heart. Mary's tears were not those of unmixed anguish; the display of his virtues gave her extreme delight—yet human nature prevailed; she trembled to think they would soon unfold themselves in a more genial clime.

CHAPTER TWENTY-NINE

SHE found Henry very ill. The physician had some weeks before declared he never knew a person with a similar pulse recover. Henry was certain he could not live long; all the rest he could obtain, was procured by opiates. Mary now enjoyed the melancholy pleasure of nursing him, and softened by her tenderness the pains she could not remove. Every sigh did she stifle, every tear restrain, when he could see or hear them. She would boast of her resignation—yet catch eagerly at the least ray of hope. While he slept she would support his pillow, and rest her head where she could feel his breath. She loved him better than herself—she could not pray for his recovery; she could only say, The will of Heaven be done.

While she was in this state, she labored to acquire fortitude; but one tender look destroyed it all—she rather labored, indeed, to make him believe she was resigned, than really to be so.

She wished to receive the sacrament with him, as a bond of union which was to extend beyond the grave. She did so, and received comfort from it; she rose above her misery.

His end was now approaching. Mary sat on the side of the

bed. His eyes appeared fixed—no longer agitated by passion, he only felt that it was a fearful thing to die. The soul retired to the citadel; but it was not now solely filled by the image of her who in silent despair watched for his last breath. Collected, a frightful calmness stilled every turbulent emotion.

The mother's grief was more audible. Henry had for some time only attended to Mary—Mary pitied the parent, whose stings of conscience increased her sorrow; she whispered him, 'Thy mother weeps, disregarded by thee; oh! comfort her!—My mother, thy son blesses thee.—' The oppressed parent left the room. And Mary *waited* to see him die.

She pressed with trembling eagerness his parched lips—he opened his eyes again; the spreading film retired, and love relumed them—he gave a look—it was never forgotten. My Mary, will you be comforted?

Yes, yes, she exclaimed in a firm voice; you go to be happy—I am not a complete wretch! The words almost choked her.

He was a long time silent; the opiate produced a kind of stupor. At last, in an agony, he cried, It is dark; I cannot see thee; raise me up. Where is Mary? did she not say she delighted to support me? let me die in her arms.

Her arms were opened to receive him; they trembled not. Again he was obliged to lie down, resting on her: as the agonies increased he leaned towards her: the soul seemed flying to her, as it escaped out of its prison. The breathing was interrupted; she heard distinctly the last sigh—and lifting up to Heaven her eyes, Father, receive his spirit, she calmly cried.

The attendants gathered round; she moved not, nor heard the clamor; the hand seemed yet to press hers; it still was warm. A ray of light from an opened window discovered the pale face.

She left the room, and retired to one very near it; and sitting down on the floor, fixed her eyes on the door of the apartment which contained the body. Every event of her life rushed across her mind with wonderful rapidity—yet all was still—fate had given the finishing stroke. She sat till midnight.——Then rose in a phrensy, went into the apartment, and desired those who watched the body to retire.

She knelt by the bed side;——an enthusiastic devotion overcame the dictates of despair.—She prayed most ardently to be supported, and dedicated herself to the service of that Being into whose hands, she had committed the spirit she almost adored—again—and again,—she prayed wildly—and fervently—but attempting to touch the lifeless hand—her head swum—she sunk——

CHAPTER THIRTY

THREE months after, her only friend, the mother of her lost Henry began to be alarmed, at observing her altered appearance; and made her own health a pretext for travelling. These complaints roused Mary out of her torpid state; she imagined a new duty now forced her to exert herself—a duty love made sacred!—

They went to Bath, from that to Bristol; but the latter place they quickly left; the sight of the sick that resort there, they neither of them could bear. From Bristol they flew to Southampton. The road was pleasant—yet Mary shut her eyes;—or if they were open, green fields and commons, passed in quick succession, and left no more traces behind than if they had been waves of the sea.

Some time after they were settled at Southampton, they met the man who took so much notice of Mary, soon after her return to England. He renewed his acquaintance; he was really interested in her fate, as he had heard her uncommon story; besides, he knew her husband; knew him to be a good-natured, weak man. He saw him soon after his arrival in his native country, and prevented his hastening to enquire into the reasons of Mary's strange conduct. He desired him not to be too precipitate, if he ever wished to possess an invaluable treasure. He was guided by him, and allowed him to follow Mary to Southampton, and speak first to her friend.

This friend determined to trust to her native strength of mind, and informed her of the circumstance; but she overrated it: Mary was not able, for a few days after the intelligence, to fix on the mode of conduct she ought now to pursue. But at last she conquered her disgust, and wrote her *husband* an account of what had passed since she had dropped his correspondence.

He came in person to answer the letter. Mary fainted when he approached her unexpectedly. Her disgust returned with additional force, in spite of previous reasonings, whenever he appeared;—yet she was prevailed on to promise to live with him, if he would permit her to pass one year, travelling from place to place; he was not to accompany her.

The time too quickly elapsed, and she gave him her hand—the struggle was almost more than she could endure. She tried to appear calm; time mellowed her grief, and mitigated her torments; but when her husband would take her hand, or mention any thing like love, she would instantly feel a sickness, a faintness at her heart, and wish, involuntarily, that the earth would open and swallow her.

CHAPTER THIRTY-ONE

MARY visited the continent, and sought health in different climates; but her nerves were not to be restored to their former state. She then retired to her house in the country, established manufactories, threw the estate into small farms; and continually employed herself this way to dissipate care, and banish unavailing regret. She visited the sick, supported the old, and educated the young.

These occupations engrossed her mind; but there were hours when all her former woes would return and haunt her.—Whenever she did, or said, any thing she thought Henry would have approved of—she could not avoid thinking with anguish, of the rapture his approbation ever conveyed to her heart—a heart in which there was a void, that even benevolence and religion could not fill. The latter taught her to struggle for resignation; and the former rendered life supportable.

Her delicate state of health did not promise long life. In moments of solitary sadness, a gleam of joy would dart across her mind—She thought she was hastening to that world *where there is neither marrying*, nor giving in marriage.

END.

THE
WRONGS OF
WOMAN:
OR,
MARIA.
A FRAGMENT

IN TWO VOLUMES

———

VOLUME I

PREFACE

THE public are here presented with the last literary attempt of an author, whose fame has been uncommonly extensive, and whose talents have probably been most admired, by the persons by whom talents are estimated with the greatest accuracy and discrimination. There are few, to whom her writings could in any case have given pleasure, that would have wished that this fragment should have been suppressed, because it is a fragment. There is a sentiment, very dear to minds of taste and imagination, that finds a melancholy delight in contemplating these unfinished productions of genius, these sketches of what, if they had been filled up in a manner adequate to the writer's conception, would perhaps have given a new impulse to the manners of a world.

The purpose and structure of the following work, had long formed a favourite subject of meditation with its author, and she judged them capable of producing an important effect. The composition had been in progress for a period of twelve months. She was anxious to do justice to her conception, and recommenced and revised the manuscript several different times. So much of it as is here given to the public, she was far from considering as finished, and, in a letter to a friend[1] directly written on this subject, she says, 'I am perfectly aware that some of the incidents ought to be transposed, and heightened by more harmonious shading; and I wished in some degree to avail myself of criticism, before I began to adjust my events into a story, the outline of which I had sketched in my mind*.' The only friends to whom the author communicated her manuscript, were Mr. Dyson, the translator of the Sorcerer,[2] and the present editor; and it was impossible for the most inexperienced author to display a stronger desire of profiting by the censures and sentiments that might be suggested†.

*A more copious extract of this letter is subjoined to the author's preface.
†The part communicated consisted of the first fourteen chapters.

In revising these sheets for the press,[1] it was necessary for the editor, in some places, to connect the more finished parts with the pages of an older copy, and a line or two in addition sometimes appeared requisite for that purpose. Wherever such a liberty has been taken, the additional phrases will be found inclosed in brackets; it being the editor's most earnest desire, to intrude nothing of himself into the work, but to give to the public the words, as well as ideas, of the real author.

What follows in the ensuing pages, is not a preface regularly drawn out by the author, but merely hints for a preface, which, though never filled up in the manner the writer intended, appeared to be worth preserving.

W. GODWIN.

AUTHOR'S PREFACE

THE Wrongs of Woman, like the wrongs of the oppressed part of mankind, may be deemed necessary by their oppressors: but surely there are a few, who will dare to advance before the improvement of the age, and grant that my sketches are not the abortion of a distempered fancy, or the strong delineations of a wounded heart.

In writing this novel, I have rather endeavoured to pourtray passions than manners.

In many instances I could have made the incidents more dramatic, would I have sacrificed my main object, the desire of exhibiting the misery and oppression, peculiar to women, that arise out of the partial laws and customs of society.

In the invention of the story, this view restrained my fancy; and the history ought rather to be considered, as of woman, than of an individual.

The sentiments I have embodied.[1]

In many works of this species, the hero is allowed to be mortal, and to become wise and virtuous as well as happy, by a train of events and circumstances. The heroines, on the contrary, are to be born immaculate; and to act like goddesses of wisdom, just come forth highly finished Minervas from the head of Jove.

———

[The following is an extract of a letter from the author to a friend,[2] to whom she communicated her manuscript.]

———

For my part, I cannot suppose any situation more distressing, than for a woman of sensibility, with an improving mind, to be bound to such a man as I have described for life; obliged to renounce all the humanizing affections, and to avoid cultivating her taste, lest her perception of grace and refinement of sentiment, should sharpen to agony the pangs of disappointment. Love, in which the imagination mingles its bewitching colouring, must be fostered by delicacy.[1] I should despise, or rather call her an ordinary woman, who could endure such a husband as I have sketched.

These appear to me (matrimonial despotism of heart and conduct) to be the peculiar Wrongs of Woman, because they degrade the mind. What are termed great misfortunes, may more forcibly impress the mind of common readers; they have more of what may justly be termed *stage-effect*; but it is the delineation of finer sensations, which, in my opinion, constitutes the merit of our best novels.[2] This is what I have in view; and to show the wrongs of different classes of women, equally oppressive, though, from the difference of education, necessarily various.

THE WRONGS OF WOMAN
CHAPTER ONE

ABODES of horror have frequently been described, and castles, filled with spectres and chimeras, conjured up by the magic spell of genius to harrow the soul, and absorb the wondering mind. But, formed of such stuff as dreams are made of,[1] what were they to the mansion of despair, in one corner of which Maria sat, endeavouring to recal her scattered thoughts!

Surprise, astonishment, that bordered on distraction, seemed to have suspended her faculties, till, waking by degrees to a keen sense of anguish, a whirlwind of rage and indignation roused her torpid pulse. One recollection with frightful velocity following another, threatened to fire her brain, and make her a fit companion for the terrific inhabitants, whose groans and shrieks were no unsubstantial sounds of whistling winds, or startled birds, modulated by a romantic fancy, which amuse while they affright; but such tones of misery as carry a dreadful certainty directly to the heart. What effect must they then have produced on one, true to the touch of sympathy, and tortured by maternal apprehension!

Her infant's image was continually floating on Maria's sight, and the first smile of intelligence remembered, as none but a mother, an unhappy mother, can conceive. She heard her speaking half cooing, and felt the little twinkling fingers on her burning bosom—a bosom bursting with the nutriment for which this cherished child might now be pining in vain. From a stranger she could indeed receive the maternal aliment, Maria was grieved at the thought—but who would watch her with a mother's tenderness, a mother's self-denial?

The retreating shadows of former sorrows rushed back in a gloomy train, and seemed to be pictured on the walls of her prison, magnified by the state of mind in which they were viewed—Still she mourned for her child, lamented she was a daughter, and anticipated the aggravated ills of life that her sex rendered almost inevitable, even while dreading she was no more. To think that she was blotted out of existence was agony, when the imagination had been long employed to expand her faculties; yet to suppose her turned adrift on an unknown sea, was scarcely less afflicting.

After being two days the prey of impetuous, varying emotions, Maria began to reflect more calmly on her present situation, for she had actually been rendered incapable of sober reflection, by the discovery of the act of atrocity of which she was the victim. She could not have imagined, that, in all the fermentation of civilized depravity, a similar plot could have entered a human mind. She had been stunned by an unexpected blow; yet life, however joyless, was not to be indolently resigned, or misery endured without exertion, and proudly termed patience. She had hitherto meditated only to point the dart of anguish, and suppressed the heart heavings of indignant nature merely by the force of contempt. Now she endeavoured to brace her mind to fortitude, and to ask herself what was to be her employment in her dreary cell? Was it not to effect her escape, to fly to the succour of her child, and to baffle the selfish schemes of her tyrant—her husband?

These thoughts roused her sleeping spirit, and the self-possession returned, that seemed to have abandoned her in the infernal solitude into which she had been precipitated. The first emotions of overwhelming impatience began to subside, and resentment gave place to tenderness, and more tranquil meditation; though anger once more stopt the calm current of reflection, when she attempted to move her manacled arms. But this was an outrage that could only excite momentary feelings of scorn which evaporated in a faint smile; for Maria was far from thinking a personal insult the most difficult to endure with magnanimous indifference.

She approached the small grated window of her chamber, and for a considerable time only regarded the blue expanse; though it commanded a view of a desolate garden, and of part of a huge pile of buildings,[1] that, after having been suffered, for half a century, to fall to decay, had undergone some clumsy repairs, merely to render it habitable. The ivy had been torn off the turrets, and the stones not wanted to patch up the breaches of time, and exclude the warring elements, left in heaps in the disordered court. Maria contemplated this scene she knew not how long; or rather gazed on the walls, and pondered on her situation. To the master of this most horrid of prisons, she had, soon after her entrance, raved of injustice, in accents that would have justified his treatment, had not a malignant smile, when she appealed to his judgment, with a dreadful conviction stifled her remonstrating complaints. By force, or openly, what could be done? But surely some expedient might occur to an active mind, without any other employment, and possessed of sufficient resolution to put the risk of life into the balance with the chance of freedom.

A woman entered in the midst of these reflections, with a firm, deliberate step, strongly marked features, and large black eyes, which she fixed steadily on Maria's, as if she designed to intimidate her, saying at the same time—'You had better sit down and eat your dinner, than look at the clouds.'

'I have no appetite,' replied Maria, who had previously determined to speak mildly; 'why then should I eat?'

'But, in spite of that, you must and shall eat something. I have had many ladies under my care, who have resolved to starve themselves; but, soon or late, they gave up their intent, as they recovered their senses.'

'Do you really think me mad?' asked Maria, meeting the searching glance of her eye.

'Not just now. But what does that prove?—only that you must be the more carefully watched, for appearing at times so reasonable. You have not touched a morsel since you entered the house.'—Maria sighed intelligibly.—'Could any thing but madness produce such a disgust for food?'

'Yes, grief; you would not ask the question if you knew what it was.' The attendant shook her head; and a ghastly smile of desperate fortitude served as a forcible reply, and made Maria pause, before she added—'Yet I will take some

refreshment: I mean not to die.—No; I will preserve my
senses; and convince even you, sooner than you are aware of,
that my intellects have never been disturbed, though the
exertion of them may have been suspended by some infernal
drug.'

Doubt gathered still thicker on the brow of her guard, as
she attempted to convict her of mistake.

'Have patience!' exclaimed Maria, with a solemnity that
inspired awe. 'My God! how have I been schooled into the
practice!' A suffocation of voice betrayed the agonizing
emotions she was labouring to keep down; and conquering a
qualm of disgust, she calmly endeavoured to eat enough to
prove her docility, perpetually turning to the suspicious
female, whose observation she courted, while she was making
the bed and adjusting the room.

'Come to me often,' said Maria, with a tone of persuasion,
in consequence of a vague plan that she had hastily adopted,
when, after surveying this woman's form and features, she felt
convinced that she had an understanding above the common
standard; 'and believe me mad, till you are obliged to
acknowledge the contrary.' The woman was no fool, that is,
she was superior to her class; nor had misery quite petrified
the life's-blood of humanity, to which reflections on our own
misfortunes only give a more orderly course. The manner,
rather than the expostulations, of Maria made a slight
suspicion dart into her mind with corresponding sympathy,
which various other avocations, and the habit of banishing
compunction, prevented her, for the present, from examining
more minutely.

But when she was told that no person, excepting the
physician appointed by her family, was to be permitted to see
the lady at the end of the gallery, she opened her keen eyes still
wider, and uttered a—'hem!' before she enquired—'Why?'
She was briefly told, in reply, that the malady was hereditary,
and the fits not occurring but at very long and irregular
intervals, she must be carefully watched; for the length of
these lucid periods only rendered her more mischievous,

when any vexation or caprice brought on the paroxysm of phrensy.

Had her master trusted her, it is probable that neither pity nor curiosity would have made her swerve from the straight line of her interest; for she had suffered too much in her intercourse with mankind, not to determine to look for support, rather to humouring their passions, than courting their approbation by the integrity of her conduct. A deadly blight had met her at the very threshold of existence; and the wretchedness of her mother seemed a heavy weight fastened on her innocent neck, to drag her down to perdition. She could not heroically determine to succour an unfortunate; but, offended at the bare supposition that she could be deceived with the same ease as a common servant, she no longer curbed her curiosity;[1] and, though she never seriously fathomed her own intentions, she would sit, every moment she could steal from observation, listening to the tale, which Maria was eager to relate with all the persuasive eloquence of grief.

It is so cheering to see a human face, even if little of the divinity of virtue beam in it, that Maria anxiously expected the return of the attendant, as of a gleam of light to break the gloom of idleness. Indulged sorrow, she perceived, must blunt or sharpen the faculties to the two opposite extremes; producing stupidity, the moping melancholy of indolence; or the restless activity of a disturbed imagination. She sunk into one state, after being fatigued by the other: till the want of occupation became even more painful than the actual pressure or apprehension of sorrow; and the confinement that froze her into a nook of existence, with an unvaried prospect before her, the most insupportable of evils. The lamp of life seemed to be spending itself to chase the vapours of a dungeon which no art could dissipate.—And to what purpose did she rally all her energy?—Was not the world a vast prison, and women born slaves?

Though she failed immediately to rouse a lively sense of injustice in the mind of her guard, because it had been sophisticated[2] into misanthropy, she touched her heart.

Jemima[1] (she had only a claim to a Christian name,[2] which had not procured her any Christian privileges) could patiently hear of Maria's confinement on false pretences; she had felt the crushing hand of power, hardened by the exercise of injustice, and ceased to wonder at the perversions of the understanding, which systematize oppression; but, when told that her child, only four months old, had been torn from her, even while she was discharging the tenderest maternal office, the woman[3] awoke in a bosom long estranged from feminine emotions, and Jemima determined to alleviate all in her power, without hazarding the loss of her place, the sufferings of a wretched mother, apparently injured, and certainly unhappy. A sense of right seems to result from the simplest act of reason,[4] and to preside over the faculties of the mind, like the master sense of feeling, to rectify the rest; but (for the comparison may be carried still farther) how often is the exquisite sensibility of both weakened or destroyed by the vulgar occupations, and ignoble pleasures of life?

The preserving her situation was, indeed, an important object to Jemima, who had been hunted from hole to hole, as if she had been a beast of prey, or infected with a moral plague. The wages she received, the greater part of which she hoarded, as her only chance for independence,[5] were much more considerable than she could reckon on obtaining any where else, were it possible that she, an outcast from society, could be permitted to earn a subsistence in a reputable family. Hearing Maria perpetually complain of listlessness, and the not being able to beguile grief by resuming her customary pursuits, she was easily prevailed on, by compassion, and that involuntary respect for abilities, which those who possess them can never eradicate, to bring her some books and implements for writing. Maria's conversation had amused and interested her, and the natural consequence was a desire, scarcely observed by herself, of obtaining the esteem of a person she admired. The remembrance of better days was rendered more lively; and the sentiments then acquired appearing less romantic than they had for a long period, a spark of hope roused her mind to new activity.

How grateful[1] was her attention to Maria! Oppressed by a dead weight of existence, or preyed on by the gnawing worm of discontent, with what eagerness did she endeavour to shorten the long days, which left no traces behind! She seemed to be sailing on the vast ocean of life, without seeing any land-mark to indicate the progress of time; to find employment was then to find variety, the animating principle of nature.

CHAPTER TWO

EARNESTLY as Maria endeavoured to soothe, by reading, the anguish of her wounded mind, her thoughts would often wander from the subject she was led to discuss, and tears of maternal tenderness obscured the reasoning page. She descanted on 'the ills which flesh is heir to,'[2] with bitterness, when the recollection of her babe was revived by a tale of fictitious woe, that bore any resemblance to her own; and her imagination was continually employed, to conjure up and embody the various phantoms of misery, which folly and vice had let loose on the world. The loss of her babe was the tender string; against other cruel remembrances she laboured to steel her bosom; and even a ray of hope, in the midst of her gloomy reveries, would sometimes gleam on the dark horizon of futurity, while persuading herself that she ought to cease to hope, since happiness was no where to be found. —But of her child, debilitated by the grief with which its mother had been assailed before it saw the light, she could not think without an impatient struggle.

'I, alone, by my active tenderness, could have saved,' she would exclaim, 'from an early blight, this sweet blossom; and, cherishing it, I should have had something still to love.'

In proportion as other expectations were torn from her, this tender one had been fondly clung to, and knit into her heart.

The books she had obtained, were soon devoured, by one who had no other resource to escape from sorrow, and the feverish dreams of ideal wretchedness or felicity, which equally weaken the intoxicated sensibility. Writing was then the only alternative, and she wrote some rhapsodies descriptive of the state of her mind; but the events of her past life pressing on her, she resolved circumstantially to relate them, with the sentiments that experience, and more matured reason, would naturally suggest. They might perhaps instruct her daughter, and shield her from the misery, the tyranny, her mother knew not how to avoid.

This thought gave life to her diction, her soul flowed into it, and she soon found the task of recollecting almost obliterated impressions very interesting. She lived again in the revived emotions of youth, and forgot her present in the retrospect of sorrows that had assumed an unalterable character.

Though this employment lightened the weight of time, yet, never losing sight of her main object, Maria did not allow any opportunity to slip of winning on the affections of Jemima; for she discovered in her a strength of mind, that excited her esteem, clouded as it was by the misanthropy of despair.

An insulated being, from the misfortune of her birth, she despised and preyed on the society by which she had been oppressed, and loved not her fellow-creatures, because she had never been beloved. No mother had ever fondled her, no father or brother had protected her from outrage; and the man who had plunged her into infamy, and deserted her when she stood in greatest need of support, deigned not to smooth with kindness the road to ruin. Thus degraded, was she let loose on the world; and virtue, never nurtured by affection, assumed the stern aspect of selfish independence.

This general view of her life, Maria gathered from her exclamations and dry remarks. Jemima indeed displayed a strange mixture of interest and suspicion; for she would listen to her with earnestness, and then suddenly interrupt the conversation, as if afraid of resigning, by giving way to her sympathy, her dear-bought knowledge of the world.

Maria alluded to the possibility of an escape, and ' mentioned a compensation, or reward; but the style in which she was repulsed made her cautious, and determine not to renew the subject, till she knew more of the character she had to work on. Jemima's countenance, and dark hints, seemed to say, 'You are an extraordinary woman; but let me consider, this may only be one of your lucid intervals.' Nay, the very energy of Maria's character, made her suspect that the extraordinary animation she perceived might be the effect of madness. 'Should her husband then substantiate his charge, and get possession of her estate, from whence would come the promised annuity, or more desired protection? Besides, might not a woman, anxious to escape, conceal some of the circumstances which made against her? Was truth to be expected from one who had been entrapped, kidnapped, in the most fradulent manner?'

In this train Jemima continued to argue, the moment after compassion and respect seemed to make her swerve; and she still resolved not to be wrought on to do more than soften the rigour of confinement, till she could advance on surer ground.

Maria was not permitted to walk in the garden; but sometimes, from her window, she turned her eyes from the gloomy walls, in which she pined life away, on the poor wretches who strayed along the walks, and contemplated the most terrific of ruins—that of a human soul. What is the view of the fallen column, the mouldering arch, of the most exquisite workmanship, .when compared with this living memento of the fragility, the instability, of reason, and the wild luxuriancy of noxious passions? Enthusiasm turned adrift, like some rich stream overflowing its banks, rushes forward with destructive velocity, inspiring a sublime concentration of thought.[1] Thus thought Maria—These are the ravages over which humanity must ever mournfully ponder, with a degree of anguish not excited by crumbling marble, or cankering brass, unfaithful to the trust of monumental fame. It is not over the decaying productions of the mind, embodied with the happiest art, we grieve most bitterly. The view of what has been done by man, produces a melancholy, yet aggrandizing, sense of what remains to be achieved by human intellect; but a mental convulsion, which, like the devastation of an earthquake, throws all the elements of thought and imagination into confusion, makes contemplation giddy, and we fearfully ask on what ground we ourselves stand.

Melancholy and imbecility marked the features of the wretches allowed to breathe at large; for the frantic, those who in a strong imagination had lost a sense of woe, were closely confined. The playful tricks and mischievous devices of their disturbed fancy, that suddenly broke out, could not be guarded against, when they were permitted to enjoy any portion of freedom; for, so active was their imagination, that every new object which accidentally struck their senses, awoke to phrenzy their restless passions; as Maria learned from the burden of their incessant ravings.

Sometimes, with a strict injunction of silence, Jemima would allow Maria, at the close of evening, to stray along the narrow avenues that separated the dungeon-like apartments, leaning on her arm. What a change of scene! Maria wished to pass the threshold of her prison, yet, when by chance she met the eye of rage glaring on her, yet unfaithful to its office, she shrunk back with more horror and affright, than if she had stumbled over a mangled corpse. Her busy fancy pictured the misery of a fond heart, watching over a friend thus estranged, absent, though present—over a poor wretch lost to reason and the social joys of existence; and losing all consciousness of misery in its excess. What a task, to watch the light of reason quivering in the eye, or with agonizing expectation to catch the beam of recollection; tantalized by hope, only to feel despair more keenly, at finding a much loved face or voice, suddenly remembered, or pathetically implored, only to be immediately forgotten, or viewed with indifference or abhorrence!

The heart-rending sigh of melancholy sunk into her soul; and when she retired to rest, the petrified figures she had encountered, the only human forms she was doomed to observe, haunting her dreams with tales of mysterious wrongs, made her wish to sleep to dream no more.[1]

Day after day rolled away, and tedious as the present moment appeared, they passed in such an unvaried tenor, Maria was surprised to find that she had already been six weeks buried alive, and yet had such faint hopes of effecting her enlargement. She was, earnestly as she had sought for employment, now angry with herself for having been amused by writing her narrative; and grieved to think that she had for an instant thought of any thing, but contriving to escape.

Jemima had evidently pleasure in her society: still, though she often left her with a glow of kindness, she returned with the same chilling air; and, when her heart appeared for a moment to open, some suggestion of reason forcibly closed it, before she could give utterance to the confidence Maria's conversation inspired.

Discouraged by these changes, Maria relapsed into despondency, when she was cheered by the alacrity with which Jemima brought her a fresh parcel of books; assuring her, that she had taken some pains to obtain them from one of the keepers, who attended a gentleman confined in the opposite corner of the gallery.

Maria took up the books with emotion. 'They come,' said she, 'perhaps, from a wretch condemned, like me, to reason on the nature of madness, by having wrecked minds continually under his eye; and almost to wish himself—as I do—mad, to escape from the contemplation of it.' Her heart throbbed with sympathetic alarm; and she turned over the leaves with awe, as if they had become sacred from passing through the hands of an unfortunate being, oppressed by a similar fate.

Dryden's Fables, Milton's Paradise Lost,[2] with several modern productions, composed the collection. It was a mine of treasure. Some marginal notes, in Dryden's Fables, caught her attention: they were written with force and taste; and, in one of the modern pamphlets, there was a fragment left, containing various observations on the present state of society and government, with a comparative view of the politics of Europe and America. These remarks were written with a degree of generous warmth, when alluding to the enslaved state of the labouring majority, perfectly in unison with Maria's mode of thinking.

She read them over and over again; and fancy, treacherous fancy, began to sketch a character, congenial with her own, from these shadowy outlines.—'Was he mad?' She re-perused the marginal notes, and they seemed the production of an animated, but not of a disturbed imagination. Confined to this speculation, every time she re-read them, some fresh refinement of sentiment, or accuteness of thought impressed her, which she was astonished at herself for not having before observed.

What a creative power has an affectionate heart! There are beings who cannot live without loving, as poets love; and who feel the electric spark of genius, wherever it awakens sentiment or grace. Maria had often thought, when disciplining her wayward heart, 'that to charm, was to be virtuous.' 'They who make me wish to appear the most amiable and good in their eyes, must possess in a degree,' she would exclaim, 'the graces and virtues they call into action.'

She took up a book on the powers of the human mind; but, her attention strayed from cold arguments on the nature of what she felt, while she was feeling, and she snapt the chain of the theory to read Dryden's Guiscard and Sigismunda.[1]

Maria, in the course of the ensuing day, returned some of the books, with the hope of getting others—and more marginal notes. Thus shut out from human intercourse, and compelled to view nothing but the prison of vexed spirits, to meet a wretch in the same situation, was more surely to find a friend, than to imagine a countryman one, in a strange land, where the human voice conveys no information to the eager ear.

'Did you ever see the unfortunate being to whom these books belong?' asked Maria, when Jemima brought her supper. 'Yes. He sometimes walks out, between five and six, before the family is stirring, in the morning, with two keepers; but even then his hands are confined.'

'What! is he so unruly?' enquired Maria, with an accent of disappointment.

'No, not that I perceive,' replied Jemima; 'but he has an untamed look, a vehemence of eye, that excites apprehension. Were his hands free, he looks as if he could soon manage both his guards: yet he appears tranquil.'

'If he be so strong, he must be young,' observed Maria.

'Three or four and thirty, I suppose; but there is no judging of a person in his situation.'

'Are you sure that he is mad?' interrupted Maria with eagerness. Jemima quitted the room, without replying.

'No, no, he certainly is not!' exclaimed Maria, answering herself; 'the man who could write those observations was not disordered in his intellects.'

She sat musing, gazing at the moon, and watching its motion as it seemed to glide under the clouds. Then, preparing for bed, she thought, 'Of what use could I be to him, or he to me, if it be true that he is unjustly confined?—Could he aid me to escape, who is himself more closely watched?—Still I should like to see him.' She went to bed, dreamed of her child, yet woke exactly at half after five o'clock, and starting up, only wrapped a gown around her, and ran to the window. The morning was chill, it was the latter end of September; yet she did not retire to warm herself and think in bed, till the sound of the servants, moving about the house, convinced her that the unknown would not walk in the garden that morning. She was ashamed at feeling disappointed; and began to reflect, as an excuse to herself, on the little objects which attract attention when there is nothing to divert the mind; and how difficult it was for women to avoid growing romantic, who have no active duties or pursuits.[1]

At breakfast, Jemima enquired whether she understood French? for, unless she did, the stranger's stock of books was exhausted. Maria replied in the affirmative; but forbore to ask any more questions respecting the person to whom they belonged. And Jemima gave her a new subject for contemplation, by describing the person of a lovely maniac, just brought into an adjoining chamber. She was singing the pathetic ballad of old Robin Gray,[1] with the most heart-melting falls and pauses. Jemima had half-opened the door, when she distinguished her voice, and Maria stood close to it, scarcely daring to respire, lest a modulation should escape her, so exquisitely sweet, so passionately wild. She began with sympathy to pourtray to herself another victim, when the lovely warbler flew, as it were, from the spray, and a torrent of unconnected exclamations and questions burst from her, interrupted by fits of laughter, so horrid, that Maria shut the door, and, turning her eyes up to heaven, exclaimed—'Gracious God!'

Several minutes elapsed before Maria could enquire respecting the rumour of the house (for this poor wretch was obviously not confined without a cause); and then Jemima could only tell her, that it was said, 'she had been married, against her inclination, to a rich old man, extremely jealous (no wonder, for she was a charming creature); and that, in consequence of his treatment, or something which hung on her mind, she had, during her first lying-in, lost her senses.'[2]

What a subject of meditation—even to the very confines of madness.

'Woman, fragile flower! why were you suffered to adorn a world exposed to the inroad of such stormy elements?' thought Maria, while the poor maniac's strain was still breathing on her ear, and sinking into her very soul.

Towards the evening, Jemima brought her Rousseau's *Heloïse*; and she sat reading with eyes and heart, till the return of her guard to extinguish the light. One instance of her kindness was, the permitting Maria to have one, till her own hour of retiring to rest. She had read this work long since; but now it seemed to open a new world to her—the only one worth inhabiting.[3] Sleep was not to be wooed; yet, far from being fatigued by the restless rotation of thought, she rose and opened her window, just as the thin watery clouds of twilight made the long silent shadows visible. The air swept across her face with a voluptuous freshness that thrilled[1] to her heart, awakening indefinable emotions; and the sound of a waving branch, or the twittering of a startled bird, alone broke the stillness of reposing nature. Absorbed by the sublime sensibility which renders the consciousness of existence felicity, Maria was happy, till an autumnal scent, wafted by the breeze of morn from the fallen leaves of the adjacent wood, made her recollect that the season had changed since her confinement; yet life afforded no variety to solace an afflicted heart. She returned dispirited to her couch, and thought of her child till the broad glare of day again invited her to the window. She looked not for the unknown, still how great was her vexation at perceiving the back of a man, certainly he, with his two attendants, as he turned into a side-path which led to the house! A confused recollection of having seen somebody who resembled him, immediately occurred, to puzzle and torment her with endless conjectures.[2] Five minutes sooner, and she should have seen his face, and been out of suspense—was ever any thing so unlucky! His steady, bold step, and the whole air of his person, bursting as it were from a cloud, pleased her, and gave an outline to the imagination to sketch the individual form she wished to recognize.

Feeling the disappointment more severely than she was willing to believe, she flew to Rousseau, as her only refuge from the idea of him, who might prove a friend, could she but find a way to interest him in her fate; still the personification of Saint Preux,[3] or of an ideal lover far superior, was after this imperfect model, of which merely a glance had been caught, even to the minutiæ of the coat and hat of the stranger. But if she lent St. Preux, or the demi-god of her fancy, his form, she richly repaid him by the donation of all St. Preux's sentiments and feelings, culled to gratify her own, to which he seemed to have an undoubted right, when she read on the margin of an impassioned letter, written in the well-known hand—'Rousseau alone, the true Prometheus[4] of sentiment, possessed the fire of genius necessary to pourtray the passion, the truth of which goes so directly to the heart.'

Maria was again true to the hour, yet had finished Rousseau, and begun to transcribe some selected passages; unable to quit either the author or the window, before she had a glimpse of the countenance she daily longed to see; and, when seen, it conveyed no distinct idea to her mind where she had seen it before. He must have been a transient acquaintance; but to discover an acquaintance was fortunate, could she contrive to attract his attention, and excite his sympathy.

Every glance afforded colouring for the picture she was delineating on her heart; and once, when the window was half open, the sound of his voice reached her. Conviction flashed on her; she had certainly, in a moment of distress, heard the same accents. They were manly, and characteristic of a noble mind; nay, even sweet—or sweet they seemed to her attentive ear.

She started back, trembling, alarmed at the emotion a strange coincidence of circumstances inspired, and wondering why she thought so much of a stranger, obliged as she had been by his timely interference; [for she recollected, by degrees, all the circumstances of their former meeting.][1] She found however that she could think of nothing else; or, if she thought of her daughter, it was to wish that she had a father whom her mother could respect and love.[2]

CHAPTER THREE

WHEN perusing the first parcel of books, Maria had, with her pencil, written in one of them a few exclamations, expressive of compassion and sympathy, which she scarcely remembered, till turning over the leaves of one of the volumes, lately brought to her, a slip of paper dropped out, which Jemima hastily snatched up.

'Let me see it,' demanded Maria impatiently, 'You surely are not afraid of trusting me with the effusions of a madman?' 'I must consider,' replied Jemima; and withdrew, with the paper in her hand.

In a life of such seclusion,[1] the passions gain undue force; Maria therefore felt a great degree of resentment and vexation, which she had not time to subdue, before Jemima, returning, delivered the paper.

'Whoever you are, who partake of my fate, accept my sincere commiseration—I would have said protection; but the privilege of man is denied me.

'My own situation forces a dreadful suspicion on my mind—I may not always languish in vain for freedom—say are you—I cannot ask the question; yet I will remember you when my remembrance can be of any use. I will enquire, *why* you are so mysteriously detained—and I *will* have an answer.

'HENRY DARNFORD.'[2]

By the most pressing intreaties, Maria prevailed on Jemima to permit her to write a reply to this note. Another and another succeeded, in which explanations were not allowed relative to their present situation; but Maria, with sufficient explicitness, alluded to a former obligation;[3] and they insensibly entered on an interchange of sentiments on the most important subjects. To write these letters was the business of the day, and to receive them the moment of sunshine. By some means, Darnford having discovered Maria's window, when she next appeared at it, he made her, behind his keepers, a profound bow of respect and recognition.

Two or three weeks glided away in this kind of intercourse, during which period Jemima, to whom Maria had given the necessary information respecting her family, had evidently gained some intelligence, which increased her desire of pleasing her charge, though she could not yet determine to liberate her. Maria took advantage of this favourable change, without too minutely enquiring into the cause; and such was her eagerness to hold human converse, and to see her former protector, still a stranger to her, that she incessantly requested her guard to gratify her more than curiosity.

Writing to Darnford, she was led from the sad objects before her, and frequently rendered insensible to the horrid noises around her, which previously had continually employed her feverish fancy. Thinking it selfish to dwell on her own sufferings, when in the midst of wretches, who had not only lost all that endears life, but their very selves,[1] her imagination was occupied with melancholy earnestness to trace the mazes of misery, through which so many wretches must have passed to this gloomy receptacle of disjointed souls, to the grand source of human corruption. Often at midnight was she waked by the dismal shrieks of demoniac rage, or of excruciating despair, uttered in such wild tones of indescribable anguish as proved the total absence of reason, and roused phantoms of horror in her mind, far more terrific than all that dreaming superstition ever drew. Besides, there was frequently something so inconceivably picturesque in the varying gestures of unrestrained passion, so irresistibly comic in their sallies, or so heart-piercingly pathetic in the little airs they would sing, frequently bursting out after an awful silence, as to fascinate the attention, and amuse the fancy, while torturing the soul. It was the uproar of the passions which she was compelled to observe; and to mark the lucid beam of reason, like a light trembling in a socket, or like the flash which divides the threatening clouds of angry heaven only to display the horrors which darkness shrouded.

Jemima would labour to beguile the tedious evenings, by describing the persons and manners of the unfortunate beings, whose figures or voices awoke sympathetic sorrow in Maria's bosom; and the stories she told were the more interesting, for perpetually leaving room to conjecture something extraordinary. Still Maria, accustomed to generalize her observations, was led to conclude from all she heard, that it was a vulgar error to suppose that people of abilities were the most apt to lose the command of reason. On

Reason vs passion

the contrary, from most of the instances she could investigate, she thought it resulted, that the passions only appeared strong and disproportioned, because the judgment was weak and unexercised; and that they gained strength by the decay of reason, as the shadows lengthen during the sun's decline.

Maria impatiently wished to see her fellow-sufferer; but Darnford was still more earnest to obtain an interview. Accustomed to submit to every impulse of passion, and never taught, like women, to restrain the most natural, and acquire, instead of the bewitching frankness of nature, a factitious propriety of behaviour, every desire became a torrent that bore down all opposition.[1]

His travelling trunk, which contained the books lent to Maria, had been sent to him, and with a part of its contents he bribed his principal keeper; who, after receiving the most solemn promise that he would return to his apartment without attempting to explore any part of the house, conducted him, in the dusk of the evening, to Maria's room.

Jemima had apprized her charge of the visit, and she expected with trembling impatience, inspired by a vague hope that he might again prove her deliverer, to see a man who had before rescued her from oppression. He entered with an animation of countenance, formed to captivate an enthusiast; and, hastily turned his eyes from her to the apartment, which he surveyed with apparent emotions of compassionate indignation. Sympathy illuminated his eye, and, taking her hand, he respectfully bowed on it, exclaiming—'This is extraordinary!—again to meet you, and in such circumstances!' Still, impressive as was the coincidence of events which brought them once more together, their full hearts did not overflow.—*

*The copy which had received the author's last corrections, breaks off in this place, and the pages which follow, to the end of Chap. IV, are printed from a copy in a less finished state.[2]

[And though, after this first visit, they were permitted frequently to repeat their interviews, they were for some time employed in] a reserved conversation, to which all the world might have listened; excepting, when discussing some literary subject, flashes of sentiment, inforced by each relaxing feature, seemed to remind them that their minds were already acquainted.

[By degrees, Darnford entered into the particulars of his story.] In a few words, he informed her that he had been a thoughtless, extravagant young man; yet, as he described his faults, they appeared to be the generous luxuriancy of a noble mind. Nothing like meanness tarnished the lustre of his youth, nor had the worm of selfishness lurked in the unfolding bud, even while he had been the dupe of others. Yet he tardily acquired the experience necessary to guard him against future imposition.

'I shall weary you,' continued he, 'by my egotism; and did not powerful emotions draw me to you,'—his eyes glistened as he spoke, and a trembling seemed to run through his manly frame,—'I would not waste these precious moments in talking of myself.

'My father and mother were people of fashion; married by their parents. He was fond of the turf, she of the card-table. I, and two or three other children since dead, were kept at home till we became intolerable. My father and mother had a visible dislike to each other, continually displayed: the servants were of the depraved kind usually found in the houses of people of fortune. My brothers and parents all dying, I was left to the care of guardians, and sent to Eton. I never knew the sweets of domestic affection, but I felt the want of indulgence and frivolous respect at school. I will not disgust you with a recital of the vices of my youth, which can scarcely be comprehended by female delicacy. I was taught to love by a creature I am ashamed to mention; and the other women with whom I afterwards became intimate, were of a class of which you can have no knowledge. I formed my acquaintance with them at the theatres; and, when vivacity danced in their eyes, I was not easily disgusted by the vulgarity which flowed from their lips. Having spent, a few years after I was of age, [the whole of] a considerable patrimony, excepting a few hundreds, I had no resource but to purchase a commission in a new-raised regiment, destined to subjugate America. The regret I felt to renounce a life of pleasure, was counterbalanced by the curiosity I had to see America, or rather to travel; [nor had any of those circumstances occurred to my youth, which might have been calculated] to bind my country to my heart. I shall not trouble you with the details of a military life. My blood was still kept in motion; till, towards the close of the contest, I was wounded and taken prisoner.[1]

'Confined to my bed, or chair, by a lingering cure, my only refuge from the preying activity of my mind, was books, which I read with great avidity, profiting by the conversation of my host, a man of sound understanding. My political sentiments now underwent a total change; and, dazzled by the hospitality of the Americans, I determined to take up my abode with freedom. I, therefore, with my usual impetuosity,[2] sold my commission, and travelled[3] into the interior parts of the country, to lay out my money to advantage. Added to this, I did not much like the puritanical manners of the large towns. Inequality of condition was there most disgustingly galling. The only pleasure wealth afforded, was to make an ostentatious display of it; for the cultivation of the fine arts, or literature, had not introduced into the first circles that polish of manners which renders the rich so essentially superior to the poor in Europe. Added to this, an influx of vices had been let in by the Revolution, and the most rigid principles of religion shaken to the centre, before the understanding could be gradually emancipated from the prejudices which led their ancestors undauntedly to seek an inhospitable clime and unbroken soil. The resolution, that led them, in pursuit of independence, to embark on rivers like seas, to search for unknown shores, and to sleep under the hovering mists of endless forests, whose baleful damps agued their limbs, was now turned into commercial speculations,[4] till the national character exhibited a phenomenon in the history of the human mind—a head enthusiastically enterprising, with cold selfishness of heart. And woman, lovely woman!—they charm every where—still there is a degree of prudery, and a want of taste and ease in the manners of the American women, that renders them, in spite of their roses and lilies, far inferior to our European charmers. In the country, they have often a bewitching simplicity of character; but, in the cities, they have all the airs and ignorance of the ladies who give the tone to the circles of the large trading towns in England. They are fond of their ornaments, merely because they are good, and not because they embellish their persons; and are more gratified to inspire the women with jealousy of these exterior advantages, than the men with love. All the frivolity which often (excuse me, Madam) renders the society of modest women so stupid in England, here seemed to throw still more leaden fetters on their charms. Not being an adept in gallantry, I found that I could only keep myself awake in their company by making downright love to them.

'But, not to intrude on your patience, I retired to the track¹ of land which I had purchased in the country, and my time passed pleasantly enough while I cut down the trees, built my house, and planted my different crops. But winter and idleness came, and I longed for more elegant society, to hear what was passing in the world, and to do something better than vegetate with the animals that made a very considerable part of my household. Consequently, I determined to travel. Motion was a substitute for variety of objects; and, passing over immense tracks of country, I exhausted my exuberant spirits, without obtaining much experience. I every where saw industry the fore-runner and not the consequence, of luxury; but this country, every thing being on an ample scale, did not afford those picturesque views, which a certain degree of cultivation is necessary gradually to produce. The eye wandered without an object to fix upon over immeasurable plains, and lakes that seemed replenished by the ocean, whilst eternal forests of small clustering trees, obstructed the circulation of air, and embarrassed the path, without gratifying the eye of taste. No cottage smiling in the waste, no travellers hailed us, to give life to silent nature; or, if perchance we saw the print of a footstep in our path, it was a dreadful warning to turn aside; and the head ached as if assailed by the scalping knife. The Indians who hovered on the skirts of the European settlements had only learned of their neighbours to plunder, and they stole their guns from them to do it with more safety.

'From the woods and back settlements, I returned to the towns, and learned to eat and drink most valiantly; but without entering into commerce (and I detested commerce) I found I could not live there; and, growing heartily weary of the land of liberty and vulgar aristocracy, seated on her bags of dollars, I resolved once more to visit Europe. I wrote to a distant relation in England, with whom I had been educated, mentioning the vessel in which I intended to sail. Arriving in London, my senses were intoxicated. I ran from street to street, from theatre to theatre, and the women of the town (again I must beg pardon for my habitual frankness) appeared to me like angels.

'A week was spent in this thoughtless manner, when, returning very late to the hotel in which I had lodged ever since my arrival, I was knocked down in a private street, and hurried, in a state of insensibility, into a coach, which brought me hither, and I only recovered my senses to be treated like one who had lost them. My keepers are deaf to my remonstrances and enquiries, yet assure me that my confinement shall not last long. Still I cannot guess, though I weary myself with conjectures, why I am confined, or in what part of England this house is situated. I imagine sometimes that I hear the sea roar, and wished myself again on the Atlantic, till I had a glimpse of you*.'

---

*The introduction of Darnford as the deliverer of Maria in a former instance, appears to have been an after-thought of the author. This has occasioned the omission of any allusion to that circumstance in the preceding narration.

EDITOR.

A few moments were only allowed to Maria to comment on this narrative, when Darnford left her to her own thoughts, to the 'never ending, still beginning,'[1] task of weighing his words, recollecting his tones of voice, and feeling them reverberate on her heart.

CHAPTER FOUR

PITY, and the forlorn seriousness of adversity, have both been considered as dispositions favourable to love, while satirical writers have attributed the propensity to the relaxing effect of idleness; what chance then had Maria of escaping, when pity, sorrow, and solitude all conspired to soften her mind, and nourish romantic wishes, and, from a natural progress, romantic expectations?

Maria was six-and-twenty. But, such was the native soundness of her constitution, that time had only given to her countenance the character of her mind. Revolving thought, and exercised affections had banished some of the playful graces of innocence, producing insensibly that irregularity of features which the struggles of the understanding to trace or govern the strong emotions of the heart, are wont to imprint on the yielding mass. Grief and care had mellowed, without obscuring, the bright tints of youth, and the thoughtfulness which resided on her brow did not take from the feminine softness of her features; nay, such was the sensibility which often mantled over it, that she frequently appeared, like a large proportion of her sex, only born to feel;[2] and the activity of her well-proportioned, and even almost voluptuous figure,[3] inspired the idea of strength of mind, rather than of body. There was a simplicity sometimes indeed in her manner, which bordered on infantine ingenuousness, that led people of common discernment to under-rate her talents, and smile at the flights of her imagination. But those who could not comprehend the delicacy of her sentiments, were attached by her unfailing sympathy, so that she was very generally beloved by characters of very different descriptions; still, she was too much under the influence of an ardent imagination to adhere to common rules.

There are mistakes of conduct which at five-and-twenty prove the strength of the mind, that, ten or fifteen years after, would demonstrate its weakness, its incapacity to acquire a sane judgment. The youths who are satisfied with the ordinary pleasures of life, and do not sigh after ideal phantoms of love and friendship, will never arrive at great maturity of understanding; but if these reveries are cherished, as is too frequently the case with women, when experience ought to have taught them in what human happiness consists, they become as useless as they are wretched. Besides, their pains and pleasures are so dependent on outward circumstances, on the objects of their affections, that they seldom act from the impulse of a nerved mind, able to choose its own pursuit.

Having had to struggle incessantly with the vices of mankind, Maria's imagination found repose in pourtraying the possible virtues the world might contain. Pygmalion[1] formed an ivory maid, and longed for an informing soul. She, on the contrary, combined all the qualities of a hero's mind, and fate presented a statue in which she might enshrine them.

We mean not to trace the progress of this passion, or recount how often Darnford and Maria were obliged to part in the midst of an interesting conversation. Jemima ever watched on the tip-toe of fear, and frequently separated them on a false alarm, when they would have given worlds to remain a little longer together.

A magic lamp now seemed to be suspended in Maria's prison, and fairy landscapes flitted round the gloomy walls, late so blank. Rushing from the depth of despair, on the seraph wing of hope, she found herself happy.—She was beloved, and every emotion was rapturous.

To Darnford she had not shown a decided affection; the fear of outrunning his, a sure proof of love, made her often assume a coldness and indifference foreign from her character; and, even when giving way to the playful emotions of a heart just loosened from the frozen bond of grief, there was a delicacy in her manner of expressing her sensibility, which made him doubt whether it was the effect of love.[1]

One evening, when Jemima left them, to listen to the sound of a distant footstep, which seemed cautiously to approach, he seized Maria's hand—it was not withdrawn. They conversed with earnestness of their situation; and, during the conversation, he once or twice gently drew her towards him. He felt the fragrance of her breath, and longed, yet feared, to touch the lips from which it issued; spirits of purity seemed to guard them, while all the enchanting graces of love sported on her cheeks, and languished in her eyes.

Jemima entering, he reflected on his diffidence with poignant regret, and, she once more taking alarm, he ventured, as Maria stood near his chair, to approach her lips with a declaration of love. She drew back with solemnity, he hung down his head abashed; but lifting his eyes timidly, they met her's; she had determined, during that instant, and suffered their rays to mingle. He took, with more ardour, reassured, a half-consenting, half-reluctant kiss, reluctant only from modesty; and there was a sacredness in her dignified manner of reclining her glowing face on his shoulder, that powerfully impressed him. Desire was lost in more ineffable emotions, and to protect her from insult and sorrow—to make her happy, seemed not only the first wish of his heart, but the most noble duty of his life. Such angelic confidence demanded the fidelity of honour; but could he, feeling her in every pulsation, could he ever change, could he be a villain? The emotion with which she, for a moment, allowed herself to be pressed to his bosom, the tear of rapturous sympathy, mingled with a soft melancholy sentiment of recollected disappointment, said—more of truth and faithfulness, than the tongue could have given utterance to in hours! They were silent—yet discoursed, how eloquently? till, after a moment's reflection, Maria drew her chair by the side of his, and, with a composed sweetness of voice, and supernatural benignity of countenance, said, 'I must open my whole heart to you; you must be told who I am, why I am here, and why, telling you I am a wife, I blush not to'—the blush spoke the rest.

Jemima was again at her elbow, and the restraint of her presence did not prevent an animated conversation, in which love, sly urchin, was ever at bo-peep.

So much of heaven did they enjoy, that paradise bloomed around them; or they, by a powerful spell, had been transported into Armida's garden.[1] Love, the grand enchanter, 'lapt them in Elysium,'[2] and every sense was harmonized to joy and social extacy. So animated, indeed, were their accents of tenderness, in discussing what, in other circumstances, would have been commonplace subjects, that Jemima felt, with surprise, a tear of pleasure trickling down her rugged cheeks. She wiped it away, half ashamed; and when Maria kindly enquired the cause, with all the eager solicitude of a happy being wishing to impart to all nature its overflowing felicity, Jemima owned that it was the first tear that social enjoyment had ever drawn from her. She seemed indeed to breathe more freely; the cloud of suspicion cleared away from her brow; she felt herself, for once in her life, treated like a fellow-creature.

Imagination! who can paint thy power; or reflect the evanescent tints of hope fostered by thee? A despondent gloom had long obscured Maria's horizon—now the sun broke forth, the rainbow appeared, and every prospect was fair. Horror still reigned in the darkened cells, suspicion lurked in the passages, and whispered along the walls. The yells of men possessed, sometimes made them pause, and wonder that they felt so happy, in a tomb of living death. They even chid themselves for such apparent insensibility; still the world contained not three happier beings. And Jemima, after again patrolling the passage, was so softened by the air of confidence which breathed around her, that she voluntarily began an account of herself.[3]

'MY father,' said Jemima, 'seduced my mother, a pretty girl, with whom he lived fellow-servant; and she no sooner perceived the natural, the dreaded consequence, than the terrible conviction flashed on her—that she was ruined.[1] Honesty, and a regard for her reputation, had been the only principles inculcated by her mother; and they had been so forcibly impressed, that she feared shame, more than the poverty to which it would lead. Her incessant importunities to prevail upon my father to screen her from reproach by marrying her, as he had promised in the fervour of seduction, estranged him from her so completely, that her very person became distasteful to him; and he began to hate, as well as despise me, before I was born.

'My mother, grieved to the soul by his neglect, and unkind treatment, actually resolved to famish herself; and injured her health by the attempt; though she had not sufficient resolution to adhere to her project, or renounce it entirely. Death came not at her call; yet sorrow, and the methods she adopted to conceal her condition, still doing the work of a house-maid, had such an effect on her constitution, that she died in the wretched garret, where her virtuous mistress had forced her to take refuge in the very pangs of labour, though my father, after a slight reproof, was allowed to remain in his place—allowed by the mother of six children, who, scarcely permitting a footstep to be heard, during her month's indulgence, felt no sympathy for the poor wretch, denied every comfort required by her situation.

'The day my mother died, the ninth after my birth, I was consigned to the care of the cheapest nurse my father could find; who suckled her own child at the same time, and lodged as many more as she could get, in two cellar-like apartments.

'Poverty, and the habit of seeing children die off her hands, had so hardened her heart, that the office of a mother did not awaken the tenderness of a woman; nor were the feminine caresses which seem a part of the rearing of a child, ever bestowed on me. The chicken has a wing to shelter under; but I had no bosom to nestle in, no kindred warmth to foster me. Left in dirt, to cry with cold and hunger till I was weary, and sleep without ever being prepared by exercise, or lulled by kindness to rest; could I be expected to become any thing but a weak and rickety babe? Still, in spite of neglect, I continued to exist, to learn to curse existence,' her countenance grew ferocious as she spoke, 'and the treatment that rendered me miserable, seemed to sharpen my wits. Confined then in a damp hovel, to rock the cradle of the succeeding tribe, I looked like a little old woman, or a hag shrivelling into nothing. The furrows of reflection and care contracted the youthful cheek, and gave a sort of supernatural wildness to the ever watchful eye. During this period, my father had married another fellow-servant, who loved him less, and knew better how to manage his passion,[1] than my mother. She likewise proving with child, they agreed to keep a shop: my step-mother, if, being an illegitimate offspring, I may venture thus to characterize her, having obtained a sum of a rich relation, for that purpose.

'Soon after her lying-in, she prevailed on my father to take me home, to save the expence of maintaining me, and of hiring a girl to assist her in the care of the child. I was young, it was true, but appeared a knowing little thing, and might be made handy. Accordingly I was brought to her house; but not to a home—for a home I never knew. Of this child, a daughter, she was extravagantly fond; and it was a part of my employment, to assist to spoil her, by humouring all her whims, and bearing all her caprices. Feeling her own consequence, before she could speak, she had learned the art of tormenting me, and if I ever dared to resist, I received blows, laid on with no compunctious hand, or was sent to bed dinnerless, as well as supperless. I said that it was a part of my daily labour to attend this child, with the servility of a slave; still it was but a part. I was sent out in all seasons, and from place to place, to

carry burdens far above my strength, without being allowed
to draw near the fire, or ever being cheered by encouragement
or kindness. No wonder then, treated like a creature of
another species, that I began to envy, and at length to hate, the
darling of the house. Yet, I perfectly remember, that it was the
caresses, and kind expressions of my step-mother, which first
excited my jealous discontent. Once, I cannot forget it, when
she was calling in vain her wayward child to kiss her, I ran to
her, saying, "I will kiss you, ma'am!" and how did my heart,
which was in my mouth, sink, what was my debasement of
soul, when pushed away with—"I do not want you, pert
thing!" Another day, when a new gown had excited the
highest good humour, and she uttered the appropriate *dear*,
addressed unexpectedly to me, I thought I could never do
enough to please her; I was all alacrity, and rose
proportionably in my own estimation.

'As her daughter grew up, she was pampered with cakes
and fruit, while I was, literally speaking, fed with the refuse of
the table, with her leavings. A liquorish[1] tooth is, I believe,
common to children, and I used to steal any thing sweet, that I
could catch up with a chance of concealment. When detected,
she was not content to chastize me herself at the moment, but,
on my father's return in the evening (he was a shopman), the
principal discourse was to recount my faults, and attribute
them to the wicked disposition which I had brought into the
world with me, inherited from my mother. He did not fail to
leave the marks of his resentment on my body, and then
solaced himself by playing with my sister.—I could have
murdered her at those moments. To save myself from these
unmerciful corrections, I resorted to falshood, and the
untruths which I sturdily maintained, were brought in
judgment against me, to support my tyrant's inhuman charge
of my natural propensity to vice. Seeing me treated with
contempt, and always being fed and dressed better, my sister
conceived a contemptuous opinion of me, that proved an
obstacle to all affection; and my father, hearing continually of
my faults, began to consider me as a curse entailed on him for

his sins: he was therefore easily prevailed on to bind me apprentice to one of my step-mother's friends, who kept a slop-shop[1] in Wapping. I was represented (as it was said) in my true colours; but she, "warranted," snapping her fingers, "that she should break my spirit or heart."

'My mother replied, with a whine, "that if any body could make me better, it was such a clever woman as herself; though, for her own part, she had tried in vain; but good-nature was her fault."

'I shudder with horror, when I recollect the treatment I had now to endure. Not only under the lash of my task-mistress, but the drudge of the maid, apprentices and children, I never had a taste of human kindness to soften the rigour of perpetual labour. I had been introduced as an object of abhorrence into the family; as a creature of whom my step-mother, though she had been kind enough to let me live in the house with her own child, could make nothing. I was described as a wretch, whose nose must be kept to the grinding stone—and it was held there with an iron grasp. It seemed indeed the privilege of their superior nature to kick me about, like the dog or cat. If I were attentive, I was called fawning, if refractory, an obstinate mule, and like a mule I received their censure on my loaded back. Often has my mistress, for some instance of forgetfulness, thrown me from one side of the kitchen to the other, knocked my head against the wall, spit in my face, with various refinements on barbarity that I forbear to enumerate, though they were all acted over again by the servant, with additional insults, to which the appellation of *bastard*, was commonly added, with taunts or sneers. But I will not attempt to give you an adequate idea of my situation, lest you, who probably have never been drenched with the dregs of human misery, should think I exaggerate.

'I stole now, from absolute necessity,—bread; yet whatever else was taken, which I had it not in my power to take, was ascribed to me. I was the filching cat, the ravenous dog, the dumb brute, who must bear all; for if I endeavoured to exculpate myself, I was silenced, without any enquiries being made, with "Hold your tongue, you never tell truth." Even the very air I breathed was tainted with scorn; for I was sent to the neighbouring shops with Glutton, Liar, or Thief, written on my forehead. This was, at first, the most bitter punishment; but sullen pride, or a kind of stupid desperation, made me, at length, almost regardless of the contempt, which had wrung from me so many solitary tears at the only moments when I was allowed to rest.

'Thus was I the mark of cruelty till my sixteenth year; and then I have only to point out a change of misery; for a period[1] I never knew. Allow me first to make one observation. Now I look back, I cannot help attributing the greater part of my misery, to the misfortune of having been thrown into the world without the grand support of life—a mother's affection.[2] I had no one to love me; or to make me respected, to enable me to acquire respect. I was an egg dropped on the sand; a pauper by nature, hunted from family to family, who belonged to nobody—and nobody cared for me. I was despised from my birth, and denied the chance of obtaining a footing for myself in society. Yes; I had not even the chance of being considered as a fellow-creature—yet all the people with whom I lived, brutalized as they were by the low cunning of trade, and the despicable shifts of poverty, were not without bowels, though they never yearned for me. I was, in fact, born a slave, and chained by infamy to slavery during the whole of existence, without having any companions to alleviate it by sympathy, or teach me how to rise above it by their example. But, to resume the thread of my tale—

'At sixteen, I suddenly grew tall, and something like comeliness appeared on a Sunday, when I had time to wash my face, and put on clean clothes. My master had once or twice caught hold of me in the passage; but I instinctively avoided his disgusting caresses. One day however, when the family were at a methodist meeting,[3] he contrived to be alone in the house with me, and by blows—yes; blows and menaces, compelled me to submit to his ferocious desire; and, to avoid my mistress's fury, I was obliged in future to comply, and skulk to my loft at his command, in spite of increasing loathing.

'The anguish which was now pent up in my bosom, seemed to open a new world to me: I began to extend my thoughts beyond myself, and grieve for human misery, till I discovered, with horror—ah! what horror!—that I was with child. I know not why I felt a mixed sensation of despair and tenderness, excepting that, ever called a bastard, a bastard appeared to me an object of the greatest compassion in creation.

'I communicated this dreadful circumstance to my master, who was almost equally alarmed at the intelligence; for he feared his wife, and public censure at the meeting. After some weeks of deliberation had elapsed, I in continual fear that my altered shape would be noticed, my master gave me a medicine in a phial, which he desired me to take, telling me, without any circumlocution, for what purpose it was designed.[1] I burst into tears, I thought it was killing myself—yet was such a self as I worth preserving? He cursed me for a fool, and left me to my own reflections. I could not resolve to take this infernal potion; but I wrapped it up in an old gown, and hid it in a corner of my box.

'Nobody yet suspected me, because they had been accustomed to view me as a creature of another species. But the threatening storm at last broke over my devoted head—never shall I forget it! One Sunday evening when I was left, as usual, to take care of the house, my master came home intoxicated, and I became the prey of his brutal appetite. His extreme intoxication made him forget his customary caution, and my mistress entered and found us in a situation that could not have been more hateful to her than me. Her husband was "pot-valiant," he feared her not at the moment, nor had he then much reason, for she instantly turned the whole force of her anger another way. She tore off my cap, scratched, kicked, and buffetted me, till she had exhausted her strength, declaring, as she rested her arm, "that I had wheedled her husband from her.—But, could anything better be expected from a wretch, whom she had taken into her house out of pure charity?" What a torrent of abuse rushed out? till, almost breathless, she concluded with saying, "that I was born a strumpet; it ran in my blood, and nothing good could come to those who harboured me."

'My situation was, of course, discovered, and she declared that I should not stay another night under the same roof with an honest family. I was therefore pushed out of doors, and my trumpery thrown after me, when it had been contemptuously examined in the passage, lest I should have stolen anything.

'Behold me then in the street, utterly destitute![1] Whither could I creep for shelter? To my father's roof I had no claim, when not pursued by shame—now I shrunk back as from death, from my mother's cruel reproaches, my father's execrations. I could not endure to hear him curse the day I was born, though life had been a curse to me. Of death I thought, but with a confused emotion of terror, as I stood leaning my head on a post, and starting at every footstep, lest it should be my mistress coming to tear my heart out. One of the boys of the shop passing by, heard my tale, and immediately repaired to his master, to give him a description of my situation; and he touched the right key—the scandal it would give rise to, if I were left to repeat my tale to every enquirer. This plea came home to his reason, who had been sobered by his wife's rage, the fury of which fell on him when I was out of her reach, and he sent the boy to me with half-a-guinea, desiring him to conduct me to a house, where beggars, and other wretches, the refuse of society, nightly lodged.

'This night was spent in a state of stupefaction, or desperation. I detested mankind, and abhorred myself.

'In the morning I ventured out, to throw myself in my master's way, at his usual hour of going abroad. I approached him, he "damned me for a b——, declared I had disturbed the peace of the family, and that he had sworn to his wife, never to take any more notice of me." He left me; but, instantly returning, he told me that he should speak to his friend, a parish-officer,[2] to get a nurse for the brat I laid to him; and advised me, if I wished to keep out of the house of correction, not to make free with his name.

'I hurried back to my hole, and, rage giving place to despair, sought for the potion that was to procure abortion, and swallowed it, with a wish that it might destroy me, at the same time that it stopped the sensations of new-born life, which I felt with indescribable emotion. My head turned round, my heart grew sick, and in the horrors of approaching dissolution, mental anguish was swallowed up. The effect of the medicine was violent, and I was confined to my bed several days; but, youth and a strong constitution prevailing, I once more crawled out, to ask myself the cruel question, "Whither I should go?" I had but two shillings left in my pocket, the rest had been expended, by a poor woman who slept in the same room, to pay for my lodging, and purchase the necessaries of which she partook.

'With this wretch I went into the neighbouring streets to beg, and my disconsolate appearance drew a few pence from the idle, enabling me still to command a bed; till, recovering from my illness, and taught to put on my rags to the best advantage, I was accosted from different motives, and yielded to the desire of the brutes I met, with the same detestation that I had felt for my still more brutal master. I have since read in novels of the blandishments of seduction, but I had not even the pleasure of being enticed into vice.[1]

'I shall not,' interrupted Jemima, 'lead your imagination into all the scenes of wretchedness and depravity, which I was condemned to view; or mark the different stages of my debasing misery. Fate dragged me through the very kennels of society; I was still a slave, a bastard, a common property. Become familiar with vice, for I wish to conceal nothing from you, I picked the pockets of the drunkards who abused me; and proved by my conduct, that I deserved the epithets, with which they loaded me at moments when distrust ought to cease.

'Detesting my nightly occupation, though valuing, if I may so use the word, my independence, which only consisted in choosing the street in which I should wander, or the roof, when I had money, in which I should hide my head, I was some time before I could prevail on myself to accept of a place in a house of ill fame, to which a girl, with whom I had accidentally conversed in the street, had recommended me. I had been hunted almost into a fever, by the watchmen[1] of the quarter of the town I frequented; one, whom I had unwittingly offended, giving the word to the whole pack. You can scarcely conceive the tyranny exercised by these wretches: considering themselves as the instruments of the very laws they violate, the pretext which steels their conscience, hardens their heart. Not content with receiving from us, outlaws of society (let other women talk of favours) a brutal gratification gratuitously as a privilege of office, they extort a tithe of prostitution, and harrass with threats the poor creatures whose occupation affords not the means to silence the growl of avarice. To escape from this persecution, I once more entered into servitude.

'A life of comparative regularity restored my health; and—do not start—my manners were improved, in a situation where vice sought to render itself alluring, and taste was cultivated to fashion the person, if not to refine the mind. Besides, the common civility of speech, contrasted with the gross vulgarity to which I had been accustomed, was something like the polish of civilization. I was not shut out from all intercourse of humanity. Still I was galled by the yoke of service, and my mistress often flying into violent fits of passion, made me dread a sudden dismission, which I understood was always the case. I was therefore prevailed on, though I felt a horror of men, to accept the offer of a gentleman,[2] rather in the decline of years, to keep his house, pleasantly situated in a little village near Hampstead.

'He was a man of great talents, and of brilliant wit; but, a worn-out votary of voluptuousness, his desires became fastidious in proportion as they grew weak, and the native tenderness of his heart was undermined by a vitiated imagination. A thoughtless career of libertinism and social enjoyment, had injured his health to such a degree, that, whatever pleasure his conversation afforded me (and my esteem was ensured by proofs of the generous humanity of his disposition), the being his mistress was purchasing it at a very dear rate. With such a keen perception of the delicacies of sentiment, with an imagination invigorated by the exercise of genius, how could he sink into the grossness of sensuality![1]

'But, to pass over a subject which I recollect with pain, I must remark to you, as an answer to your often-repeated question, "Why my sentiments and language were superior to my station?" that I now began to read, to beguile the tediousness of solitude, and to gratify an inquisitive, active mind. I had often, in my childhood, followed a ballad-singer, to hear the sequel of a dismal story, though sure of being severely punished for delaying to return with whatever I was sent to purchase. I could just spell and put a sentence together, and I listened to the various arguments, though often mingled with obscenity, which occurred at the table where I was allowed to preside: for a literary friend or two frequently came home with my master, to dine and pass the night. Having lost the privileged respect of my sex, my presence, instead of restraining, perhaps gave the reins to their tongues; still I had the advantage of hearing discussions, from which, in the common course of life, women are excluded.

'You may easily imagine, that it was only by degrees that I could comprehend some of the subjects they investigated, or acquire from their reasoning what might be termed a moral sense. But my fondness of reading increasing, and my master occasionally shutting himself up in this retreat, for weeks together, to write, I had many opportunities of improvement. At first, considering money (I was right!' exclaimed Jemima, altering her tone of voice) 'as the only means, after my loss of reputation, of obtaining respect, or even the toleration of humanity, I had not the least scruple to secrete a part of the sums intrusted to me, and to screen myself from detection by a system of falshood. But, acquiring new principles, I began to have the ambition of returning to the respectable part of society, and was weak enough to suppose it possible. The attention of my unassuming instructor, who, without being ignorant of his own powers, possessed great simplicity of manners, strengthened the illusion. Having sometimes caught up hints for thought, from my untutored remarks, he often led me to discuss the subjects he was treating, and would read to me his productions, previous to their publication, wishing to profit by the criticism of unsophisticated feeling. The aim of his writings was to touch the simple springs of the heart; for he despised the would-be oracles, the self-elected philosophers, who fright away fancy, while sifting each grain of thought to prove that slowness of comprehension is wisdom.[1]

'I should have distinguished this as a moment of sunshine, a happy period in my life, had not the repugnance the disgusting libertinism of my protector inspired, daily become more painful.—And, indeed, I soon did recollect it as such with agony, when his sudden death (for he had recourse to the most exhilarating cordials to keep up the convivial tone of his spirits) again threw me into the desert of human society. Had he had any time for reflection, I am certain he would have left the little property in his power to me: but, attacked by the fatal apoplexy in town, his heir, a man of rigid morals, brought his wife with him to take possession of the house and effects, before I was even informed of his death,—"to prevent," as she took care indirectly to tell me, "such a creature as she supposed me to be,[2] from purloining any of them, had I been apprized of the event in time."

'The grief I felt at the sudden shock the information gave me, which at first had nothing selfish in it, was treated with contempt, and I was ordered to pack up my clothes; and a few trinkets and books, given me by the generous deceased, were contested, while they piously hoped, with a reprobating shake of the head, "that God would have mercy on his sinful soul!" With some difficulty, I obtained my arrears of wages; but asking—such is the spirit-grinding consequence of poverty and infamy—for a character for honesty and economy, which God knows I merited, I was told by this—why must I call her woman?—"that it would go against her conscience to recommend a kept mistress." Tears started in my eyes, burning tears; for there are situations in which a wretch is humbled by the contempt they are conscious they do not deserve.

'I returned to the metropolis; but the solitude of a poor lodging was inconceivably dreary, after the society I had enjoyed. To be cut off from human converse, now I had been taught to relish it, was to wander a ghost among the living. Besides, I foresaw, to aggravate the severity of my fate, that my little pittance would soon melt away. I endeavoured to obtain needlework; but, not having been taught early, and my hands being rendered clumsy by hard work, I did not sufficiently excel to be employed by the ready-made linen shops,[1] when so many women, better qualified, were suing for it. The want of a character prevented my getting a place; for, irksome as servitude would have been to me, I should have made another trial, had it been feasible. Not that I disliked employment, but the inequality of condition to which I must have submitted. I had acquired a taste for literature, during the five years I had lived with a literary man, occasionally conversing with men of the first abilities of the age; and now to descend to the lowest vulgarity, was a degree of wretchedness not to be imagined unfelt. I had not, it is true, tasted the charms of affection, but I had been familiar with the graces of humanity.

'One of the gentlemen, whom I had frequently dined in company with, while I was treated like a companion, met me in the street, and enquired after my health. I seized the occasion, and began to describe my situation; but he was in haste to join, at dinner, a select party of choice spirits; therefore, without waiting to hear me, he impatiently put a guinea into my hand, saying, "It was a pity such a sensible woman should be in distress—he wished me well from his soul."

'To another I wrote, stating my case, and requesting advice. He was an advocate for unequivocal sincerity; and had often, in my presence, descanted on the evils which arise in society from the despotism of rank and riches.

'In reply, I received a long essay on the energy of the human mind, with continual allusions to his own force of character. He added, "That the woman who could write such a letter as I had sent him, could never be in want of resources, were she to look into herself, and exert her powers; misery was the consequence of indolence, and, as to my being shut out from society, it was the lot of man to submit to certain privations."

'How often have I heard,' said Jemima, interrupting her narrative, 'in conversation, and read in books, that every person willing to work may find employment? It is the vague assertion, I believe, of insensible indolence, when it relates to men; but, with respect to women, I am sure of its fallacy, unless they will submit to the most menial bodily labour; and even to be employed at hard labour is out of the reach of many, whose reputation misfortune or folly has tainted.

'How writers, professing to be friends to freedom, and the improvement of morals, can assert that poverty is no evil, I cannot imagine.'[1]

'No more can I,' interrupted Maria, 'yet they even expatiate on the peculiar happiness of indigence, though in what it can consist, excepting in brutal rest, when a man can barely earn a subsistence, I cannot imagine. The mind is necessarily imprisoned in its own little tenement; and, fully occupied by keeping it in repair, has not time to rove abroad for improvement. The book of knowledge is closely clasped, against those who must fulfil their daily task of severe manual labour or die; and curiosity, rarely excited by thought or information, seldom moves on the stagnate lake of ignorance.'

'As far as I have been able to observe,' replied Jemima, 'prejudices, caught up by chance, are obstinately maintained by the poor, to the exclusion of improvement; they have not time to reason or reflect to any extent, or minds sufficiently exercised to adopt the principles of action, which form perhaps the only basis of contentment in every station*.'

_____

'And independence,' said Darnford, 'they are necessarily strangers to, even the independence of despising their persecutors. If the poor are happy, or can be happy, *things are very well as they are*.[1] And I cannot conceive on what principle those writers contend for a change of system, who support this opinion. The authors on the other side of the question are much more consistent, who grant the fact; yet, insisting that it is the lot of the majority to be oppressed in this life, kindly turn them over to another,[2] to rectify the false weights and measures of this, as the only way to justify the dispensations of Providence. I have not,' continued Darnford, 'an opinion more firmly fixed by observation in my mind, than that, though riches may fail to produce proportionate happiness, poverty most commonly excludes it, by shutting up all the avenues to improvement.'[3]

'And as for the affections,' added Maria, with a sigh, 'how gross, and even tormenting do they become, unless regulated by an improving mind! The culture of the heart ever, I believe, keeps pace with that of the mind. But pray go on,' addressing Jemima, 'though your narrative gives rise to the most painful reflections on the present state of society.'

'Not to trouble you,' continued she, 'with a detailed description of all the painful feelings of unavailing exertion, I have only to tell you, that at last I got recommended to wash in a few families, who did me the favour to admit me into their houses, without the most strict enquiry, to wash from one in the morning till eight at night, for eighteen or twenty-pence a day.[4] On the happiness to be enjoyed over a washing-tub I need not comment; yet you will allow me to observe, that this was a wretchedness of situation peculiar to my sex. A man with half my industry, and, I may say, abilities, could have procured a decent livelihood, and discharged some of the

_____

*The copy which appears to have received the author's last corrections, ends at this place.

duties which knit mankind together; whilst I, who had
acquired a taste for the rational, nay, in honest pride let me
assert it, the virtuous enjoyments of life, was cast aside as the
filth of society. Condemned to labour, like a machine, only to
earn bread, and scarcely that, I became melancholy and
desperate.

'I have now to mention a circumstance which fills me with
remorse, and fear it will entirely deprive me of your esteem.
A tradesman became attached to me, and visited me
frequently,—and I at last obtained such a power over him,
that he offered to take me home to his house.—Consider, dear
madam, I was famishing: wonder not that I became a
wolf!—The only reason for not taking me home immediately,
was the having a girl in the house, with child by him—and this
girl—I advised him—yes, I did! would I could forget it!—to
turn out of doors: and one night he determined to follow my
advice. Poor wretch! she fell upon her knees, reminded him
that he had promised to marry her, that her parents were
honest!—What did it avail?—She was turned out.

'She approached her father's door, in the skirts of
London,—listened at the shutters,—but could not knock. A
watchman had observed her go and return several
times—Poor wretch!—' The remorse Jemima spoke of,
seemed to be stinging her to the soul, as she proceeded.

'She left it, and, approaching a tub where horses were
watered, she sat down in it, and, with desperate resolution,
remained in that attitude—till resolution was no longer
necessary!

'I happened that morning to be going out to wash,
anticipating the moment when I should escape from such
hard labour. I passed by, just as some men, going to work,
drew out the stiff, cold corpse—Let me not recal the horrid
moment!—I recognized her pale visage; I listened to the tale
told by the spectators, and my heart did not burst. I thought
of my own state, and wondered how I could be such a
monster!—I worked hard; and, returning home, I was
attacked by a fever. I suffered both in body and mind. I

determined not to live with the wretch. But he did not try me; he left the neighbourhood. I once more returned to the wash-tub.

'Still this state, miserable as it was, admitted of aggravation. Lifting one day a heavy load, a tub fell against my shin, and gave me great pain. I did not pay much attention to the hurt, till it became a serious wound; being obliged to work as usual, or starve. But, finding myself at length unable to stand for any time, I thought of getting into an hospital.[1] Hospitals, it should seem (for they are comfortless abodes for the sick) were expressly endowed for the reception of the friendless; yet I, who had on that plea a right to assistance, wanted the recommendation of the rich and respectable, and was several weeks languishing for admittance; fees were demanded on entering; and, what was still more unreasonable, security for burying me, that expence not coming into the letter of the charity. A guinea was the stipulated sum—I could as soon have raised a million; and I was afraid to apply to the parish for an order, lest they should have passed me,[2] I knew not whither. The poor woman at whose house I lodged, compassionating my state, got me into the hospital; and the family where I received the hurt, sent me five shillings, three and six-pence of which I gave at my admittance—I know not for what.

'My leg grew quickly better; but I was dismissed before my cure was completed, because I could not afford to have my linen washed to appear decently, as the virago of a nurse said, when the gentlemen (the surgeons) came. I cannot give you an adequate idea of the wretchedness of an hospital; every thing is left to the care of people intent on gain. The attendants seem to have lost all feeling of compassion in the bustling discharge of their offices; death is so familiar to them, that they are not anxious to ward it off. Every thing appeared to be conducted for the accommodation of the medical men and their pupils, who came to make experiments on the poor, for the benefit of the rich. One of the physicians, I must not forget to mention, gave me half-a-crown, and ordered me some wine, when I was at the lowest ebb. I thought of making my case known to the lady-like matron; but her forbidding countenance prevented me. She condescended to look on the patients, and make general enquiries, two or three times a week; but the nurses knew the hour when the visit of ceremony would commence, and every thing was as it should be.

'After my dismission, I was more at a loss than ever for a subsistence, and, not to weary you with a repetition of the same unavailing attempts, unable to stand at the washing-tub, I began to consider the rich and poor as natural enemies, and became a thief from principle.[1] I could not now cease to reason, but I hated mankind. I despised myself, yet I justified my conduct. I was taken, tried, and condemned to six months' imprisonment in a house of correction. My soul recoils with horror from the remembrance of the insults I had to endure, till, branded with shame, I was turned loose in the street, pennyless. I wandered from street to street, till, exhausted by hunger and fatigue, I sunk down senseless at a door, where I had vainly demanded a morsel of bread. I was sent by the inhabitant to the work-house, to which he had surlily bid me go, saying, he "paid enough in conscience to the poor," when, with parched tongue, I implored his charity.[2] If those well-meaning people who exclaim against beggars, were acquainted with the treatment the poor receive in many of these wretched asylums,[3] they would not stifle so easily involuntary sympathy, by saying that they have all parishes to go to, or wonder that the poor dread to enter the gloomy walls. What are the common run of work-houses, but prisons, in which many respectable old people, worn out by immoderate labour, sink into the grave in sorrow, to which they are carried like dogs!'

Alarmed by some indistinct noise, Jemima rose hastily to listen, and Maria, turning to Darnford, said, 'I have indeed been shocked beyond expression when I have met a pauper's funeral. A coffin carried on the shoulders of three or four ill-looking wretches, whom the imagination might easily convert into a band of assassins, hastening to conceal the corpse, and

quarrelling about the prey on their way. I know it is of little
consequence how we are consigned to the earth; but I am led
by this brutal insensibility, to what even the animal creation
appears forcibly to feel, to advert to the wretched, deserted
manner in which they died.'

'True,' rejoined Darnford, 'and, till the rich will give more
than a part of their wealth, till they will give time and attention
to the wants of the distressed, never let them boast of charity.
Let them open their hearts, and not their purses, and employ
their minds in the service, if they are really actuated by
humanity; or charitable institutions will always be the prey of
the lowest order of knaves.'

Jemima returning, seemed in haste to finish her tale. 'The
overseer farmed the poor[1] of different parishes, and out of the
bowels of poverty was wrung the money with which he
purchased this dwelling, as a private receptacle for madness.
He had been a keeper at a house of the same description, and
conceived that he could make money much more readily in his
old occupation. He is a shrewd—shall I say it?—villain. He
observed something resolute in my manner, and offered to
take me with him, and instruct me how to treat the disturbed
minds he meant to intrust to my care. The offer of forty
pounds a year, and to quit a workhouse, was not to be
despised, though the condition of shutting my eyes and
hardening my heart was annexed to it.

'I agreed to accompany him; and four years have I been
attendant on many wretches, and'—she lowered voice,—'the
witness of many enormities. In solitude my mind seemed to
recover its force, and many of the sentiments which I imbibed
in the only tolerable period of my life, returned with their full
force. Still what should induce me to be the champion for
suffering humanity?—Who ever risked any thing for
me?—Who ever acknowledged me to be a fellow-creature?'—

Maria took her hand, and Jemima, more overcome by
kindness than she had ever been by cruelty, hastened out of
the room to conceal her emotions.

Darnford soon after heard his summons, and, taking leave

of him, Maria promised to gratify his curiosity, with respect to herself, the first opportunity.

CHAPTER SIX

ACTIVE as love was in the heart of Maria, the story she had just heard made her thoughts take a wider range. The opening buds of hope closed, as if they had put forth too early, and the happiest day of her life was overcast by the most melancholy reflections. Thinking of Jemima's peculiar fate and her own, she was led to consider the oppressed state of women, and to lament that she had given birth to a daughter. Sleep fled from her eyelids, while she dwelt on the wretchedness of unprotected infancy, till sympathy with Jemima changed to agony, when it seemed probable that her own babe might even now be in the very state she so forcibly described.

Maria thought, and thought again. Jemima's humanity had rather been benumbed than killed, by the keen frost she had to brave at her entrance into life; an appeal then to her feelings, on this tender point, surely would not be fruitless; and Maria began to anticipate the delight it would afford her to gain intelligence of her child. This project was now the only subject of reflection; and she watched impatiently for the dawn of day, with that determinate purpose which generally insures success.

At the usual hour, Jemima brought her breakfast, and a tender note from Darnford. She ran her eye hastily over it, and her heart calmly hoarded up the rapture a fresh assurance of affection, affection such as she wished to inspire, gave her, without diverting her mind a moment from its design. While Jemima waited to take away the breakfast, Maria alluded to the reflections, that had haunted her during the night to the exclusion of sleep. She spoke with energy of Jemima's unmerited sufferings, and of the fate of a number of deserted females, placed within the sweep of a whirlwind, from which it was next to impossible to escape. Perceiving the effect her conversation produced on the countenance of her guard, she grasped the arm of Jemima with that irresistible warmth which defies repulse, exclaiming—'With your heart, and such dreadful experience, can you lend your aid to deprive my babe of a mother's tenderness, a mother's care? In the name of God, assist me to snatch her from destruction! Let me but give her an education—let me but prepare her body and mind to encounter the ills which await her sex, and I will teach her to consider you as her second mother, and herself as the prop of your age. Yes, Jemima, look at me—observe me closely, and read my very soul; you merit a better fate;' she held out her hand with a firm gesture of assurance; 'and I will procure it for you, as a testimony of my esteem, as well as of my gratitude.'

Jemima had not power to resist this persuasive torrent; and, owning that the house in which she was confined, was situated on the banks of the Thames, only a few miles from London, and not on the sea-coast, as Darnford had supposed, she promised to invent some excuse for her absence, and go herself to trace the situation, and enquire concerning the health, of this abandoned daughter. Her manner implied an intention to do something more, but she seemed unwilling to impart her design; and Maria, glad to have obtained the main point, thought it best to leave her to the workings of her own mind; convinced that she had the power of interesting her still more in favour of herself and child, by a simple recital of facts.

In the evening, Jemima informed the impatient mother, that on the morrow she should hasten to town before the family hour of rising, and received all the information necessary, as a clue to her search. The 'Good night!' Maria uttered was peculiarly solemn and affectionate. Glad expectation sparkled in her eye; and, for the first time since her detention, she pronounced the name of her child with pleasureable fondness; and, with all the garrulity of a nurse, described her first smile when she recognized her mother. Recollecting herself, a still kinder 'Adieu!' with a 'God bless you!'—that seemed to include a maternal benediction, dismissed Jemima.

The dreary solitude of the ensuing day, lengthened by impatiently dwelling on the same idea, was intolerably wearisome. She listened for the sound of a particular clock, which some directions of the wind allowed her to hear distinctly. She marked the shadow gaining on the wall; and, twilight thickening into darkness, her breath seemed oppressed while she anxiously counted nine.—The last sound was a stroke of despair on her heart; for she expected every moment, without seeing Jemima, to have her light extinguished by the savage female who supplied her place. She was even obliged to prepare for bed, restless as she was, not to disoblige her new attendant. She had been cautioned not to speak too freely to her; but the caution was needless, her countenance would still more emphatically have made her shrink back. Such was the ferocity of manner, conspicuous in every word and gesture of this hag, that Maria was afraid to enquire, why Jemima, who had faithfully promised to see her before her door was shut for the night, came not?—and, when the key turned in the lock, to consign her to a night of suspence, she felt a degree of anguish which the circumstances scarcely justified.

Continually on the watch, the shutting of a door, or the sound of a footstep, made her start and tremble with apprehension, something like what she felt, when, at her entrance, dragged along the gallery, she began to doubt whether she were not surrounded by demons?

Fatigued by an endless rotation of thought and wild alarms, she looked like a spectre, when Jemima entered in the morning; especially as her eyes darted out of her head, to read in Jemima's countenance, almost as pallid, the intelligence she dared not trust her tongue to demand. Jemima put down the tea-things, and appeared very busy in arranging the table. Maria took up a cup with trembling hand, then forcibly recovering her fortitude, and restraining the convulsive movement which agitated the muscles of her mouth, she said,

'Spare yourself the pain of preparing me for your information, I adjure you!—My child is dead!' Jemima solemnly answered, 'Yes;' with a look expressive of compassion and angry emotions. 'Leave me,' added Maria, making a fresh effort to govern her feelings, and hiding her face in her handkerchief, to conceal her anguish—'It is enough—I know that my babe is no more—I will hear the particulars when I am'—*calmer*, she could not utter; and Jemima, without importuning her by idle attempts to console her, left the room.

Plunged in the deepest melancholy, she would not admit Darnford's visits; and such is the force of early associations even on strong minds, that, for a while, she indulged the superstitious notion that she was justly punished by the death of her child, for having for an instant ceased to regret her loss. Two or three letters from Darnford, full of soothing, manly tenderness, only added poignancy to these accusing emotions; yet the passionate style in which he expressed, what he termed the first and fondest wish of his heart, 'that his affection might make her some amends for the cruelty and injustice she had endured,' inspired a sentiment of gratitude to heaven; and her eyes filled with delicious tears, when, at the conclusion of his letter, wishing to supply the place of her unworthy relations, whose want of principle he execrated, he assured her, calling her his dearest girl, 'that it should henceforth be the business of his life to make her happy.'

He begged, in a note sent the following morning, to be permitted to see her, when his presence would be no intrusion on her grief; and so earnestly intreated to be allowed, according to promise, to beguile the tedious moments of absence, by dwelling on the events of her past life, that she sent him the memoirs which had been written for her daughter, promising Jemima the perusal as soon as he returned them.

CHAPTER SEVEN

'ADDRESSING these memoirs to you, my child, uncertain whether I shall ever have an opportunity of instructing you, many observations will probably flow from my heart, which only a mother—a mother schooled in misery, could make.

'The tenderness of a father who knew the world, might be great; but could it equal that of a mother—of a mother, labouring under a portion of the misery, which the constitution of society seems to have entailed on all her kind?[1] It is, my child, my dearest daughter, only such a mother, who will dare to break through all restraint to provide for your happiness—who will voluntarily brave censure herself, to ward off sorrow from your bosom. From my narrative, my dear girl, you may gather the instruction, the counsel, which is meant rather to exercise[2] than influence your mind.—Death may snatch me from you, before you can weigh my advice, or enter into my reasoning:[3] I would then, with fond anxiety, lead you very early in life to form your grand principle of action, to save you from the vain regret of having, through irresolution, let the spring-tide of existence pass away, unimproved, unenjoyed.—Gain experience—ah! gain it—while experience is worth having, and acquire sufficient fortitude to pursue your own happiness; it includes your utility, by a direct path. What is wisdom too often, but the owl of the goddess,[4] who sits moping in a desolated heart; around me she shrieks, but I would invite all the gay warblers of spring to nestle in your blooming bosom.—Had I not wasted years in deliberating, after I ceased to doubt, how I ought to have acted—I might now be useful and happy.—For my sake, warned by my example, always appear what you are, and you will not pass through existence without enjoying its genuine blessings, love and respect.

'Born in one of the most romantic parts of England, an

enthusiastic fondness for the varying charms of nature is the first sentiment I recollect; or rather it was the first consciousness of pleasure that employed and formed my imagination.

'My father had been a captain of a man of war; but, disgusted with the service, on account of the preferment of men whose chief merit was their family connections or borough interest,[1] he retired into the country; and, not knowing what to do with himself—married. In his family, to regain his lost consequence, he determined to keep up the same passive obedience, as in the vessels in which he had commanded. His orders were not to be disputed;[2] and the whole house was expected to fly, at the word of command, as if to man the shrouds, or mount aloft in an elemental strife, big with life or death. He was to be instantaneously obeyed, especially by my mother, whom he very benevolently married for love; but took care to remind her of the obligation, when she dared, in the slightest instance, to question his absolute authority. My eldest brother,[3] it is true, as he grew up, was treated with more respect by my father; and became in due form the deputy-tyrant of the house. The representative of my father, a being privileged by nature—a boy, and the darling of my mother, he did not fail to act like an heir apparent. Such indeed was my mother's extravagant partiality, that, in comparison with her affection for him, she might be said not to love the rest of her children. Yet none of the children seemed to have so little affection for her. Extreme indulgence had rendered him so selfish, that he only thought of himself; and from tormenting insects and animals, he became the despot of his brothers, and still more of his sisters.

'It is perhaps difficult to give you an idea of the petty cares which obscured the morning of my life; continual restraint in the most trivial matters; unconditional submission to orders, which, as a mere child, I soon discovered to be unreasonable, because inconsistent and contradictory. Thus are we destined to experience a mixture of bitterness, with the recollection of our most innocent enjoyments.

'The circumstances which, during my childhood, occurred to fashion my mind, were various; yet, as it would probably afford me more pleasure to revive the fading remembrance of newborn delight, than you, my child, could feel in the perusal, I will not entice you to stray with me into the verdant meadow, to search for the flowers that youthful hopes scatter in every path; though, as I write, I almost scent the fresh green of spring—of that spring which never returns!

'I had two sisters, and one brother, younger than myself; my brother Robert was two years older, and might truly be termed the idol of his parents, and the torment of the rest of the family. Such indeed is the force of prejudice, that what was called spirit and wit in him, was cruelly repressed as forwardness in me.

'My mother had an indolence of character, which prevented her from paying much attention to our education. But the healthy breeze of a neighbouring heath,[1] on which we bounded at pleasure, volatilized the humours that improper food might have generated. And to enjoy open air and freedom, was paradise, after the unnatural restraint of our fire-side, where we were often obliged to sit three or four hours together, without daring to utter a word, when my father was out of humour, from want of employment, or of a variety of boisterous amusement. I had however one advantage, an instructor, the brother of my father,[2] who, intended for the church, had of course received a liberal education. But, becoming attached to a young lady of great beauty and large fortune, and acquiring in the world some opinions not consonant with the profession for which he was designed, he accepted, with the most sanguine expectations of success, the offer of a nobleman to accompany him to India, as his confidential secretary.

'A correspondence was regularly kept up with the object of his affection; and the intricacies of business, peculiarly wearisome to a man of a romantic turn of mind, contributed, with a forced absence, to increase his attachment. Every other passion was lost in this master-one, and only served to swell the torrent. Her relations, such were his waking dreams, who had despised him, would court in their turn his alliance, and all the blandishments of taste would grace the triumph of love.—While he basked in the warm sunshine of love, friendship also promised to shed its dewy freshness; for a friend, whom he loved next to his mistress, was the confident, who forwarded the letters from one to the other, to elude the observation of prying relations. A friend false in similar circumstances, is, my dearest girl, an old tale; yet, let not this example, or the frigid caution of cold-blooded moralists, make you endeavour to stifle hopes, which are the buds that naturally unfold themselves during the spring of life! Whilst your own heart is sincere, always expect to meet one glowing with the same sentiments; for to fly from pleasure, is not to avoid pain!

'My uncle realized, by good luck, rather than management, a handsome fortune; and returning on the wings of love, lost in the most enchanting reveries, to England, to share it with his mistress and his friend, he found them—united.

'There were some circumstances, not necessary for me to recite, which aggravated the guilt of the friend beyond measure, and the deception, that had been carried on to the last moment, was so base, it produced the most violent effect on my uncle's health and spirits. His native country, the world! lately a garden of blooming sweets, blasted by treachery, seemed changed into a parched desert, the abode of hissing serpents. Disappointment rankled in his heart; and, brooding over his wrongs, he was attacked by a raging fever, followed by a derangement of mind, which only gave place to habitual melancholy, as he recovered more strength of body.

'Declaring an intention never to marry, his relations were ever clustering about him, paying the grossest adulation to a man, who, disgusted with mankind, received them with scorn, or bitter sarcasms. Something in my countenance pleased him, when I began to prattle. Since his return, he appeared dead to affection; but I soon, by showing him innocent fondness, became a favourite; and endeavouring to enlarge and strengthen my mind, I grew dear to him in proportion as I imbibed his sentiments. He had a forcible manner of speaking, rendered more so by a certain impressive wildness of look and gesture, calculated to engage the attention of a young and ardent mind. It is not then surprising that I quickly adopted his opinions in preference, and reverenced him as one of a superior order of beings. He inculcated, with great warmth, self-respect, and a lofty consciousness of acting right, independent of the censure or applause of the world; nay, he almost taught me to brave, and even despise its censure, when convinced of the rectitude of my own intentions.

'Endeavouring to prove to me that nothing which deserved the name of love or friendship, existed in the world, he drew such animated pictures of his own feelings, rendered permanent by disappointment, as imprinted the sentiments strongly on my heart, and animated my imagination. These remarks are necessary to elucidate some peculiarities in my character, which by the world are indefinitely termed romantic.[1]

'My uncle's increasing affection led him to visit me often. Still, unable to rest in any place, he did not remain long in the country to soften domestic tyranny; but he brought me books, for which I had a passion, and they conspired with his conversation, to make me form an ideal picture of life. I shall pass over the tyranny of my father, much as I suffered from it; but it is necessary to notice, that it undermined my mother's health; and that her temper, continually irritated by domestic bickering, became intolerably peevish.

'My eldest brother was articled to a neighbouring attorney,[2] the shrewdest, and, I may add, the most un-principled man in that part of the country. As my brother generally came home every Saturday, to astonish my mother by exhibiting his attainments, he gradually assumed a right of directing the whole family, not excepting my father. He seemed to take a peculiar pleasure in tormenting and humbling me; and if I ever ventured to complain of this treatment to either my father or mother, I was rudely rebuffed for presuming to judge of the conduct of my eldest brother.

'About this period a merchant's family came to settle in our neighbourhood. A mansion-house in the village, lately purchased, had been preparing the whole spring, and the sight of the costly furniture, sent from London, had excited my mother's envy, and roused my father's pride. My sensations were very different, and all of a pleasurable kind. I longed to see new characters, to break the tedious monotony of my life; and to find a friend, such as fancy had pourtrayed. I cannot then describe the emotion I felt, the Sunday they made their appearance at church. My eyes were rivetted on the pillar round which I expected first to catch a glimpse of them, and darted forth to meet a servant who hastily preceded a group of ladies, whose white robes and waving plumes, seemed to stream along the gloomy aisle, diffusing the light, by which I contemplated their figures.

'We visited them in form; and I quickly selected the eldest daughter for my friend. The second son, George, paid me particular attention, and finding his attainments and manners superior to those of the young men of the village, I began to imagine him superior to the rest of mankind. Had my home been more comfortable, or my previous acquaintance more numerous, I should not probably have been so eager to open my heart to new affections.[1]

'Mr. Venables, the merchant, had acquired a large fortune by unremitting attention to business; but his health declining rapidly, he was obliged to retire, before his son, George, had acquired sufficient experience, to enable him to conduct their affairs on the same prudential plan, his father had invariably pursued. Indeed, he had laboured to throw off his authority, having despised his narrow plans and cautious speculation. The eldest son could not be prevailed on to enter the firm; and, to oblige his wife, and have peace in the house, Mr. Venables had purchased a commission for him in the guards.

'I am now alluding to circumstances which came to my knowledge long after; but it is necessary, my dearest child, that you should know the character of your father, to prevent your despising your mother; the only parent inclined to discharge a parent's duty. In London, George had acquired habits of libertinism, which he carefully concealed from his father and his commercial connections. The mask he wore, was so complete a covering of his real visage, that the praise his father lavished on his conduct, and, poor mistaken man! on his principles, contrasted with his brother's, rendered the notice he took of me peculiarly flattering. Without any fixed design, as I am now convinced, he continued to single me out at the dance, press my hand at parting, and utter expressions of unmeaning passion, to which I gave a meaning naturally suggested by the romantic turn of my thoughts. His stay in the country was short; his manners did not entirely please me; but, when he left us, the colouring of my picture became more vivid—Whither did not my imagination lead me? In short, I fancied myself in love—in love with the disinterestedness, fortitude, generosity, dignity, and humanity, with which I had invested the hero I dubbed. A circumstance which soon after occurred, rendered all these virtues palpable. [The incident is perhaps worth relating on other accounts, and therefore I shall describe it distinctly.]

'I had a great affection for my nurse, old Mary, for whom I used often to work, to spare her eyes. Mary had a younger sister, married to a sailor, while she was suckling me; for my mother only suckled my eldest brother, which might be the cause of her extraordinary partiality. Peggy,[1] Mary's sister, lived with her, till her husband, becoming a mate in a West-India trader, got a little before-hand in the world. He wrote to his wife from the first port in the Channel, after his most successful voyage, to request her to come to London to meet him; he even wished her to determine on living there for the future, to save him the trouble of coming to her the moment he came on shore; and to turn a penny by keeping a green-stall.[2] It was too much to set out on a journey the moment he had finished a voyage, and fifty miles by land, was worse than a thousand leagues by sea.

'She packed up her alls,[3] and came to London—but did not

meet honest Daniel. A common misfortune prevented her, and the poor are bound to suffer for the good of their country—he was pressed[1] in the river—and never came on shore.

'Peggy was miserable in London, not knowing, as she said, "the face of any living soul." Besides, her imagination had been employed, anticipating a month or six weeks' happiness with her husband. Daniel was to have gone with her to Sadler's Wells, and Westminster Abbey, and to many sights, which he knew she never heard of in the country. Peggy too was thrifty, and how could she manage to put his plan in execution alone? He had acquaintance; but she did not know the very name of their places of abode. His letters were made up of—How do you does, and God bless yous,—information was reserved for the hour of meeting.

'She too had her portion of information, near at heart. Molly and Jacky were grown such little darlings, she was almost angry that daddy did not see their tricks. She had not half the pleasure she should have had from their prattle, could she have recounted to him each night the pretty speeches of the day. Some stories, however, were stored up—and Jacky could say papa with such a sweet voice, it must delight his heart. Yet when she came, and found no Daniel to greet her, when Jacky called papa, she wept, bidding "God bless his innocent soul, that did not know what sorrow was."—But more sorrow was in store for Peggy, innocent as she was.—Daniel was killed in the first engagement, and then the *papa* was agony, sounding to the heart.

'She had lived sparingly on his wages, while there was any hope of his return; but, that gone, she returned with a breaking heart to the country, to a little market town, nearly three miles from our village. She did not like to go to service, to be snubbed about, after being her own mistress. To put her children out to nurse was impossible: how far would her wages go? and to send them to her husband's parish,[2] a distant one, was to lose her husband twice over.

'I had heard all from Mary, and made my uncle furnish a

little cottage for her, to enable her to sell—so sacred was poor Daniel's advice, now he was dead and gone—a little fruit, toys and cakes. The minding of the shop did not require her whole time, nor even the keeping her children clean, and she loved to see them clean; so she took in washing, and altogether made a shift to earn bread for her children, still weeping for Daniel, when Jacky's arch looks made her think of his father.—It was pleasant to work for her children.[1]—"Yes; from morning till night, could she have had a kiss from their father, God rest his soul! Yes; had it plased Providence to have let him come back without a leg or an arm, it would have been the same thing to her—for she did not love him because he maintained them—no; she had hands of her own."

'The country people were honest, and Peggy left her linen out to dry very late. A recruiting party, as she supposed, passing through, made free with a large wash; for it was all swept away, including her own and her children's little stock.

'This was a dreadful blow; two dozen of shirts, stocks and handkerchiefs. She gave the money which she had laid by for half a year's rent, and promised to pay two shillings a week till all was cleared; so she did not lose her employment. This two shillings a week, and the buying a few necessaries for the children, drove her so hard, that she had not a penny to pay her rent with, when a twelvemonth's became due.

'She was now with Mary, and had just told her tale, which Mary instantly repeated—it was intended for my ear. Many houses in this town, producing a borough-interest,[2] were included in the estate purchased by Mr. Venables, and the attorney with whom my brother lived, was appointed his agent, to collect and raise the rents.

'He demanded Peggy's, and, in spite of her intreaties, her poor goods had been seized and sold. So that she had not, and what was worse her children, "for she had known sorrow enough," a bed to lie on. She knew that I was good-natured—right charitable, yet not liking to ask for more than needs must, she scorned to petition while people could any how be made to wait. But now, should she be turned out of doors, she must expect nothing less than to lose all her customers, and then she must beg or starve—and what would become of her children?—"had Daniel not been pressed—but God knows best—all this could not have happened."

'I had two mattrasses on my bed; what did I want with two, when such a worthy creature must lie on the ground? My mother would be angry, but I could conceal it till my uncle came down; and then I would tell him all the whole truth, and if he absolved me, heaven would.

'I begged the house-maid to come up stairs with me (servants always feel for the distresses of poverty, and so would the rich if they knew what it was). She assisted me to tie up the mattrass; I discovering, at the same time, that one blanket would serve me till winter, could I persuade my sister, who slept with me, to keep my secret. She entering in the midst of the package, I gave her some new feathers, to silence her. We got the mattrass down the back stairs, unperceived, and I helped to carry it, taking with me all the money I had, and what I could borrow from my sister.

'When I got to the cottage, Peggy declared that she would not take what I had brought secretly; but, when, with all the eager eloquence inspired by a decided purpose, I grasped her hand with weeping eyes, assuring her that my uncle would screen me from blame, when he was once more in the country, describing, at the same time, what she would suffer in parting with her children, after keeping them so long from being thrown on the parish, she reluctantly consented.

'My project of usefulness ended not here; I determined to speak to the attorney; he frequently paid me compliments. His character did not intimidate me; but, imagining that Peggy must be mistaken, and that no man could turn a deaf ear to such a tale of complicated distress, I determined to walk to the town with Mary the next morning, and request him to wait for the rent, and keep my secret, till my uncle's return.

'My repose was sweet; and, waking with the first dawn of day, I bounded to Mary's cottage. What charms do not a light heart spread over nature! Every bird that twittered in a bush, every flower that enlivened the hedge, seemed placed there to awaken me to rapture—yes; to rapture. The present moment was full fraught with happiness; and on futurity I bestowed not a thought, excepting to anticipate my success with the attorney.

'This man of the world, with rosy face and simpering features, received me politely, nay kindly; listened with complacency to my remonstrances, though he scarcely heeded Mary's tears. I did not then suspect, that my eloquence was in my complexion, the blush of seventeen, or that, in a world where humanity to women is the chacteristic of advancing civilization, the beauty of a young girl was so much more interesting than the distress of an old one.[1] Pressing my hand, he promised to let Peggy remain in the house as long as I wished.—I more than returned the pressure—I was so grateful and so happy. Emboldened by my innocent warmth, he then kissed me—and I did not draw back—I took it for a kiss of charity.

'Gay as a lark, I went to dine at Mr. Venables'. I had previously obtained five shillings from my father, towards re-clothing the poor children of my care, and prevailed on my mother to take one of the girls into the house, whom I determined to teach to work[2] and read.

'After dinner, when the younger part of the circle retired to the music-room, I recounted with energy my tale; that is, I mentioned Peggy's distress, without hinting at the steps I had taken to relieve her. Miss Venables gave me half-a-crown; the heir five shillings; but George sat unmoved. I was cruelly distressed by the disappointment—I scarcely could remain on my chair; and, could I have got out of the room unperceived, I should have flown home, as if to run away from myself. After several vain attempts to rise, I leaned my head against the marble chimney-piece, and gazing on the evergreens that filled the fire-place, moralized on the vanity of human expectations; regardless of the company. I was roused by a gentle tap on my shoulder from behind Charlotte's chair. I turned my head, and George slid a guinea into my hand, putting his finger to his mouth, to enjoin me silence.

'What a revolution took place, not only in my train of thoughts, but feelings! I trembled with emotion—now, indeed, I was in love. Such delicacy too, to enhance his benevolence! I felt in my pocket every five minutes, only to feel the guinea; and its magic touch invested my hero with more than mortal beauty. My fancy had found a basis to erect its model of perfection on; and quickly went to work, with all the happy credulity of youth, to consider that heart as devoted to virtue, which had only obeyed a virtuous impulse. The bitter experience was yet to come, that has taught me how very distinct are the principles of virtue, from the casual feelings from which they germinate.[1]

CHAPTER EIGHT

'I HAVE perhaps dwelt too long on a circumstance, which is only of importance as it marks the progress of a deception that has been so fatal to my peace; and introduces to your notice a poor girl, whom, intending to serve, I led to ruin. Still it is probable that I was not entirely the victim of mistake; and that your father, gradually fashioned by the world, did not quickly become what I hesitate to call him—out of respect to my daughter.

'But, to hasten to the more busy scenes of my life. Mr. Venables and my mother died the same summer; and, wholly engrossed by my attention to her, I thought of little else. The neglect of her darling, my brother Robert, had a violent effect on her weakened mind; for, though boys may be reckoned the pillars of the house without doors, girls are often the only comfort within. They but too frequently waste their health and spirits attending a dying parent,[2] who leaves them in comparative poverty. After closing, with filial piety, a father's eyes, they are chased from the paternal roof, to make room for the first-born, the son,[3] who is to carry the empty family-name down to posterity; though, occupied with his own pleasures, he scarcely thought of discharging, in the decline of his parent's life, the debt contracted in his childhood. My mother's conduct led me to make these reflections. Great as was the fatigue I endured, and the affection my unceasing solicitude evinced, of which my mother seemed perfectly sensible, still, when my brother, whom I could hardly persuade to remain a quarter of an hour in her chamber, was with her alone, a short time before her death, she gave him a little hoard, which she had been some years accumulating.

'During my mother's illness, I was obliged to manage my father's temper, who, from the lingering nature of her malady, began to imagine that it was merely fancy. At this period, an artful kind of upper servant[1] attracted my father's attention, and the neighbours made many remarks on the finery, not honestly got, exhibited at evening service. But I was too much occupied with my mother to observe any change in her dress or behaviour, or to listen to the whisper of scandal.

'I shall not dwell on the death-bed scene, lively as is the remembrance, or on the emotion produced by the last grasp of my mother's cold hand; when blessing me, she added, "A little patience, and all will be over!" Ah! my child, how often have those words rung mournfully in my ears—and I have exclaimed—"A little more patience, and I too shall be at rest!"

'My father was violently affected by her death, recollected instances of his unkindness, and wept like a child.

'My mother had solemnly recommended my sisters to my care, and bid me be a mother to them.[2] They, indeed, became more dear to me as they became more forlorn; for, during my mother's illness, I discovered the ruined state of my father's circumstances,[3] and that he had only been able to keep up appearances, by the sums which he borrowed of my uncle.

'My father's grief, and consequent tenderness to his children, quickly abated, the house grew still more gloomy or riotous; and my refuge from care was again at Mr. Venables'; the young 'squire having taken his father's place, and allowing, for the present, his sister to preside at his table. George, though dissatisfied with his portion of the fortune, which had till lately been all in trade, visited the family as usual. He was now full of speculations in trade, and his brow became clouded by care. He seemed to relax in his attention to me, when the presence of my uncle gave a new turn to his behaviour. I was too unsuspecting, too disinterested, to trace these changes to their source.

'My home every day became more and more disagreeable to me; my liberty was unnecessarily abridged, and my books, on the pretext that they made me idle, taken from me. My father's mistress was with child, and he, doating on her, allowed or overlooked her vulgar manner of tyrannizing over us. I was indignant, especially when I saw her endeavouring to attract, shall I say seduce? my younger brother. By allowing women but one way of rising in the world, the fostering the libertinism of men, society makes monsters of them, and then their ignoble vices are brought forward as a proof of inferiority of intellect.[1]

'The wearisomeness of my situation can scarcely be described. Though my life had not passed in the most even tenour with my mother, it was paradise to that I was destined to endure with my father's mistress, jealous of her illegitimate authority. My father's former occasional tenderness, in spite of his violence of temper, had been soothing to me; but now he only met me with reproofs or portentous frowns. The house-keeper, as she was now termed, was the vulgar despot of the family; and assuming the new character of a fine lady, she could never forgive the contempt which was sometimes visible in my countenance, when she uttered with pomposity her bad English, or affected to be well bred.

'To my uncle I ventured to open my heart; and he, with his wonted benevolence, began to consider in what manner he could extricate me out of my present irksome situation. In spite of his own disappointment, or, most probably, actuated by the feelings that had been petrified, not cooled, in all their sanguine fervour, like a boiling torrent of lava suddenly dashing into the sea, he thought a marriage of mutual inclination (would envious stars permit it) the only chance for happiness in this disastrous world. George Venables had the reputation of being attentive to business, and my father's example gave great weight to this circumstance; for habits of order in business would, he conceived, extend to the regulation of the affections in domestic life. George seldom spoke in my uncle's company, except to utter a short, judicious question, or to make a pertinent remark, with all due deference to his superior judgment; so that my uncle seldom left his company without observing, that the young man had more in him than people supposed.

'In this opinion he was not singular; yet, believe me, and I am not swayed by resentment, these speeches so justly poized, this silent deference, when the animal spirits of other young people were throwing off youthful ebullitions, were not the effect of thought or humility, but sheer barrenness of mind, and want of imagination. A colt of mettle will curvet and shew his paces. Yes; my dear girl, these prudent young men want all the fire necessary to ferment their faculties, and are characterized as wise, only because they are not foolish. It is true, that George was by no means so great a favourite of mine as during the first year of our acquaintance; still, as he often coincided in opinion with me, and echoed my sentiments; and having myself no other attachment, I heard with pleasure my uncle's proposal; but thought more of obtaining my freedom, than of my lover. But, when George, seemingly anxious for my happiness, pressed me to quit my present painful situation, my heart swelled with gratitude—I knew not that my uncle had promised him five thousand pounds.

'Had this truly generous man mentioned his intention to me, I should have insisted on a thousand pounds being settled on each of my sisters;[1] George would have contested; I should have seen his selfish soul; and—gracious God! have been spared the misery of discovering, when too late, that I was united to a heartless, unprincipled wretch. All my schemes of usefulness would not then have been blasted. The tenderness of my heart would not have heated my imagination with visions of the ineffable delight of happy love; nor would the sweet duty of a mother have been so cruelly interrupted.

'But I must not suffer the fortitude I have so hardly acquired, to be undermined by unavailing regret. Let me hasten forward to describe the turbid stream in which I had to wade—but let me exultingly declare that it is passed—my soul holds fellowship with him no more. He cut the Gordian knot, which my principles, mistaken ones, respected; he dissolved the tie, the fetters rather, that ate into my very vitals—and I should rejoice, conscious that my mind is freed, though confined in hell itself; the only place that even fancy can imagine more dreadful than my present abode.

'These varying emotions will not allow me to proceed. I heave sigh after sigh; yet my heart is still oppressed. For what am I reserved? Why was I not born a man, or why was I born at all?'

END OF VOL. I

THE
WRONGS OF
WOMAN:
OR,
MARIA.
A FRAGMENT

IN TWO VOLUMES

———

VOLUME II

THE WRONGS OF WOMAN
CHAPTER NINE

'I RESUME my pen to fly from thought. I was married; and we hastened to London. I had purposed taking one of my sisters with me; for a strong motive for marrying, was the desire of having a home at which I could receive them,[1] now their own grew so uncomfortable, as not to deserve the cheering appellation. An objection was made to her accompanying me, that appeared plausible; and I reluctantly acquiesced. I was however willingly allowed to take with me Molly, poor Peggy's daughter. London and preferment, are ideas commonly associated in the country; and, as blooming as May, she bade adieu to Peggy with weeping eyes. I did not even feel hurt at the refusal in relation to my sister, till hearing what my uncle had done for me, I had the simplicity to request, speaking with warmth of their situation, that he would give them a thousand pounds a-piece, which seemed to me but justice. He asked me, giving me a kiss, "If I had lost my senses?" I started back, as if I had found a wasp in a rose-bush. I expostulated. He sneered; and the demon of discord entered our paradise, to poison with his pestiferous breath every opening joy.

'I had sometimes observed defects in my husband's understanding; but, led astray by a prevailing opinion, that goodness of disposition is of the first importance in the relative situations of life, in proportion as I perceived the narrowness of his understanding, fancy enlarged the boundary of his heart. Fatal error! How quickly is the so much vaunted milkiness of nature turned into gall, by an intercourse with the world, if more generous juices do not sustain the vital source of virtue!

'One trait in my character was extreme credulity; but, when my eyes were once opened, I saw but too clearly all I had before overlooked. My husband was sunk in my esteem; still there are youthful emotions, which, for a while, fill up the chasm of love and friendship. Besides, it required some time to enable me to see his whole character in a just light, or rather to allow it to become fixed. While circumstances were ripening my faculties, and cultivating my taste, commerce and gross relaxations were shutting his against any possibility of improvement, till, by stifling every spark of virtue in himself, he began to imagine that it no where existed.

'Do not let me lead you astray, my child, I do not mean to assert, that any human being is entirely incapable of feeling the generous emotions, which are the foundation of every true principle of virtue; but they are frequently, I fear, so feeble, that, like the inflammable quality which more or less lurks in all bodies, they often lie for ever dormant; the circumstances never occurring, necessary to call them into action.

'I discovered however by chance, that, in consequence of some losses in trade, the natural effect of his gambling desire to start suddenly into riches, the five thousand pounds given me by my uncle, had been paid very opportunely.[1] This discovery, strange as you may think the assertion, gave me pleasure; my husband's embarrassments endeared him to me. I was glad to find an excuse for his conduct to my sisters, and my mind became calmer.

'My uncle introduced me to some literary society; and the theatres were a never-failing source of amusement to me. My delighted eye followed Mrs. Siddons, when, with dignified delicacy, she played Calista;[2] and I involuntarily repeated after her, in the same tone, and with a long-drawn sigh,

"Hearts like our's were pair'd . . . not match'd."[3]

'These were, at first, spontaneous emotions, though, becoming acquainted with men of wit and polished manners, I could not sometimes help regretting my early marriage; and that, in my haste to escape from a temporary dependence, and expand my newly fledged wings, in an unknown sky, I had been caught in a trap, and caged for life. Still the novelty of

London, and the attentive fondness of my husband, for he had some personal regard for me, made several months glide away. Yet, not forgetting the situation of my sisters, who were still very young, I prevailed on my uncle to settle a thousand pounds on each; and to place them in a school near town, where I could frequently visit, as well as have them at home with me.

'I now tried to improve my husband's taste, but we had few subjects in common; indeed he soon appeared to have little relish for my society, unless he was hinting to me the use he could make of my uncle's wealth. When we had company, I was disgusted by an ostentatious display of riches, and I have often quitted the room, to avoid listening to exaggerated tales of money obtained by lucky hits.

'With all my attention and affectionate interest, I perceived that I could not become the friend or confident of my husband. Every thing I learned relative to his affairs I gathered up by accident; and I vainly endeavoured to establish, at our fire-side, that social converse, which often renders people of different characters dear to each other. Returning from the theatre, or any amusing party, I frequently began to relate what I had seen and highly relished; but with sullen taciturnity he soon silenced me. I seemed therefore gradually to lose, in his society, the soul, the energies of which had just been in action. To such a degree, in fact, did his cold, reserved manner affect me, that, after spending some days with him alone, I have imagined myself the most stupid creature in the world, till the abilities of some casual visitor convinced me that I had some dormant animation, and sentiments above the dust in which I had been groveling. The very countenance of my husband changed; his complexion became sallow, and all the charms of youth were vanishing with its vivacity.

'I give you one view of the subject; but these experiments and alterations took up the space of five years; during which period, I had most reluctantly extorted several sums from my uncle, to save my husband, to use his own words, from destruction. At first it was to prevent bills being noted, to the injury of his credit; then to bail him; and afterwards to prevent an execution from entering the house. I began at last to conclude, that he would have made more exertions of his own to extricate himself, had he not relied on mine, cruel as was the task he imposed on me; and I firmly determined that I would make use of no more pretexts.

'From the moment I pronounced this determination, indifference on his part was changed into rudeness, or something worse.

'He now seldom dined at home, and continually returned at a late hour, drunk, to bed. I retired to another apartment; I was glad, I own, to escape from his; for personal intimacy without affection, seemed, to me the most degrading, as well as the most painful state in which a woman of any taste, not to speak of the peculiar delicacy of fostered sensibility, could be placed. But my husband's fondness for women was of the grossest kind,[1] and imagination was so wholly out of the question, as to render his indulgences of this sort entirely promiscuous, and of the most brutal nature. My health suffered, before my heart was entirely estranged by the loathsome information; could I then have returned to his sullied arms, but as a victim to the prejudices of mankind, who have made women the property of their husbands? I discovered even, by his conversation, when intoxicated, that his favourites were wantons of the lowest class, who could by their vulgar, indecent mirth, which he called nature, rouse his sluggish spirits. Meretricious ornaments and manners were necessary to attract his attention. He seldom looked twice at a modest woman, and sat silent in their company; and the charms of youth and beauty had not the slightest effect on his senses, unless the possessors were initiated in vice. His intimacy with profligate women, and his habits of thinking, gave him a contempt for female endowments; and he would repeat, when wine had loosed his tongue, most of the common-place sarcasms levelled at them, by men who do not allow them to have minds, because mind would be an impediment to gross enjoyment. Men who are inferior to their fellow men, are always most anxious to establish their superiority over women. But where are these reflections leading me?

'Women who have lost their husband's affection, are justly reproved for neglecting their persons, and not taking the same pains to keep, as to gain a heart; but who thinks of giving the same advice to men, though women are continually stigmatized for being attached to fops; and from the nature of their education, are more susceptible of disgust? Yet why a woman should be expected to endure a sloven, with more patience than a man, and magnanimously to govern herself, I cannot conceive; unless it be supposed arrogant in her to look for respect as well as a maintenance. It is not easy to be pleased, because, after promising to love, in different circumstances, we are told that it is our duty. I cannot, I am sure (though, when attending the sick, I never felt disgust) forget my own sensations, when rising with health and spirit, and after scenting the sweet morning, I have met my husband at the breakfast table. The active attention I had been giving to domestic regulations, which were generally settled before he rose, or a walk, gave a glow to my countenance, that contrasted with his squallid appearance. The squeamishness of stomach alone, produced by the last night's intemperance, which he took no pains to conceal, destroyed my appetite. I think I now see him[1] lolling in an arm-chair, in a dirty powdering gown,[2] soiled linen, ungartered stockings, and tangled hair, yawning and stretching himself. The newspaper was immediately called for, if not brought in on the tea-board, from which he would scarcely lift his eyes while I poured out the tea, excepting to ask for some brandy to put into it, or to declare that he could not eat. In answer to any question, in his best humour, it was a drawling "What do you say, child?" But if I demanded money for the house expences, which I put off till the last moment, his customary reply, often prefaced with an oath, was, "Do you think me, madam, made of money?"—The butcher, the baker, must wait; and, what was

worse, I was often obliged to witness his surly dismission of
tradesmen, who were in want of their money, and whom I
sometimes paid with the presents my uncle gave me for my
own use.

'At this juncture my father's mistress, by terrifying his
conscience, prevailed on him to marry her; he was already
become a methodist; and my brother, who now practised for
himself, had discovered a flaw in the settlement made on my
mother's children, which set it aside,[1] and he allowed my
father, whose distress made him submit to any thing, a tithe of
his own, or rather our fortune.

'My sisters had left school, but were unable to endure home,
which my father's wife rendered as disagreeable as possible, to
get rid of girls whom she regarded as spies on her conduct.
They were accomplished, yet you can (may you never be
reduced to the same destitute state!) scarcely conceive the
trouble I had to place them in the situation of governesses,[2]
the only one in which even a well-educated woman, with more
than ordinary talents, can struggle for a subsistence; and even
this is a dependence next to menial. Is it then surprising, that
so many forlorn women, with human passions and feelings,
take refuge in infamy? Alone in large mansions, I say alone,
because they had no companions with whom they could
converse on equal terms, or from whom they could expect the
endearments of affection, they grew melancholy, and the
sound of joy made them sad; and the youngest, having a more
delicate frame, fell into a decline. It was with great difficulty
that I, who now almost supported the house by loans from my
uncle, could prevail on the *master* of it, to allow her a room to
die in. I watched her sick bed for some months, and then
closed her eyes, gentle spirit! for ever. She was pretty, with
very engaging manners; yet had never an opportunity to
marry, excepting to a very old man.[3] She had abilities
sufficient to have shone in any profession, had there been any
professions for women, though she shrunk at the name of
milliner or mantua-maker as degrading to a gentlewoman. I
would not term this feeling false pride to any one but you, my

child, whom I fondly hope to see (yes; I will indulge the hope for a moment!) possessed of that energy of character which gives dignity to any station; and with that clear, firm spirit that will enable you' to choose a situation for yourself, or submit to be classed in the lowest, if it be the only one in which you can be the mistress of your own actions.[1]

'Soon after the death of my sister, an incident occurred, to prove to me that the heart of a libertine is dead to natural affection; and to convince me, that the being who has appeared all tenderness, to gratify a selfish passion, is as regardless of the innocent fruit of it, as of the object, when the fit is over. I had casually observed an old, mean-looking woman, who called on my husband every two or three months to receive some money. One day entering the passage of his little counting-house, as she was going out, I heard her say, "The child is very weak; she cannot live long, she will soon die out of your way, so you need not grudge her a little physic."

' "So much the better," he replied, "and pray mind your own business, good woman."

'I was struck by his unfeeling, inhuman tone of voice, and drew back, determined when the woman came again, to try to speak to her, not out of curiosity, I had heard enough, but with the hope of being useful to a poor, outcast girl.

'A month or two elapsed before I saw this woman again; and then she had a child in her hand that tottered along, scarcely able to sustain her own weight. They were going away, to return at the hour Mr. Venables was expected; he was now from home. I desired the woman to walk into the parlour. She hesitated, yet obeyed. I assured her that I should not mention to my husband (the word seemed to weigh on my respiration), that I had seen her, or his child. The woman stared at me with astonishment; and I turned my eyes on the squalid object [that accompanied her.] She could hardly support herself, her complexion was sallow, and her eyes inflamed, with an indescribable look of cunning, mixed with the wrinkles produced by the peevishness of pain.

' "Poor child!" I exclaimed. "Ah! you may well say poor

child," replied the woman. "I brought her here to see whether
he would have the heart to look at her, and not get some
advice. I do not know what they deserve who nursed her.
Why, her legs bent under her like a bow when she came to me,
and she has never been well since; but, if they were not better
paid than I am, it is not to be wondered at, sure enough."

'On further enquiry I was informed, that this miserable
spectacle was the daughter of a servant, a country girl, who
caught Mr. Venables' eye, and whom he seduced. On his
marriage he sent her away, her situation being too visible.
After her delivery, she was thrown on the town; and died in an
hospital within the year. The babe was sent to a parish-
nurse,[1] and afterwards to this woman, who did not seem
much better; but what was to be expected from such a close
bargain? She was only paid three shillings a week for board
and washing.

'The woman begged me to give her some old clothes for the
child, assuring me, that she was almost afraid to ask master for
money to buy even a pair of shoes.

'I grew sick at heart. And, fearing Mr. Venables might
enter, and oblige me to express my abhorrence, I hastily
enquired where she lived, promised to pay her two shillings a
week more, and to call on her in a day or two; putting a trifle
into her hand as a proof of my good intention.

'If the state of this child affected me, what were my feelings
at a discovery I made respecting Peggy————?*

*The manuscript is imperfect here. An episode seems to have been
intended, which was never committed to paper.   EDITOR.

CHAPTER TEN

'MY father's situation was now so distressing, that I prevailed
on my uncle to accompany me to visit him; and to lend me his
assistance; to prevent the whole property of the family from
becoming the prey of my brother's rapacity; for, to extricate

himself out of present difficulties, my father was totally regardless of futurity. I took down with me some presents for my step-mother; it did not require an effort for me to treat her with civility, or to forget the past.

'This was the first time I had visited my native village,[1] since my marriage. But with what different emotions did I return from the busy world, with a heavy weight of experience benumbing my imagination, to scenes, that whispered recollections of joy and hope most eloquently to my heart! The first scent of the wild flowers from the heath, thrilled through my veins, awakening every sense to pleasure. The icy hand of despair seemed to be removed from my bosom; and—forgetting my husband—the nurtured visions of a romantic mind, bursting on me with all their original wildness and gay exuberance, were again hailed as sweet realities. I forgot, with equal facility, that I ever felt sorrow, or knew care in the country; while a transient rainbow stole athwart the cloudy sky of despondency. The picturesque form of several favourite trees, and the porches of rude cottages, with their smiling hedges, were recognized with the gladsome playfulness of childish vivacity. I could have kissed the chickens that pecked on the common; and longed to pat the cows, and frolic with the dogs that sported on it. I gazed with delight on the windmill, and thought it lucky that it should be in motion, at the moment I passed by; and entering the dear green-lane, which led directly to the village, the sound of the well-known rookery gave that sentimental tinge to the varying sensations of my active soul, which only served to heighten the lustre of the luxuriant scenery. But, spying, as I advanced, the spire, peeping over the withered tops of the aged elms that composed the rookery, my thoughts flew immediately to the church-yard, and tears of affection, such was the effect of my imagination, bedewed my mother's grave. Sorrow gave place to devotional feelings. I wandered through the church in fancy, as I used sometimes to do on a Saturday evening. I recollected with what fervour I addressed the God of my youth: and once more with rapturous love looked above my sorrows to the Father of nature. I pause—feeling forcibly all the emotions I am describing; and (reminded, as I register my sorrows, of the sublime calm I have felt, when in some tremendous solitude, my soul rested on itself, and seemed to fill the universe) I insensibly breathe soft, hushing every wayward emotion, as if fearing to sully with a sigh, a contentment so extatic.

'Having settled my father's affairs, and, by my exertions in his favour, made my brother my sworn foe, I returned to London. My husband's conduct was now changed; I had during my absence, received several affectionate, penitential letters from him; and he seemed on my arrival, to wish by his behaviour to prove his sincerity. I could not then conceive why he acted thus; and, when the suspicion darted into my head, that it might arise from observing my increasing influence with my uncle, I almost despised myself for imagining that such a degree of debasing selfishness could exist.

'He became, unaccountable as was the change, tender and attentive; and, attacking my weak side, made a confession of his follies, and lamented the embarrassments in which I, who merited a far different fate, might be involved. He besought me to aid him with my counsel, praised my understanding, and appealed to the tenderness of my heart.

'This conduct only inspired me with compassion. I wished to be his friend; but love had spread his rosy pinions, and fled far, far away; and had not (like some exquisite perfumes, the fine spirit of which is continually mingling with the air) left a fragrance behind, to mark where he had shook his wings. My husband's renewed caresses then became hateful to me; his brutality was tolerable, compared to his distasteful fondness. Still, compassion, and the fear of insulting his supposed feelings, by a want of sympathy, made me dissemble, and do violence to my delicacy. What a task!

'Those who support a system of what I term false refinement, and will not allow great part of love in the female, as well as male breast, to spring in some respects

involuntarily, may not admit that charms are as necessary to
feed the passion, as virtues to convert the mellowing spirit
into friendship. To such observers I have nothing to say, any
more than to the moralists, who insist that women ought to,
and can love their husbands, because it is their duty. To you,
my child, I may add, with a heart tremblingly alive to your
future conduct, some observations, dictated by my present
feelings, on calmly reviewing this period of my life. When
novelists or moralists praise as a virtue, a woman's coldness of
constitution, and want of passion; and make her yield to the
ardour of her lover out of sheer compassion, or to promote a
frigid plan of future comfort, I am disgusted.[1] They may be
good women, in the ordinary acceptation of the phrase, and do
no harm; but they appear to me not to have those "finely
fashioned nerves,"[2] which render the senses exquisite. They
may possess tenderness; but they want that fire of the
imagination, which produces *active* sensibility, and *positive*
virtue. How does the woman deserve to be characterized, who
marries one man, with a heart and imagination devoted to
another? Is she not an object of pity or contempt, when thus
sacrilegiously violating the purity of her own feelings? Nay, it
is as indelicate, when she is indifferent, unless she be
constitutionally insensible; then indeed it is a mere affair of
barter; and I have nothing to do with the secrets of trade. Yes;
eagerly as I wish you to possess true rectitude of mind, and
purity of affection, I must insist that a heartless conduct is the
contrary of virtuous. Truth is the only basis of virtue; and we
cannot, without depraving our minds, endeavour to please a
lover or husband, but in proportion as he pleases us. Men,
more effectually to enslave us, may inculcate this partial
morality, and lose sight of virtue in subdividing it into the
duties of particular stations; but let us not blush for nature
without a cause!

'After these remarks, I am ashamed to own, that I was
pregnant. The greatest sacrifice of my principles in my whole
life, was the allowing my husband again to be familiar with my
person, though to this cruel act of self-denial, when I wished

the earth to open and swallow me, you owe your birth; and I the unutterable pleasure of being a mother. There was something of delicacy in my husband's bridal attentions; but now his tainted breath, pimpled face, and blood-shot eyes, were not more repugnant to my senses, than his gross manners, and loveless familiarity to my taste.

'A man would only be expected to maintain; yes, barely grant a subsistence, to a woman rendered odious by habitual intoxication; but who would expect him, or think it possible to love her? And unless "youth, and genial years were flown,"[1] it would be thought equally unreasonable to insist, [under penalty of] forfeiting almost every thing reckoned valuable in life, that he should not love another: whilst woman, weak in reason, impotent in will, is required to moralize, sentimentalize herself to stone, and pine her life away, labouring to reform her embruted mate. He may even spend in dissipation, and intemperance, the very intemperance which renders him so hateful, her property, and by stinting her expences, not permit her to beguile in society, a wearisome, joyless life; for over their mutual fortune she has no power, it must all pass through his hand. And if she be a mother, and in the present state of women, it is a great misfortune to be prevented from discharging the duties, and cultivating the affections of one, what has she not to endure?—But I have suffered the tenderness of one to lead me into reflections that I did not think of making, to interrupt my narrative—yet the full heart will overflow.

'Mr. Venables' embarrassments did not now endear him to me; still, anxious to befriend him, I endeavoured to prevail on him to retrench his expences; but he had always some plausible excuse to give, to justify his not following my advice. Humanity, compassion, and the interest produced by a habit of living together, made me try to relieve, and sympathize with him; but, when I recollected that I was bound to live with such a being for ever—my heart died within me; my desire of improvement became languid, and baleful, corroding melancholy took possession of my soul. Marriage had bastilled[1] me for life. I discovered in myself a capacity for the enjoyment of the various pleasures existence affords; yet, fettered by the partial laws of society, this fair globe was to me an universal blank.

'When I exhorted my husband to economy, I referred to himself. I was obliged to practice the most rigid, or contract debts, which I had too much reason to fear would never be paid. I despised this paltry privilege of a wife, which can only be of use to the vicious or inconsiderate, and determined not to increase the torrent that was bearing him down. I was then ignorant of the extent of his fraudulent speculations, whom I was bound to honour and obey.

'A woman neglected by her husband, or whose manners form a striking contrast with his, will always have men on the watch to soothe and flatter her. Besides, the forlorn state of a neglected woman, not destitute of personal charms, is particularly interesting, and rouses that species of pity, which is so near akin, it easily slides into love. A man of feeling thinks not of seducing, he is himself seduced by all the noblest emotions of his soul. He figures to himself all the sacrifices a woman of sensibility must make, and every situation in which his imagination places her, touches his heart, and fires his passions. Longing to take to his bosom the shorn lamb, and bid the drooping buds of hope revive, benevolence changes into passion: and should he then discover that he is beloved, honour binds him fast, though foreseeing that he may afterwards be obliged to pay severe damages to the man, who never appeared to value his wife's society, till he found that there was a chance of his being indemnified for the loss of it.

'Such are the partial laws enacted by men; for, only to lay a stress on the dependent state of a woman in the grand question of the comforts arising from the possession of property, she is [even in this article] much more injured by the loss of the husband's affection, than he by that of his wife; yet where is she, condemned to the solitude of a deserted home, to look for a compensation from the woman, who seduces him from her? She cannot drive an unfaithful husband from his house, nor separate, or tear, his children from him, however culpable he may be; and he, still the master of his own fate, enjoys the smiles of a world, that would brand her with infamy, did she, seeking consolation, venture to retaliate.

'These remarks are not dictated by experience; but merely by the compassion I feel for many amiable women, the *outlaws*[1] of the world. For myself, never encouraging any of the advances that were made to me, my lovers dropped off like the untimely shoots of spring. I did not even coquet with them; because I found, on examining myself, I could not coquet with a man without loving him a little; and I perceived that I should not be able to stop at the line of what are termed *innocent freedoms*, did I suffer any. My reserve was then the consequence of delicacy. Freedom of conduct has emancipated many women's minds; but my conduct has most rigidly been governed by my principles, till the improvement of my understanding has enabled me to discern the fallacy of prejudices at war with nature and reason.

'Shortly after the change I have mentioned in my husband's conduct, my uncle was compelled by his declining health, to seek the succour of a milder climate, and embark for Lisbon. He left his will in the hands of a friend, an eminent solicitor; he had previously questioned me relative to my situation and state of mind, and declared very freely, that he could place no reliance on the stability of my husband's professions. He had been deceived in the unfolding of his character; he now thought it fixed in a train of actions that would inevitably lead to ruin and disgrace.

'The evening before his departure, which we spent alone together, he folded me to his heart, uttering the endearing appellation of "child."—My more than father![2] why was I not permitted to perform the last duties of one, and smooth the pillow of death? He seemed by his manner to be convinced that he should never see me more; yet requested me, most earnestly, to come to him, should I be obliged to leave my husband. He had before expressed his sorrow at hearing of my pregnancy, having determined to prevail on me to accompany him, till I informed him of that circumstance. He expressed himself unfeignedly sorry that any new tie should bind me to a man whom he thought so incapable of estimating my value; such was the kind language of affection.

'I must repeat his own words; they made an indelible impression on my mind:

' "The marriage state is certainly that in which women, generally speaking, can be most useful; but I am far from thinking that a woman, once married, ought to consider the engagement as indissoluble (especially if there be no children to reward her for sacrificing her feelings) in case her husband merits neither her love, nor esteem. Esteem will often supply the place of love; and prevent a woman from being wretched, though it may not make her happy. The magnitude of a sacrifice ought always to bear some proportion to the utility in view; and for a woman to live with a man, for whom she can cherish neither affection nor esteem, or even be of any use to him, excepting in the light of a house-keeper, is an abjectness of condition, the enduring of which no concurrence of circumstances can ever make a duty in the sight of God or just men. If indeed she submits to it merely to be maintained in idleness, she has no right to complain bitterly of her fate; or to act, as a person of independent character might, as if she had a title to disregard general rules.

' "But the misfortune is, that many women only submit in appearance, and forfeit their own respect to secure their reputation in the world.[1] The situation of a woman separated from her husband, is undoubtedly very different from that of a man who has left his wife. He, with lordly dignity, has shaken off a clog; and the allowing her food and raiment, is thought sufficient to secure his reputation from taint. And, should she have been inconsiderate, he will be celebrated for his generosity and forbearance. Such is the respect paid to the master-key of property! A woman, on the contrary, resigning what is termed her natural protector (though he never was so, but in name) is despised and shunned, for asserting the independence of mind distinctive of a rational being, and spurning at slavery."

'During the remainder of the evening, my uncle's tenderness led him frequently to revert to the subject, and utter, with increasing warmth, sentiments to the same purport. At length it was necessary to say "Farewell!"—and we parted—gracious God! to meet no more.

CHAPTER ELEVEN

'A GENTLEMAN of large fortune and of polished manners, had lately visited very frequently at our house, and treated me, if possible, with more respect than Mr. Venables paid him; my pregnancy was not yet visible. His society was a great relief to me, as I had for some time past, to avoid expence, confined myself very much at home. I ever disdained unnecessary, perhaps even prudent concealments; and my husband, with great ease, discovered the amount of my uncle's parting present. A copy of a writ was the stale pretext to extort it from me; and I had soon reason to believe that it was fabricated for the purpose. I acknowledge my folly in thus suffering myself to be continually imposed on. I had adhered to my resolution not to apply to my uncle, on the part of my husband, any more; yet, when I had received a sum sufficient to supply my own wants, and to enable me to pursue a plan I had in view, to settle my younger brother in a respectable employment, I allowed myself to be duped by Mr. Venables' shallow pretences, and hypocritical professions.

'Thus did he pillage me and my family, thus frustrate all my plans of usefulness. Yet this was the man I was bound to respect and esteem: as if respect and esteem depended on an arbitrary will of our own! But a wife being as much a man's property as his horse, or his ass,[1] she has nothing she can call her own. He may use any means to get at what the law considers as his,[2] the moment his wife is in possession of it, even to the forcing of a lock, as Mr. Venables did, to search for notes in my writing-desk—and all this is done with a show of equity, because, forsooth, he is responsible for her maintenance.

'The tender mother cannot *lawfully* snatch from the gripe of the gambling spendthrift, or beastly drunkard, unmindful of his offspring, the fortune which falls to her by chance; or (so flagrant is the injustice) what she earns by her own exertions. No; he can rob her with impunity, even to waste publicly on a courtezan; and the laws of her country—if women have a country—afford her no protection or redress from the oppressor, unless she have the plea of bodily fear; yet how many ways are there of goading the soul almost to madness, equally unmanly, though not so mean? When such laws were framed, should not impartial lawgivers have first decreed, in the style of a great assembly, who recognized the existence of an *être suprême*,[1] to fix the national belief, that the husband should always be wiser and more virtuous than his wife, in order to entitle him, with a show of justice, to keep this idiot, or perpetual minor, for ever in bondage. But I must have done—on this subject, my indignation continually runs away with me.

'The company of the gentleman I have already mentioned, who had a general acquaintance with literature and subjects of taste, was grateful to me; my countenance brightened up as he approached, and I unaffectedly expressed the pleasure I felt. The amusement his conversation afforded me, made it easy to comply with my husband's request, to endeavour to render our house agreeable to him.

'His attentions became more pointed; but, as I was not of the number of women, whose virtue, as it is termed, immediately takes alarm, I endeavoured, rather by raillery than serious expostulation, to give a different turn to his conversation. He assumed a new mode of attack, and I was, for a while, the dupe of his pretended friendship.

'I had, merely in the style of *badinage*, boasted of my conquest, and repeated his lover-like compliments to my husband. But he begged me, for God's sake, not to affront his friend, or I should destroy all his projects, and be his ruin. Had I had more affection for my husband, I should have expressed my contempt of this time-serving politeness: now I imagined that I only felt pity; yet it would have puzzled a casuist to point out in what the exact difference consisted.

'This friend began now, in confidence, to discover to me the real state of my husband's affairs. "Necessity," said Mr. S——;[1] why should I reveal his name? for he affected to palliate the conduct he could not excuse, "had led him to take such steps, by accommodation bills,[2] buying goods on credit, to sell them for ready money, and similar transactions, that his character in the commerical world was gone. He was considered," he added, lowering his voice, "on 'Change as a swindler."

'I felt at that moment the first maternal pang. Aware of the evils my sex have to struggle with, I still wished, for my own consolation, to be the mother of a daughter; and I could not bear to think, that the *sins* of her father's entailed disgrace, should be added to the ills to which woman is heir.

'So completely was I deceived by these shows of friendship (nay, I believe, according to his interpretation, Mr. S—— really was my friend) that I began to consult him respecting the best mode of retrieving my husband's character: it is the good name of a woman only that sets to rise no more. I knew not that he had been drawn into a whirlpool, out of which he had not the energy to attempt to escape. He seemed indeed destitute of the power of employing his faculties in any regular pursuit. His principles of action were so loose, and his mind so uncultivated, that every thing like order appeared to him in the shape of restraint; and, like men in the savage state, he required the strong stimulus of hope or fear, produced by wild speculations, in which the interests of others went for nothing, to keep his spirits awake. He one time professed patriotism, but he knew not what it was to feel honest indignation; and pretended to be an advocate for liberty, when, with as little affection for the human race as for individuals, he thought of nothing but his own gratification. He was just such a citizen, as a father. The sums he adroitly obtained by a violation of the laws of his country, as well as those of humanity, he would allow a mistress to squander; though she was, with the same *sang froid*, consigned, as were his children, to poverty, when another proved more attractive.

'On various pretences, his friend continued to visit me; and, observing my want of money, he tried to induce me to accept of pecuniary aid; but this offer I absolutely rejected, though it was made with such delicacy, I could not be displeased.

'One day he came, as I thought accidentally, to dinner. My husband was very much engaged in business, and quitted the room soon after the cloth was removed. We conversed as usual, till confidential advice led again to love. I was extremely mortified. I had a sincere regard for him, and hoped that he had an equal friendship for me. I therefore began mildly to expostulate with him. This gentleness he mistook for coy encouragement; and he would not be diverted from the subject. Perceiving his mistake, I seriously asked him how, using such language to me, he could profess to be my husband's friend? A significant sneer excited my curiosity, and he, supposing this to be my only scruple, took a letter deliberately out of his pocket, saying, "Your husband's honour is not inflexible. How could you, with your discernment, think it so? Why, he left the room this very day on purpose to give me an opportunity to explain myself; *he* thought me too timid—too tardy."

'I snatched the letter with indescribable emotion. The purport of it was to invite him to dinner, and to ridicule his chivalrous respect for me. He assured him, "that every woman had her price," and, with gross indecency, hinted, that he should be glad to have the duty of a husband taken off his hands. These he termed *liberal sentiments*. He advised him not to shock my romantic notions, but to attack my credulous generosity, and weak pity; and concluded with requesting him to lend him five hundred pounds for a month or six weeks." I read this letter twice over; and the firm purpose it inspired, calmed the rising tumult of my soul. I rose deliberately, requested Mr. S———— to wait a moment, and instantly going into the counting-house, desired Mr. Venables to return with me to the dining-parlour.

'He laid down his pen, and entered with me, without observing any change in my countenance. I shut the door, and, giving him the letter, simply asked, "whether he wrote it, or was it a forgery?"

'Nothing could equal his confusion. His friend's eye met his, and he muttered something about a joke—But I interrupted him—"It is sufficient—We part for ever."

'I continued, with solemnity, "I have borne with your tyranny and infidelities. I disdain to utter what I have borne with. I thought you unprincipled, but not so decidedly vicious. I formed a tie, in the sight of heaven—I have held it sacred; even when men, more conformable to my taste, have made me feel—I despise all subterfuge!—that I was not dead to love. Neglected by you, I have resolutely stifled the enticing emotions, and respected the plighted faith you outraged. And you dare now to insult me, by selling me to prostitution!—Yes—equally lost to delicacy and principle—you dared sacrilegiously to barter the honour of the mother of your child."

'Then, turning to Mr. S————, I added, "I call on you, Sir, to witness," and I lifted my hands and eyes to heaven, "that, as solemnly as I took his name, I now abjure it," I pulled off my ring, and put it on the table; "and that I mean immediately to quit his house, never to enter it more. I will provide for myself and child. I leave him as free as I am determined to be myself—he shall be answerable for no debts of mine."

'Astonishment closed their lips, till Mr. Venables, gently pushing his friend, with a forced smile, out of the room, nature for a moment prevailed, and, appearing like himself, he turned round, burning with rage, to me: but there was no terror in the frown, excepting when contrasted with the malignant smile which preceded it. He bade me "leave the house at my peril; told me he despised my threats; I had no resource; I could not swear the peace against him!—I was not afraid of my life!—he had never struck me!"[1]

'He threw the letter in the fire, which I had incautiously left in his hands; and, quitting the room, locked the door on me.

'When left alone, I was a moment or two before I could recollect myself. One scene had succeeded another with such rapidity, I almost doubted whether I was reflecting on a real event. "Was it possible? Was I, indeed, free?"—Yes; free I termed myself, when I decidedly perceived the conduct I ought to adopt.[2] How had I panted for liberty—liberty, that I would have purchased at any price, but that of my own esteem! I rose, and shook myself; opened the window, and methought the air never smelled so sweet. The face of heaven grew fairer as I viewed it, and the clouds seemed to flit away obedient to my wishes, to give my soul room to expand. I was all soul, and (wild as it may appear) felt as if I could have dissolved in the soft balmy gale that kissed my cheek, or have glided below the horizon on the glowing, descending beams. A seraphic satisfaction animated, without agitating my spirits; and my imagination collected, in visions sublimely terrible, or soothingly beautiful, an immense variety of the endless images, which nature affords, and fancy combines, of the grand and fair. The lustre of these bright picturesque sketches faded with the setting sun; but I was still alive to the calm delight they had diffused through my heart.

'There may be advocates for matrimonial obedience, who, making a distinction between the duty of a wife and of a human being, may blame my conduct.—To them I write not—my feelings are not for them to analyze; and may you, my child, never be able to ascertain, by heart-rending experience, what your mother felt before the present emancipation of her mind!

'I began to write a letter to my father, after closing one to my uncle; not to ask advice, but to signify my determination; when I was interrupted by the entrance of Mr. Venables. His

manner was changed. His views on my uncle's fortune made
him averse to my quitting his house, or he would, I am
convinced, have been glad to have shaken off even the slight
restraint my presence imposed on him; the restraint of
showing me some respect. So far from having an affection for
me, he really hated me, because he was convinced that I must
despise him.

'He told me, that, "As I now had had time to cool and
reflect, he did not doubt but that my prudence, and nice sense
of propriety, would lead me to overlook what was passed."

' "Reflection," I replied, "had only confirmed my purpose,
and no power on earth could divert me from it."

'Endeavouring to assume a soothing voice and look, when
he would willingly have tortured me, to force me to feel his
power, his countenance had an infernal expression, when he
desired me, "not to expose myself to the servants, by obliging
him to confine me in my apartment; if then I would give my
promise not to quit the house precipitately, I should be
free—and—." I declared, interrupting him, "that I would
promise nothing. I had no measures to keep with him—I was
resolved, and would not condescend to subterfuge."

'He muttered, "that I should soon repent of these
preposterous airs;" and, ordering tea to be carried into my
little study, which had a communication with my bed-
chamber, he once more locked the door upon me, and left me
to my own meditations. I had passively followed him up
stairs, not wishing to fatigue myself with unavailing exertion.

'Nothing calms the mind like a fixed purpose. I felt as if I
had heaved a thousand weight from my heart; the atmosphere
seemed lightened; and, if I execrated the institutions of
society, which thus enable men to tyrannize over women, it
was almost a disinterested sentiment. I disregarded present
inconveniences, when my mind had done struggling with
itself,—when reason and inclination had shaken hands and
were at peace. I had no longer the cruel task before me, in
endless perspective, aye, during the tedious for ever of life, of
labouring to overcome my repugnance—of labouring to

extinguish the hopes, the maybes of a lively imagination. Death I had hailed as my only chance for deliverance; but, while existence had still so many charms, and life promised happiness, I shrunk from the icy arms of an unknown tyrant, though far more inviting than those of the man, to whom I supposed myself bound without any other alternative; and was content to linger a little longer, waiting for I knew not what, rather than leave "the warm precincts of the cheerful day,"[1] and all the unenjoyed affection of my nature.

'My present situation gave a new turn to my reflection; and I wondered (now the film seemed to be withdrawn, that obscured the piercing sight of reason) how I could, previously to the deciding outrage, have considered myself as everlastingly united to vice and folly! "Had an evil genius cast a spell at my birth; or a demon stalked out of chaos, to perplex my understanding, and enchain my will, with delusive prejudices?"

'I pursued this train of thinking; it led me out of myself, to expatiate on the misery peculiar to my sex. "Are not," I thought, "the despots for ever stigmatized, who, in the wantonness of power, commanded even the most atrocious criminals to be chained to dead bodies? though surely those laws are much more inhuman, which forge adamantine fetters to bind minds together, that never can mingle in social communion! What indeed can equal the wretchedness of that state, in which there is no alternative, but to extinguish the affections, or encounter infamy?"

CHAPTER TWELVE

'TOWARDS midnight Mr. Venables entered my chamber; and, with calm audacity preparing to go to bed, he bade me make haste, "for that was the best place for husbands and wives to end their differences." He had been drinking plentifully to aid his courage.

'I did not at first deign to reply. But perceiving that he affected to take my silence for consent, I told him that, "If he would not go to another bed, or allow me, I should sit up in my study all night." He attempted to pull me into the chamber, half joking. But I resisted; and, as he had determined not to give me any reason for saying that he used violence, after a few more efforts, he retired, cursing my obstinacy, to bed.

'I sat musing some time longer; then, throwing my cloak around me, prepared for sleep on a sopha. And, so fortunate seemed my deliverance, so sacred the pleasure of being thus wrapped up in myself, that I slept profoundly, and woke with a mind composed to encounter the struggles of the day. Mr. Venables did not wake till some hours after; and then he came to me half-dressed, yawning and stretching, with haggard eyes, as if he scarcely recollected what had passed the preceding evening. He fixed his eyes on me for a moment, then, calling me a fool, asked "How long I intended to continue this pretty farce? For his part, he was devilish sick of it; but this was the plague of marrying women who pretended to know something."

'I made no other reply to this harangue, than to say, "That he ought to be glad to get rid of a woman so unfit to be his companion—and that any change in my conduct would be mean dissimulation; for maturer reflection only gave the sacred seal of reason to my first resolution."

'He looked as if he could have stamped with impatience, at being obliged to stifle his rage; but, conquering his anger (for weak people, whose passions seem the most ungovernable, restrain them with the greatest ease, when they have a sufficient motive), he exclaimed, "Very pretty, upon my soul! very pretty, theatrical flourishes! Pray, fair Roxana,[1] stoop from your altitudes, and remember that you are acting a part in real life."

'He uttered this speech with a self-satisfied air, and went down stairs to dress.

'In about an hour he came to me again; and in the same tone

said, "That he came as my gentleman-usher to hand me down to breakfast."

' "Of the black rod?"[1] asked I.

'This question, and the tone in which I asked it, a little disconcerted him. To say the truth, I now felt no resentment; my firm resolution to free myself from my ignoble thraldom, had absorbed the various emotions which, during six years, had racked my soul. The duty pointed out by my principles seemed clear; and not one tender feeling intruded to make me swerve. The dislike which my husband had inspired was strong; but it only led me to wish to avoid, to wish to let him drop out of my memory; there was no misery, no torture that I would not deliberately have chosen, rather than renew my lease of servitude.

'During the breakfast, he attempted to reason with me on the folly of romantic sentiments; for this was the indiscriminate epithet he gave to every mode of conduct or thinking superior to his own. He asserted, "that all the world were governed by their own interest; those who pretended to be actuated by different motives, were only deeper knaves, or fools crazed by books, who took for gospel all the rodomantade nonsense written by men who knew nothing of the world. For his part, he thanked God, he was no hypocrite; and, if he stretched a point sometimes, it was always with an intention of paying every man his own."

'He then artfully insinuated, "that he daily expected a vessel to arrive, a successful speculation, that would make him easy for the present, and that he had several other schemes actually depending, that could not fail. He had no doubt of becoming rich in a few years, though he had been thrown back by some unlucky adventures at the setting out."

'I mildly replied, "That I wished he might not involve himself still deeper."

'He had no notion that I was governed by a decision of judgment, not to be compared with a mere spurt of resentment. He knew not what it was to feel indignation against vice, and often boasted of his placable temper, and readiness to forgive injuries. True; for he only considered the being deceived, as an effort of skill he had not guarded against; and then, with a cant of candour, would observe, "that he did not know how he might himself have been tempted to act in the same circumstances." And, as his heart never opened to friendship, it never was wounded by disappointment. Every new acquaintance he protested, it is true, was "the cleverest fellow in the world;" and he really thought so; till the novelty of his conversation or manners ceased to have any effect on his sluggish spirits. His respect for rank or fortune was more permanent, though he chanced to have no design of availing himself of the influence of either to promote his own views.

'After a prefatory conversation,—my blood (I thought it had been cooler) flushed over my whole countenance as he spoke—he alluded to my situation. He desired me to reflect—"and act like a prudent woman, as the best proof of my superior understanding; for he must own I had sense, did I know how to use it. I was not," he laid a stress on his words, "without my passions; and a husband was a convenient cloke.—He was liberal in his way of thinking; and why might not we, like many other married people, who were above vulgar prejudices, tacitly consent to let each other follow their own inclination?—He meant nothing more, in the letter I made the ground of complaint; and the pleasure which I seemed to take in Mr. S.'s company, led him to conclude, that he was not disagreeable to me."

'A clerk brought in the letters of the day, and I, as I often did, while he was discussing subjects of business, went to the *piano forte*, and began to play a favourite air to restore myself, as it were, to nature, and drive the sophisticated sentiments I had just been obliged to listen to, out of my soul.

'They had excited sensations similar to those I have felt, in viewing the squalid inhabitants of some of the lanes and back streets of the metropolis, mortified at being compelled to consider them as my fellow-creatures, as if an ape had claimed kindred with me. Or, as when surrounded by a mephitical fog,

I have wished to have a volley of cannon fired, to clear the incumbered atmosphere, and give me room to breathe and move.

'My spirits were all in arms, and I played a kind of extemporary prelude. The cadence was probably wild and impassioned, while, lost in thought, I made the sounds a kind of echo to my train of thinking.

'Pausing for a moment, I met Mr. Venables' eyes. He was observing me with an air of conceited satisfaction, as much as to say—"My last insinuation has done the business—she begins to know her own interest." Then gathering up his letters, he said, "That he hoped he should hear no more romantic stuff, well enough in a miss just come from boarding school;" and went, as was his custom, to the counting-house. I still continued playing; and, turning to a sprightly lesson, I executed it with uncommon vivacity. I heard footsteps approach the door, and was soon convinced that Mr. Venables was listening; the consciousness only gave more animation to my fingers. He went down into the kitchen, and the cook, probably by his desire, came to me, to know what I would please to order for dinner. Mr. Venables came into the parlour again, with apparent carelessness. I perceived that the cunning man was over-reaching himself; and I gave my directions as usual, and left the room.

'While I was making some alteration in my dress, Mr. Venables peeped in, and, begging my pardon for interrupting me, disappeared. I took up some work (I could not read), and two or three messages were sent to me, probably for no other purpose, but to enable Mr. Venables to ascertain what I was about.

'I listened whenever I heard the street-door open; at last I imagined I could distinguish Mr. Venables' step, going out. I laid aside my work; my heart palpitated; still I was afraid hastily to enquire; and I waited a long half hour, before I ventured to ask the boy whether his master was in the counting-house?

'Being answered in the negative, I bade him call me a coach, and collecting a few necessaries hastily together, with a little parcel of letters and papers which I had collected the preceding evening, I hurried into it, desiring the coachman to drive to a distant part of the town.[1]

'I almost feared that the coach would break down before I got out of the street; and, when I turned the corner, I seemed to breathe a freer air. I was ready to imagine that I was rising above the thick atmosphere of earth; or I felt, as wearied souls might be supposed to feel on entering another state of existence.

'I stopped at one or two stands of coaches to elude pursuit, and then drove round the skirts of the town to seek for an obscure lodging, where I wished to remain concealed, till I could avail myself of my uncle's protection. I had resolved to assume my own name immediately, and openly to avow my determination, without any formal vindication, the moment I had found a home, in which I could rest free from the daily alarm of expecting to see Mr. Venables enter.

'I looked at several lodgings; but finding that I could not, without a reference to some acquaintance, who might inform my tyrant, get admittance into a decent apartment—men have not all this trouble—I thought of a woman whom I had assisted to furnish a little haberdasher's shop, and who I knew had a first floor to let.

'I went to her, and though I could not persuade her, that the quarrel between me and Mr. Venables would never be made up, still she agreed to conceal me for the present; yet assuring me at the same time, shaking her head, that, when a woman was once married, she must bear every thing. Her pale face, on which appeared a thousand haggard lines and delving wrinkles, produced by what is emphatically termed fretting, inforced her remark; and I had afterwards an opportunity of observing the treatment she had to endure, which grizzled[2] her into patience. She toiled from morning till night; yet her husband would rob the till, and take away the money reserved for paying bills; and, returning home drunk, he would beat her if she chanced to offend him, though she had a child at the breast.

'These scenes awoke me at night; and, in the morning, I heard her, as usual, talk to her dear Johnny—he, forsooth, was her master; no slave in the West Indies had one more despotic; but fortunately she was of the true Russian breed of wives.[1]

'My mind, during the few past days, seemed, as it were, disengaged from my body; but, now the struggle was over, I felt very forcibly the effect which perturbation of spirits produces on a woman in my situation.

'The apprehension of a miscarriage, obliged me to confine myself to my apartment near a fortnight; but I wrote to my uncle's friend for money, promising "to call on him, and explain my situation, when I was well enough to go out; mean time I earnestly intreated him, not to mention my place of abode to any one, lest my husband—such the law considered him—should disturb the mind he could not conquer. I mentioned my intention of setting out for Lisbon, to claim my uncle's protection, the moment my health would permit."

'The tranquillity however, which I was recovering, was soon interrupted. My landlady came up to me one day, with eyes swollen with weeping, unable to utter what she was commanded to say. She declared, "That she was never so miserable in her life; that she must appear an ungrateful monster; and that she would readily go down on her knees to me, to intreat me to forgive her, as she had done to her husband to spare her the cruel task." Sobs prevented her from proceeding, or answering my impatient enquiries, to know what she meant.

'When she became a little more composed, she took a newspaper out her pocket, declaring, "that her heart smote her, but what could she do?—she must obey her husband." I snatched the paper from her. An advertisement quickly met my eye, purporting, that "Maria Venables had, without any assignable cause, absconded from her husband; and any person harbouring her, was menaced with the utmost severity of the law."

'Perfectly acquainted with Mr. Venables' meanness of soul, this step did not excite my surprise, and scarcely my contempt. Resentment in my breast, never survived love. I bade the poor woman, in a kind tone, wipe her eyes, and request her husband to come up, and speak to me himself.

'My manner awed him. He respected a lady, though not a woman; and began to mutter out an apology.

' "Mr. Venables was a rich gentleman; he wished to oblige me, but he had suffered enough by the law already, to tremble at the thought; besides, for certain, we should come together again, and then even I should not thank him for being accessary to keeping us asunder.—A husband and wife were, God knows, just as one,—and all would come round at last." He uttered a drawling "Hem!" and then with an arch look, added—"Master might have had his little frolics—but—Lord bless your heart!—men would be men while the world stands."

'To argue with this privileged first-born of reason, I perceived, would be vain. I therefore only requested him to let me remain another day at his house, while I sought for a lodging; and not to inform Mr. Venables that I had ever been sheltered there.

'He consented, because he had not the courage to refuse a person for whom he had an habitual respect; but I heard the pent-up choler burst forth in curses, when he met his wife, who was waiting impatiently at the foot of the stairs, to know what effect my expostulations would have on him.

'Without wasting any time in the fruitless indulgence of vexation, I once more set out in search of an abode in which I could hide myself for a few weeks.

'Agreeing to pay an exorbitant price, I hired an apartment, without any reference being required relative to my character: indeed, a glance at my shape seemed to say, that my motive for concealment was sufficiently obvious. Thus was I obliged to shroud my head in infamy.

'To avoid all danger of detection—I use the appropriate word, my child, for I was hunted out like a felon—I determined to take possession of my new lodgings that very evening.

'I did not inform my landlady where I was going. I knew that she had a sincere affection for me, and would willingly have run any risk to show her gratitude; yet I was fully convinced, that a few kind words from Johnny would have found the woman in her, and her dear benefactress, as she termed me in an agony of tears, would have been sacrificed, to recompense her tyrant for condescending to treat her like an equal. He could be kind-hearted, as she expressed it, when he pleased. And this thawed sternness, contrasted with his habitual brutality, was the more acceptable, and could not be purchased at too dear a rate.

'The sight of the advertisement made me desirous of taking refuge with my uncle, let what would be the consequence; and I repaired in a hackney coach (afraid of meeting some person who might chance to know me, had I walked) to the chambers of my uncle's friend.

'He received me with great politeness (my uncle had already prepossessed him in my favour), and listened, with interest, to my explanation of the motives which had induced me to fly from home, and skulk in obscurity, with all the timidity of fear that ought only to be the companion of guilt. He lamented, with rather more gallantry than, in my situation, I thought delicate, that such a woman should be thrown away on a man insensible to the charms of beauty or grace. He seemed at a loss what to advise me to do, to evade my husband's search, without hastening to my uncle, whom, he hesitating said, I might not find alive. He uttered this intelligence with visible regret; requested me, at least, to wait for the arrival of the next packet; offered me what money I wanted, and promised to visit me.

'He kept his word; still no letter arrived to put an end to my painful state of suspense. I procured some books and music, to beguile the tedious solitary days.

"Come, ever smiling Liberty,
And with thee bring thy jocund train:"[1]

I sung—and sung till, saddened by the strain of joy, I bitterly lamented the fate that deprived me of all social pleasure. Comparative liberty indeed I had possessed myself of; but the jocund train lagged far behind!

CHAPTER THIRTEEN

'BY watching my only visitor, my uncle's friend, or by some other means, Mr. Venables discovered my residence, and came to enquire for me. The maid-servant assured him there was no such person in the house. A bustle ensued—I caught the alarm—listened—distinguished his voice, and immediately locked the door. They suddenly grew still; and I waited near a quarter of an hour, before I heard him open the parlour door, and mount the stairs with the mistress of the house, who obsequiously declared that she knew nothing of me.

'Finding my door locked, she requested me to "open it, and prepare to go home with my husband, poor gentleman! to whom I had already occasioned sufficient vexation." I made no reply. Mr. Venables then, in an assumed tone of softness, intreated me, "to consider what he suffered, and my own reputation, and get the better of childish resentment." He ran on in the same strain, pretending to address me, but evidently adapting his discourse to the capacity of the landlady; who, at every pause, uttered an exclamation of pity; or "Yes, to be sure—Very true, sir."

'Sick of the farce, and perceiving that I could not avoid the hated interview, I opened the door, and he entered. Advancing with easy assurance to take my hand, I shrunk from his touch, with an involuntary start, as I should have done from a noisome reptile, with more disgust than terror.

His conductress was retiring, to give us, as she said, an opportunity to accommodate matters. But I bade her come in, or I would go out; and curiosity impelled her to obey me.

'Mr. Venables began to expostulate; and this woman, proud of his confidence, to second him. But I calmly silenced her, in the midst of a vulgar harangue, and turning to him, asked, "Why he vainly tormented me? declaring that no power on earth should force me back to his house."

'After a long altercation, the particulars of which, it would be to no purpose to repeat, he left the room. Some time was spent in loud conversation in the parlour below, and I discovered that he had brought his friend, an attorney, with him. *The tumult on the landing place, brought out a gentleman, who had recently taken apartments in the house; he enquired why I was thus assailed*? The voluble attorney instantly repeated the trite tale. The stranger turned to me, observing, with the most soothing politeness and manly interest, that "my countenance told a very different story." He added, "that I should not be insulted, or forced out of the house, by any body."

' "Not by her husband?" asked the attorney.

' "No, sir, not by her husband." Mr. Venables advanced towards him—But there was a decision in his attitude, that so well seconded that of his voice, * They left the house: at the same time protesting, that any one that should dare to protect me, should be prosecuted with the utmost rigour.

---

*The introduction of Darnford as the deliverer of Maria, in an early stage of the history, is already stated (Chap. III.) to have been an afterthought of the author. This has probably caused the imperfectness of the manuscript in the above passage; though, at the same time, it must be acknowledged to be somewhat uncertain, whether Darnford is the stranger intended in this place. It appears from Chap. XVII, that an interference of a more decisive nature was designed to be attributed to him.

EDITOR.

'They were scarcely out of the house, when my landlady came up to me again, and begged my pardon, in a very different tone. For, though Mr. Venables had bid her, at her peril, harbour me, he had not attended, I found, to her broad hints, to discharge the lodging. I instantly promised to pay her, and make her a present to compensate for my abrupt departure, if she would procure me another lodging, at a sufficient distance; and she, in return, repeating Mr. Venables' plausible tale, I raised her indignation, and excited her sympathy, by telling her briefly the truth.

'She expressed her commiseration with such honest warmth, that I felt soothed; for I have none of that fastidious sensitiveness, which a vulgar accent or gesture can alarm to the disregard of real kindness. I was ever glad to perceive in others the humane feelings I delighted to exercise;[1] and the recollection of some ridiculous characteristic circumstances, which have occurred in a moment of emotion, has convulsed me with laughter, though at the instant I should have thought it sacrilegious to have smiled. Your improvement, my dearest girl, being ever present to me while I write, I note these feelings, because women, more accustomed to observe manners than actions, are too much alive to ridicule. So much so, that their boasted sensibility is often stifled by false delicacy. True sensibility, the sensibility which is the auxiliary of virtue, and the soul of genius, is in society so occupied with the feelings of others, as scarcely to regard its own sensations. With what reverence have I looked up at my uncle, the dear parent of my mind! when I have seen the sense of his own sufferings, of mind and body, absorbed in a desire to comfort those, whose misfortunes were comparatively trivial. He would have been ashamed of being as indulgent to himself, as he was to others. "Genuine fortitude," he would assert, "consisted in governing our own emotions, and making allowance for the weaknesses in our friends, that we would not tolerate in ourselves." But where is my fond regret leading me!

' "Women must be submissive," said my landlady.

"Indeed what could most women do? Who had they to maintain them, but their husbands? Every woman, and especially a lady, could not go through rough and smooth, as she had done, to earn a little bread."

'She was in a talking mood, and proceeded to inform me how she had been used in the world.[1] "She knew what it was to have a bad husband, or she did not know who should." I perceived that she would be very much mortified, were I not to attend to her tale, and I did not attempt to interrupt her, though I wished her, as soon as possible, to go out in search of a new abode for me, where I could once more hide my head.

'She began by telling me, "That she had saved a little money in service; and was over-persuaded (we must all be in love once in our lives) to marry a likely man, a footman in the family, not worth a groat. My plan," she continued, "was to take a house, and let out lodgings; and all went on well, till my husband got acquainted with an impudent slut, who chose to live on other people's means—and then all went to rack and ruin. He ran in debt to buy her fine clothes, such clothes as I never thought of wearing myself, and—would you believe it?—he signed an execution[2] on my very goods, bought with the money I worked so hard to get; and they came and took my bed from under me, before I heard a word of the matter. Aye, madam, these are misfortunes that you gentlefolks know nothing of;—but sorrow is sorrow, let it come which way it will.

' "I sought for a service again—very hard, after having a house of my own!—but he used to follow me, and kick up such a riot when he was drunk, that I could not keep a place; nay, he even stole my clothes, and pawned them; and when I went to the pawnbroker's, and offered to take my oath that they were not bought with a farthing of his money, they said, "It was all as one, my husband had a right to whatever I had."

' "At last he listed for a soldier, and I took a house, making an agreement to pay for the furniture by degrees; and I almost starved myself, till I once more got before-hand in the world.

' "After an absence of six years (God forgive me! I thought

he was dead) my husband returned; found me out, and came with such a penitent face, I forgave him, and clothed him from head to foot. But he had not been a week in the house, before some of his creditors arrested him; and, he selling my goods, I found myself once more reduced to beggary; for I was not as well able to work, go to bed late, and rise early, as when I quitted service; and then I thought it hard enough. He was soon tired of me, when there was nothing more to be had, and left me again.

' "I will not tell you how I was buffeted about, till, hearing for certain that he had died in an hospital abroad, I once more returned to my old occupation; but have not yet been able to get my head above water: so, madam, you must not be angry if I am afraid to run any risk, when I know so well, that women have always the worst of it, when law is to decide."

'After uttering a few more complaints, I prevailed on my landlady to go out in quest of a lodging; and, to be more secure, I condescended to the mean shift of changing my name.

'But why should I dwell on similar incidents!—I was hunted,[1] like an infected beast, from three different apartments, and should not have been allowed to rest in any, had not Mr. Venables, informed of my uncle's dangerous state of health, been inspired with the fear of hurrying me out of the world as I advanced in my pregnancy, by thus tormenting and obliging me to take sudden journeys to avoid him; and then his speculations on my uncle's fortune must prove abortive.

'One day, when he had pursued me to an inn, I fainted, hurrying from him; and, falling down, the sight of my blood alarmed him, and obtained a respite for me. It is strange that he should have retained any hope, after observing my unwavering determination; but, from the mildness of my behaviour, when I found all my endeavours to change his disposition unavailing, he formed an erroneous opinion of my character, imagining that, were we once more together, I should part with the money he could not legally force from me, with the same facility as formerly. My forbearance and occasional sympathy he had mistaken for weakness of character; and, because he perceived that I disliked resistance, he thought my indulgence and compassion mere selfishness, and never discovered that the fear of being unjust, or of unnecessarily wounding the feelings of another, was much more painful to me, than any thing I could have to endure myself. Perhaps it was pride which made me imagine, that I could bear what I dreaded to inflict; and that it was often easier to suffer, than to see the sufferings of others.

'I forgot to mention that, during this persecution, I received a letter from my uncle, informing me, "that he only found relief from continual change of air; and that he intended to return when the spring was a little more advanced (it was now the middle of February), and then we would plan a journey to Italy, leaving the fogs and cares of England far behind." He approved of my conduct, promised to adopt my child, and seemed to have no doubt of obliging Mr. Venables to hear reason. He wrote to his friend, by the same post, desiring him to call on Mr. Venables in his name; and, in consequence of the remonstrances he dictated, I was permitted to lie-in tranquilly.

'The two or three weeks previous, I had been allowed to rest in peace; but, so accustomed was I to pursuit and alarm, that I seldom closed my eyes without being haunted by Mr. Venables' image, who seemed to assume terrific or hateful forms to torment me, wherever I turned.—Sometimes a wild cat, a roaring bull, or hideous assassin, whom I vainly attempted to fly; at others he was a demon, hurrying me to the brink of a precipice, plunging me into dark waves, or horrid gulfs; and I woke, in violent fits of trembling anxiety, to assure myself that it was all a dream, and to endeavour to lure my waking thoughts to wander to the delightful Italian vales, I hoped soon to visit; or to picture some august ruins, where I reclined in fancy on a mouldering column, and escaped, in the contemplation of the heart-enlarging virtues of antiquity,[1] from the turmoil of cares that had depressed all the daring purposes of my soul. But I was not long allowed to calm my mind by the exercise of my imagination; for the third day after your birth, my child, I was surprised by a visit from my elder brother; who came in the most abrupt manner, to inform me of the death of my uncle. He had left the greater part of his fortune to my child, appointing me its guardian; in short, every step was taken to enable me to be mistress of his fortune, without putting any part of it in Mr. Venables' power. My brother came to vent his rage on me, for having, as he expressed himself, "deprived him, my uncle's eldest nephew, of his inheritance;" though my uncle's property, the fruit of his own exertion, being all in the funds, or on landed securities, there was not a shadow of justice in the charge.

'As I sincerely loved my uncle, this intelligence brought on a fever, which I struggled to conquer with all the energy of my mind; for, in my desolate state, I had it very much at heart to suckle you, my poor babe. You seemed my only tie to life, a cherub, to whom I wished to be a father, as well as a mother; and the double duty appeared to me to produce a proportionate increase of affection. But the pleasure I felt, while sustaining you, snatched from the wreck of hope, was cruelly damped by melancholy reflections on my widowed state—widowed by the death of my uncle. Of Mr. Venables I thought not, even when I thought of the felicity of loving your father, and how a mother's pleasure might be exalted, and her care softened by a husband's tenderness.—"Ought to be!" I exclaimed; and I endeavoured to drive away the tenderness that suffocated me; but my spirits were weak, and the unbidden tears would flow. "Why was I," I would ask thee, but thou didst not heed me,—"cut off from the participation of the sweetest pleasure of life?" I imagined with what extacy, after the pains of child-bed, I should have presented my little stranger, whom I had so long wished to view, to a respectable father, and with what maternal fondness I should have pressed them both to my heart!—Now I kissed her with less delight, though with the most endearing compassion, poor helpless one! when I perceived a slight resemblance of him, to whom she owed her existence; or, if any gesture reminded me

of him, even in his best days, my heart heaved, and I pressed
the innocent to my bosom, as if to purify it—yes, I blushed to
think that its purity had been sullied, by allowing such a man
to be its father.

'After my recovery, I began to think of taking a house in the
country, or of making an excursion on the continent, to avoid
Mr. Venables; and to open my heart to new pleasures and
affection. The spring was melting into summer, and you, my
little companion, began to smile—that smile made hope bud
out afresh, assuring me the world was not a desert. Your
gestures were ever present to my fancy; and I dwelt on the joy
I should feel when you would begin to walk and lisp.
Watching your wakening mind, and shielding from every
rude blast my tender blossom, I recovered my spirits—I
dreamed not of the frost—"the killing frost,"[1] to which you
were destined to be exposed.—But I lose all patience—and
execrate the injustice of the world—folly! ignorance!—I
should rather call it; but, shut up from a free circulation of
thought, and always pondering on the same griefs, I writhe
under the torturing apprehensions, which ought to excite only
honest indignation, or active compassion; and would, could I
view them as the natural consequence of things. But, born a
woman—and born to suffer, in endeavouring to repress my
own emotions, I feel more acutely the various ills my sex are
fated to bear—I feel that the evils they are subject to endure,
degrade them so far below their oppressors, as almost to
justify their tyranny; leading at the same time superficial
reasoners to term that weakness the cause, which is only the
consequence of short-sighted despotism.[2]

CHAPTER FOURTEEN

'As my mind grew calmer, the visions of Italy again returned
with their former glow of colouring; and I resolved on
quitting the kingdom for a time, in search of the cheerfulness,
that naturally results from a change of scene, unless we carry

the barbed arrow with us, and only see what we feel.

'During the period necessary to prepare for a long absence, I sent a supply to pay my father's debts, and settled my brothers in eligible situations;[1] but my attention was not wholly engrossed by my family, though I do not think it necessary to enumerate the common exertions of humanity. The manner in which my uncle's property was settled, prevented me from making the addition to the fortune of my surviving sister, that I could have wished; but I had prevailed on him to bequeath her two thousand pounds, and she determined to marry a lover, to whom she had been some time attached. Had it not been for this engagement, I should have invited her to accompany me in my tour; and I might have escaped the pit, so artfully dug in my path, when I was the least aware of danger.

'I had thought of remaining in England, till I weaned my child; but this state of freedom was too peaceful to last, and I had soon reason to wish to hasten my departure. A friend of Mr. Venables, the same attorney who had accompanied him in several excursions to hunt me from my hiding places, waited on me to propose a reconciliation. On my refusal, he indirectly advised me to make over to my husband—for husband he would term him—the greater part of the property I had at command, menacing me with continual persecution unless I complied; and that, as a last resort, he would claim the child.[2] I did not, though intimidated by the last insinuation, scruple to declare, that I would not allow him to squander the money left to me for far different purposes, but offered him five hundred pounds, if he would sign a bond not to torment me any more. My maternal anxiety made me thus appear to waver from my first determination, and probably suggested to him, or his diabolical agent, the infernal plot, which has succeeded but too well.

'The bond was executed; still I was impatient to leave England. Mischief hung in the air when we breathed the same; I wanted seas to divide us, and waters to roll between, till he had forgotten that I had the means of helping him through a new scheme. Disturbed by the late occurrences, I instantly prepared for my departure. My only delay was waiting for a maid-servant, who spoke French fluently, and had been warmly recommended to me. A valet I was advised to hire, when I fixed on my place of residence for any time.

'My God, with what a light heart did I set out for Dover!¹—It was not my country, but my cares, that I was leaving behind. My heart seemed to bound with the wheels, or rather appeared the centre on which they twirled. I clasped you to my bosom, exclaiming "And you will be safe—quite safe—when—we are once on board the packet.—Would we were there!" I smiled at my idle fears, as the natural effect of continual alarm; and I scarcely owned to myself that I dreaded Mr. Venables's cunning, or was conscious of the horrid delight he would feel, at forming stratagem after stratagem to circumvent me. I was already in the snare—I never reached the packet—I never saw thee more.—I grow breathless. I have scarcely patience to write down the details. The maid—the plausible woman I had hired—put, doubtless, some stupifying potion in what I ate or drank, the morning I left town. All I know is, that she must have quitted the chaise, shameless wretch! and taken (from my breast) my babe with her. How could a creature in a female form see me caress thee, and steal thee from my arms! I must stop, stop to repress a mother's anguish; lest, in bitterness of soul, I imprecate the wrath of heaven on this tiger, who tore my only comfort from me.

'How long I slept I know not; certainly many hours, for I woke at the close of day, in a strange confusion of thought. I was probably roused to recollection by some one thundering at a huge, unwieldy gate. Attempting to ask where I was, my voice died away, and I tried to raise it in vain, as I have done in a dream. I looked for my babe with affright; feared that it had fallen out of my lap, while I had so strangely forgotten her; and, such was the vague intoxication, I can give it no other name, in which I was plunged, I could not recollect

when or where I last saw you; but I sighed, as if my heart
wanted room to clear my head.

'The gates opened heavily, and the sullen sound of many
locks and bolts drawn back, grated on my very soul, before I
was appalled by the creeking of the dismal hinges, as they
closed after me. The gloomy pile was before me, half in
ruins; some of the aged trees of the avenue were cut down,
and left to rot where they fell; and as we approached some
mouldering steps, a monstrous dog darted forwards to the
length of his chain, and barked and growled infernally.

'The door was opened slowly, and a murderous visage
peeped out, with a lantern. "Hush!" he uttered, in a
threatning tone, and the affrighted animal stole back to his
kennel. The door of the chaise flew back, the stranger put
down the lantern, and clasped his dreadful arms around me.
It was certainly the effect of the soporific draught, for,
instead of exerting my strength, I sunk without motion,
though not without sense, on his shoulder, my limbs refusing
to obey my will. I was carried up the steps into a close-shut
hall. A candle flaring in the socket, scarcely dispersed the
darkness, though it displayed to me the ferocious countenance
of the wretch who held me.

'He mounted a wide staircase. Large figures painted on the
walls seemed to start on me, and glaring eyes to meet me at
every turn. Entering a long gallery, a dismal shriek made me
spring out of my conductor's arms, with I know not what
mysterious emotion of terror; but I fell on the floor, unable
to sustain myself.

'A strange-looking female started out of one of the
recesses, and observed me with more curiosity than interest;
till, sternly bid retire, she flitted back like a shadow. Other
faces, strongly marked, or distorted, peeped through the
half-opened doors, and I heard some incoherent sounds. I
had no distinct idea where I could be—I looked on all sides,
and almost doubted whether I was alive or dead.

'Thrown on a bed, I immediately sunk into insensibility
again; and next day, gradually recovering the use of reason, I

began, starting affrighted from the conviction, to discover where I was confined—I insisted on seeing the master of the mansion—I saw him—and perceived that I was buried alive.[1]—

'Such, my child, are the events of thy mother's life to this dreadful moment—Should she ever escape from the fangs of her enemies, she will add the secrets of her prison-house—and—'

Some lines were here crossed out, and the memoirs broke off abruptly with the names of Jemima and Darnford.

APPENDIX

[ADVERTISEMENT.

THE performance, with a fragment of which the reader has now been presented, was designed to consist of three parts. The preceding sheets were considered as constituting one of those parts. Those persons who in the perusal of the chapters, already written and in some degree finished by the author, have felt their hearts awakened, and their curiosity excited as to the sequel of the story, will, of course, gladly accept even of the broken paragraphs and half-finished sentences, which have been found committed to paper, as materials for the remainder. The fastidious and cold-hearted critic may perhaps feel himself repelled by the incoherent form in which they are presented. But an inquisitive temper willingly accepts the most imperfect and mutilated information, where better is not to be had: and readers, who in any degree resemble the author in her quick apprehension of sentiment, and of the pleasures and pains of imagination, will, I believe, find gratification, in contemplating sketches, which were designed in a short time to have received the finishing touches of her genius; but which must now for ever remain a mark to record the triumphs of mortality, over schemes of usefulness, and projects of public interest.]

CHAPTER FIFTEEN

DARNFORD returned the memoirs to Maria, with a most affectionate letter, in which he reasoned on 'the absurdity of the laws respecting matrimony, which, till divorces could be more easily obtained, was,' he declared, 'the most insufferable bondage. Ties of this nature could not bind minds governed by superior principles; and such beings were privileged to act above the dictates of laws they had no voice in framing, if they had sufficient strength of mind to endure the natural consequence.[1] In her case, to talk of duty, was a farce, excepting what was due to herself. Delicacy, as well as reason, forbade her ever to think of returning to her husband: was she then to restrain her charming sensibility through mere prejudice? These arguments were not absolutely impartial, for he disdained to conceal, that, when he appealed to her reason, he felt that he had some interest in her heart.—The conviction was not more transporting, than sacred—a thousand times a day, he asked himself how he had merited such happiness?—and as often he determined to purify the heart she deigned to inhabit—He intreated to be again admitted to her presence.'

He was; and the tear which glistened in his eye, when he respectfully pressed her to his bosom, rendered him peculiarly dear to the unfortunate mother. Grief had stilled the transports of love, only to render their mutual tenderness more touching. In former interviews, Darnford had contrived, by a hundred little pretexts, to sit near her, to take her hand, or to meet her eyes—now it was all soothing affection, and esteem seemed to have rivalled love.[2] He adverted to her narrative, and spoke with warmth of the oppression she had endured.—His eyes, glowing with a lambent flame, told her how much he wished to restore her to liberty and love; but he kissed her hand, as if it had been that of a saint; and spoke of the loss of her child, as if it had been

his own.—What could have been more flattering to
Maria?—Every instance of self-denial was registered in her
heart, and she loved him, for loving her too well to give way
to the transports of passion.

They met again and again; and Darnford declared, while
passion suffused his cheeks, that he never before knew what
it was to love.—

One morning Jemima informed Maria, that her master
intended to wait on her, and speak to her without witnesses.
He came, and brought a letter with him, pretending that he
was ignorant of its contents, though he insisted on having it
returned to him. It was from the attorney already mentioned,
who informed her of the death of her child, and hinted, 'that
she could not now have a legitimate heir, and that, would she
make over the half of her fortune during lif̂ she should be
conveyed to Dover, and permitted to pursue her plan of
travelling.'

Maria answered with warmth, 'That she had no terms to
make with the murderer of her babe, nor would she purchase
liberty at the price of her own respect.'

She began to expostulate with her jailor; but he sternly
bade her 'Be silent—he had not gone so far, not to go
further.'

Darnford came in the evening. Jemima was obliged to be
absent, and she, as usual, locked the door on them, to prevent
interruption or discovery. — The lovers were, at first,
embarrassed; but fell insensibly into confidential discourse.
Darnford represented, 'that they might soon be parted,' and
wished her 'to put it out of the power of fate to separate
them.'

As her husband she now received him, and he solemnly
pledged himself as her protector—and eternal friend.—

There was one peculiarity in Maria's mind: she was more
anxious not to deceive, than to guard against deception; and
had rather trust without sufficient reason, than be for ever
the prey of doubt. Besides, what are we, when the mind has,
from reflection, a certain kind of elevation, which exalts the

contemplation above the little concerns of prudence! We see what we wish, and make a world of our own—and, though reality may sometimes open a door to misery, yet the moments of happiness procured by the imagination, may, without a paradox, be reckoned among the solid comforts of life. Maria now, imagining that she had found a being of celestial mould—was happy,—nor was she deceived.—He was then plastic in her impassioned hand—and reflected all the sentiments which animated and warmed her. ————

———————————————————————
———————————————————————

CHAPTER SIXTEEN

ONE morning confusion seemed to reign in the house, and Jemima came in terror, to inform Maria, 'that her master had left it, with a determination, she was assured (and too many circumstances corroborated the opinion, to leave a doubt of its truth) of never returning. I am prepared then,' said Jemima, 'to accompany you in your flight.'

Maria started up, her eyes darting towards the door, as if afraid that some one should fasten it on her for ever.

Jemima continued, 'I have perhaps no right now to expect the performance of your promise; but on you it depends to reconcile me with the human race.'

'But Darnford!'—exclaimed Maria, mournfully—sitting down again, and crossing her arms—'I have no child to go to, and liberty has lost its sweets.'

'I am much mistaken, if Darnford is not the cause of my master's flight—his keepers assure me, that they have promised to confine him two days longer, and then he will be free—you cannot see him; but they will give a letter to him the moment he is free.—In that inform him where he may find you in London; fix on some hotel. Give me your clothes; I will send them out of the house with mine, and we will slip

out at the garden-gate. Write your letter while I make these
arrangements, but lose no time!'

In an agitation of spirit, not to be calmed, Maria began to
write to Darnford. She called him by the sacred name of
'husband,' and bade him 'hasten to her, to share her fortune,
or she would return to him.'—An hotel in the Adelphi[1] was
the place of rendezvous.

The letter was sealed and given in charge; and with light
footsteps, yet terrified at the sound of them, she descended,
scarcely breathing, and with an indistinct fear that she
should never get out at the garden gate. Jemima went first.

A being, with a visage that would have suited one
possessed by a devil, crossed the path, and seized Maria by
the arm. Maria had no fear but of being detained—'Who are
you? what are you?' for the form was scarcely human. 'If you
are made of flesh and blood,' his ghastly eyes glared on her,
'do not stop me!'

'Woman,' interrupted a sepulchral voice, 'what have I to
do with thee?'—Still he grasped her hand, muttering a curse.

'No, no; you have nothing to do with me,' she exclaimed,
'this is a moment of life and death!'—

With supernatural force she broke from him, and,
throwing her arms round Jemima, cried, 'Save me!' The
being, from whose grasp she had loosed herself, took up a
stone as they opened the door, and with a kind of hellish
sport threw it after them. They were out of his reach.

When Maria arrived in town, she drove to the hotel
already fixed on. But she could not sit still—her child was
ever before her; and all that had passed during her
confinement, appeared to be a dream. She went to the house
in the suburbs, where, as she now discovered, her babe had
been sent. The moment she entered, her heart grew sick; but
she wondered not that it had proved its grave. She made the
necessary enquiries, and the church-yard was pointed out, in
which it rested under a turf. A little frock which the nurse's
child wore (Maria had made it herself) caught her eye. The
nurse was glad to sell it for half-a-guinea, and Maria

hastened away with the relic, and, re-entering the hackney-coach which waited for her, gazed on it, till she reached her hotel.

She then waited on the attorney who had made her uncle's will, and explained to him her situation. He readily advanced her some of the money which still remained in his hands, and promised to take the whole of the case into consideration. Maria only wished to be permitted to remain in quiet—She found that several bills, apparently with her signature, had been presented to her agent, nor was she for a moment at a loss to guess by whom they had been forged; yet, equally averse to threaten or intreat, she requested her friend [the solicitor] to call on Mr. Venables. He was not to be found at home; but at length his agent, the attorney, offered a conditional promise to Maria, to leave her in peace, as long as she behaved with propriety, if she would give up the notes. Maria inconsiderately consented—Darnford was arrived, and she wished to be only alive to love; she wished to forget the anguish she felt whenever she thought of her child.

They took a ready-furnished lodging together, for she was above disguise; Jemima insisting on being considered as her house-keeper, and to receive the customary stipend. On no other terms would she remain with her friend.

Darnford was indefatigable in tracing the mysterious circumstances of his confinement. The cause was simply, that a relation, a very distant one, to whom he was heir, had died intestate, leaving a considerable fortune. On the news of Darnford's arrival [in England, a person, intrusted with the management of the property, and who had the writings in his possession, determining, by one bold stroke, to strip Darnford of the succession,] had planned his confinement;[1] and [as soon as he had taken the measures he judged most conducive to his object, this ruffian, together with his instrument,] the keeper of the private madhouse, left the kingdom. Darnford, who still pursued his enquiries, at last discovered that they had fixed their place of refuge at Paris.

Maria and he determined therefore, with the faithful

Jemima, to visit that metropolis, and accordingly were
preparing for the journey, when they were informed that Mr.
Venables had commenced an action against Darnford for
seduction and adultery.[1] The indignation Maria felt cannot
be explained; she repented of the forbearance she had
exercised in giving up the notes. Darnford could not put off
his journey, without risking the loss of his property: Maria
therefore furnished him with money for his expedition; and
determined to remain in London till the termination of this
affair.

She visited some ladies with whom she had formerly been
intimate, but was refused admittance;[2] and at the opera, or
Ranelagh, they could not recollect her. Among these ladies
there were some, not her most intimate acquaintance, who
were generally supposed to avail themselves of the cloke of
marriage, to conceal a mode of conduct, that would for ever
have damned their fame, had they been innocent, seduced
girls. These particularly stood aloof.—Had she remained
with her husband, practising insincerity, and neglecting her
child to manage an intrigue, she would still have been visited
and respected. If, instead of openly living with her lover, she
could have condescended to call into play a thousand arts,
which, degrading her own mind, might have allowed the
people who were not deceived, to pretend to be so, she would
have been caressed and treated like an honourable woman.[3]
'And Brutus* is an honourable man!' said Mark-Antony
with equal sincerity.

With Darnford she did not taste uninterrupted felicity;
there was a volatility in his manner which often distressed
her; but love gladdened the scene; besides, he was the most
tender, sympathizing creature in the world. A fondness for
the sex often gives an appearance of humanity to the
behaviour of men, who have small pretensions to the reality;
and they seem to love others, when they are only pursuing
their own gratification. Darnford appeared ever willing to

*The name in the manuscript is by mistake written Cæsar.
EDITOR.

avail himself of her taste and acquirements, while she endeavoured to profit by his decision of character, and to eradicate some of the romantic notions, which had taken root in her mind, while in adversity she had brooded over visions of unattainable bliss.

The real affections of life, when they are allowed to burst forth, are buds pregnant with joy and all the sweet emotions of the soul; yet they branch out with wild ease, unlike the artificial forms of felicity, sketched by an imagination painfully[1] alive. The substantial happiness, which enlarges and civilizes the mind, may be compared to the pleasure experienced in roving through nature at large, inhaling the sweet gale natural to the clime; while the reveries of a feverish imagination continually sport themselves in gardens full of aromatic shrubs, which cloy while they delight, and weaken the sense of pleasure they gratify. The heaven of fancy, below or beyond the stars, in this life, or in those ever-smiling regions surrounded by the unmarked ocean of futurity, have an insipid uniformity which palls. Poets have imagined scenes of bliss; but, fencing out sorrow, all the extatic emotions of the soul, and even its grandeur, seem to be equally excluded. We dose over the unruffled lake, and long to scale the rocks which fence the happy valley[2] of contentment, though serpents hiss in the pathless desert, and danger lurks in the unexplored wilds. Maria found herself more indulgent as she was happier, and discovered virtues, in characters she had before disregarded, while chasing the phantoms of elegance and excellence, which sported in the meteors that exhale in the marshes of misfortune. The heart is often shut by romance against social pleasure; and, fostering a sickly sensibility, grows callous to the soft touches of humanity.

To part with Darnford was indeed cruel.—It was to feel most painfully alone; but she rejoiced to think, that she should spare him the care and perplexity of the suit, and meet him again, all his own. Marriage, as at present constituted, she considered as leading to immorality—yet, as the odium of

society impedes usefulness, she wished to avow her affection
to Darnford, by becoming his wife according to established
rules; not to be confounded with women who act from very
different motives,[1] though her conduct would be just the
same without the ceremony as with it, and her expectations
from him not less firm. The being summoned to defend
herself from a charge which she was determined to plead
guilty to, was still galling, as it roused bitter reflections on the
situation of women in society.

CHAPTER SEVENTEEN

SUCH was her state of mind when the dogs of law were let
loose on her. Maria took the task of conducting Darnford's
defence upon herself.[2] She instructed his counsel to plead
guilty to the charge of adultery; but to deny that of
seduction.

The counsel for the plaintiff opened the cause, by
observing, 'that his client had ever been an indulgent
husband, and had borne with several defects of temper, while
he had nothing criminal to lay to the charge of his wife. But
that she left his house without assigning any cause. He could
not assert that she was then acquainted with the defendant;
yet, when he was once endeavouring to bring her back to her
home, this man put the peace-officers to flight, and took her
he knew not whither. After the birth of her child, her
conduct was so strange, and a melancholy malady having
afflicted one of the family, which delicacy forbade the
dwelling on, it was necessary to confine her. By some means
the defendant enabled her to make her escape, and they had
lived together, in despite of all sense of order and decorum.
The adultery was allowed, it was not necessary to bring any
witnesses to prove it; but the seduction, though highly
probable from the circumstances which he had the honour to

state, could not be so clearly proved.—It was of the most atrocious kind, as decency was set at defiance, and respect for reputation, which shows internal compunction, utterly disregarded.'

A strong sense of injustice had silenced every emotion, which a mixture of true and false delicacy might otherwise have excited in Maria's bosom. She only felt in earnest to insist on the privilege of her nature. The sarcasms of society, and the condemnation of a mistaken world, were nothing to her, compared with acting contrary to those feelings which were the foundation of her principles. [She therefore eagerly put herself forward, instead of desiring to be absent, on this memorable occasion.]

Convinced that the subterfuges of the law were disgraceful, she wrote a paper, which she expressly desired might be read in court:

'Married when scarcely able to distinguish the nature of the engagement, I yet submitted to the rigid laws which enslave women, and obeyed the man whom I could no longer love. Whether the duties of the state are reciprocal, I mean not to discuss; but I can prove repeated infidelities which I overlooked or pardoned. Witnesses are not wanting to establish these facts. I at present maintain the child of a maid servant, sworn to him, and born after our marriage. I am ready to allow, that education and circumstances lead men to think and act with less delicacy, than the preservation of order in society demands from women; but surely I may without assumption declare, that, though I could excuse the birth, I could not the desertion of this unfortunate babe:—and, while I despised the man, it was not easy to venerate the husband. With proper restrictions however, I revere the institution which fraternizes the world. I exclaim against the laws which throw the whole weight of the yoke on the weaker shoulders, and force women, when they claim protectorship as mothers, to sign a contract, which renders them dependent on the caprice of the tyrant, whom choice or necessity has appointed to reign over them. Various are the cases, in which a woman ought to separate herself from her husband; and mine, I may be allowed emphatically to insist, comes under the description of the most aggravated.

'I will not enlarge on those provocations which only the individual can estimate; but will bring forward such charges only, the truth of which is an insult upon humanity. In order to promote certain destructive speculations, Mr. Venables prevailed on me to borrow certain sums of a wealthy relation; and, when I refused further compliance, he thought of bartering my person; and not only allowed opportunities to, but urged, a friend from whom he borrowed money, to seduce me. On the discovery of this act of atrocity, I determined to leave him, and in the most decided manner, for ever. I consider all obligation as made void by his conduct; and hold, that schisms which proceed from want of principles, can never be healed.

'He received a fortune with me to the amount of five thousand pounds. On the death of my uncle, convinced that I could provide for my child, I destroyed the settlement of that fortune. I required none of my property to be returned to me, nor shall enumerate the sums extorted from me during six years that we lived together.

'After leaving, what the law considers as my home, I was hunted like a criminal from place to place, though I contracted no debts, and demanded no maintenance—yet, as the laws sanction such proceeding, and make women the property of their husbands, I forbear to animadvert. After the birth of my daughter, and the death of my uncle, who left a very considerable property to myself and child, I was exposed to new persecution; and, because I had, before arriving at what is termed years of discretion, pledged my faith, I was treated by the world, as bound for ever to a man whose vices were notorious. Yet what are the vices generally known, to the various miseries that a woman may be subject to, which, though deeply felt, eating into the soul, elude description, and may be glossed over! A false morality is even established, which makes all the virtue of women consist in chastity, submission, and the forgiveness of injuries.[1]

'I pardon my oppressor—bitterly as I lament the loss of my child, torn from me in the most violent manner. But nature revolts, and my soul sickens at the bare supposition, that it could ever be a duty to pretend affection, when a separation is necessary to prevent my feeling hourly aversion.

'To force me to give my fortune, I was imprisoned—yes; in a private mad-house.—There, in the heart of misery, I met the man charged with seducing me. We became attached—I deemed, and ever shall deem, myself free. The death of my babe dissolved the only tie which subsisted between me and my, what is termed, lawful husband.

'To this person, thus encountered, I voluntarily gave myself, never considering myself as any more bound to transgress the laws of moral purity, because the will of my husband might be pleaded in my excuse, than to transgress those laws to which [the policy of artificial society has] annexed [positive] punishments.——While no command of a husband can prevent a woman from suffering for certain crimes, she must be allowed to consult her conscience, and regulate her conduct, in some degree, by her own sense of right. The respect I owe to myself, demanded my strict adherence to my determination of never viewing Mr. Venables in the light of a husband, nor could it forbid me from encouraging another. If I am unfortunately united to an unprincipled man, am I for ever to be shut out from fulfilling the duties of a wife and mother?—I wish my country to approve of my conduct; but, if laws exist, made by the strong to oppress the weak, I appeal to my own sense of justice, and declare that I will not live with the individual, who has violated every moral obligation which binds man to man.

'I protest equally against any charge being brought to criminate the man, whom I consider as my husband. I was six-and-twenty when I left Mr. Venables' roof; if ever I am to be supposed to arrive at an age to direct my own actions, I must by that time have arrived at it.—I acted with deliberation.—Mr. Darnford found me a forlorn and oppressed woman, and promised the protection women in the present state of society[1] want.—But the man who now claims me—was he deprived of my society by this conduct? The question is an insult to common sense, considering where Mr. Darnford met me.—Mr. Venables' door was indeed open to me—nay, threats and intreaties were used to induce me to return; but why? Was affection or honour the motive?—I cannot, it is true, dive into the recesses of the human heart—yet I presume to assert, [borne out as I am by a variety of circumstances,] that he was merely influenced by the most rapacious avarice.

'I claim then a divorce, and the liberty of enjoying, free from molestation, the fortune left to me by a relation, who was well aware of the character of the man with whom I had to contend.—I appeal to the justice and humanity of the jury[2]—a body of men, whose private judgment must be allowed to modify laws, that must be unjust, because definite rules can never apply to indefinite circumstances[3]—and I deprecate punishment [upon the man of my choice, freeing him, as I solemnly do, from the charge of seduction.]

'I did not put myself into a situation to justify a charge of adultery, till I had, from conviction, shaken off the fetters which bound me to Mr. Venables.—While I lived with him, I defy the voice of calumny to sully what is termed the fair fame of woman.—Neglected by my husband, I never encouraged a lover; and preserved with scrupulous care, what is termed my honour, at the expence of my peace, till he, who should have been its guardian, laid traps to ensnare me. From that moment I believed myself, in the sight of heaven, free—and no power on earth shall force me to renounce my resolution.'

The judge, in summing up the evidence, alluded to 'the fallacy of letting women plead their feelings, as an excuse for the violation of the marriage-vow. For his part, he had always determined to oppose all innovation, and the new-fangled notions which incroached on the good old rules of conduct. We did not want French principles[1] in public or private life—and, if women were allowed to plead their feelings, as an excuse or palliation of infidelity, it was opening a flood-gate for immorality. What virtuous woman thought of her feelings?—It was her duty to love and obey the man chosen by her parents and relations, who were qualified by their experience to judge better for her, than she could for herself. As to the charges brought against the husband, they were vague, supported by no witnesses, excepting that of imprisonment in a private mad-house. The proofs of an insanity in the family, might render that however a prudent measure; and indeed the conduct of the lady did not appear that of a person of sane mind. Still such a mode of proceeding could not be justified, and might perhaps entitle the lady [in another court] to a sentence of separation from bed and board,[2] during the joint lives of the parties; but he hoped that no Englishman would legalize adultery, by enabling the adulteress to enrich her seducer. Too many restrictions could not be thrown in the way of divorces, if we wished to maintain the sanctity of marriage; and, though they might bear a little hard on a few, very few individuals, it was evidently for the good of the whole.'

lord sets out for France. Letters—Once more pregnant. He returns. Mysterious behaviour. Visit—Expectation—Discovery—Interview.

Sued by her husband. Damages awarded to her lover. The rack of expectation. Finds herself with child—Delighted. A discovery—A visit—A miscarriage. Conclusion.

Pregnancy. M——

CONCLUSION,

BY THE EDITOR.

VERY few hints exist respecting the plan of the remainder of the work. I find only two detached sentences, and some scattered heads for the continuation of the story. I transcribe the whole.

I

'Darnford's letters were affectionate; but circumstances occasioned delays,[1] and the miscarriage of some letters rendered the reception of wished-for answers doubtful: his return was necessary to calm Maria's mind.'

II

'As Darnford had informed her that his business was settled, his delaying to return seemed extraordinary; but love to excess, excludes fear or suspicion.'

The scattered heads for the continuation of the story, are as follow*.

I

'Trial for adultery—Maria defends herself—A separation from bed and board is the consequence—Her fortune is thrown into chancery[2]—Darnford obtains a part of his property—Maria goes into the country.'

II

'A prosecution for adultery commenced—Trial—Darn-

---

*To understand these minutes, it is necessary the reader should consider each of them as setting out from the same point in the story, viz. the point to which it is brought down in the preceding chapter.

ford sets out for France—Letters—Once more pregnant—
He returns—Mysterious behaviour—Visit—Expectation—
Discovery—Interview—Consequence.'[1]

III

'Sued by her husband—Damages awarded to
him—Separation from bed and board—Darnford goes
abroad—Maria into the country—Provides for her
father—Is shunned—Returns to London—Expects to see
her lover—The rack of expectation—Finds herself again
with child—Delighted—A discovery—A visit—A
miscarriage—Conclusion.'

IV

'Divorced by her husband—Her lover unfaithful—
Pregnancy—Miscarriage—Suicide.'

[The following passage appears in some respects to deviate
from the preceding hints. It is superscribed]

'THE END.

'She swallowed the laudanum;[2] her soul was calm—the
tempest had subsided—and nothing remained but an eager
longing to forget herself—to fly from the anguish she
endured to escape from thought—from this hell of
disappointment.

'Still her eyes closed not—one remembrance with frightful
velocity followed another—All the incidents of her life were
in arms, embodied to assail her, and prevent her sinking into
the sleep of death.—Her murdered child again appeared to
her, mourning for the babe of which she was the
tomb.—"And could it have a nobler?—Surely it is better to
die with me, than to enter on life without a mother's care!—I
cannot live!—but could I have deserted my child the

moment it was born?—thrown it on the troubled wave of life, without a hand to support it?"—She looked up: "What have I not suffered!—may I find a father where I am going!"—Her head turned; a stupor ensued; a faintness—"Have a little patience," said Maria, holding her swimming head (she thought of her mother), "this cannot last long; and what is a little bodily pain to the pangs I have endured?"

'A new vision swam before her. Jemima seemed to enter—leading a little creature, that, with tottering footsteps, approached the bed. The voice of Jemima sounding as at a distance, called her—she tried to listen, to speak, to look!

' "Behold your child!" exclaimed Jemima. Maria started off the bed, and fainted.—Violent vomiting followed.

'When she was restored to life, Jemima addressed her with great solemnity: "———— led me to suspect, that your husband and brother had deceived you, and secreted the child. I would not torment you with doubtful hopes, and I left you (at a fatal moment) to search for the child!—I snatched her from misery—and (now she is alive again) would you leave her alone in the world, to endure what I have endured?"

'Maria gazed wildly at her, her whole frame was convulsed with emotion; when the child, whom Jemima had been tutoring all the journey, uttered the word "Mamma!" She caught her to her bosom, and burst into a passion of tears—then, resting the child gently on the bed, as if afraid of killing it,—she put her hand to her eyes, to conceal as it were the agonizing struggle of her soul. She remained silent for five minutes, crossing her arms over her bosom, and reclining her head,—then exclaimed: "The conflict is over!—I will live for my child!" '

A few readers perhaps, in looking over these hints, will wonder how it could have been practicable, without tediousness, or remitting in any degree the interest of the story, to have filled, from these slight sketches, a number of pages, more considerable than those which have been already presented. But, in reality, these hints, simple as they are, are pregnant with passion and distress. It is the refuge of barren authors only, to crowd their fictions with so great a number of events, as to suffer no one of them to sink into the reader's mind. It is the province of true genius to develop events, to discover their capabilities, to ascertain the different passions and sentiments with which they are fraught, and to diversify them with incidents, that give reality to the picture, and take a hold upon the mind of a reader of taste, from which they can never be loosened. It was particularly the design of the author, in the present instance, to make her story subordinate to a great moral purpose, that 'of exhibiting the misery and oppression, peculiar to women, that arise out of the partial laws and customs of society.—This view restrained her fancy*.' It was necessary for her, to place in a striking point of view, evils that are too frequently overlooked, and to drag into light those details of oppression, of which the grosser and more insensible part of mankind make little account.

THE END.

*See author's preface.

EXPLANATORY NOTES

ABBREVIATIONS

Flexner	Eleanor Flexner, *Mary Wollstonecraft, A Biography* (1972)
Godwin and Mary	*Godwin and Mary. Letters of William Godwin and Mary Wollstonecraft*, ed. Ralph M. Wardle (1967)
Johnson	Samuel Johnson, *A Dictionary of the English Language*, 9th edn. (1806)
Memoirs	William Godwin, *Memoirs of Mary Wollstonecraft*, ed. W. Clark Durant (1927). Originally published 1798
OED	*Oxford English Dictionary*
Posthumous Works	Mary Wollstonecraft, *Posthumous Works of the Author of a Vindication of the Rights of Woman*, ed. William Godwin, 4 vols. (1798)
Rights of Men	Mary Wollstonecraft, *A Vindication of the Rights of Men, in a Letter to . . . Edmund Burke; Occasioned by his Reflections on the Revolution in France*, 2nd edn. (1790)
Rights of Woman	Mary Wollstonecraft, *A Vindication of the Rights of Woman, With Strictures on Political and Moral Subjects*, ed. Carol H. Poston (1976)

Title Page. (1) *L'exercice . . . génie*: probably taken from an anthology of quotations from Rousseau, *Les Pensées de J. J. Rousseau* (1763). M.W. reviewed two translations of this work in the *Analytical Review* (Oct. 1788), ii. 225–6.

Advertisement. (1) *a Clarissa, a Lady G—, nor a*Sophie*: characters in Richardson's *Clarissa* and *Sir Charles Grandison*, and Rousseau's *Émile*.

(2) *organs*: 'mental or spiritual faculties regarded as instruments of the mind or soul' (*OED*).

(3) *physically*: 'according to nature or the material laws of nature' (*OED*).

(4) *drawn . . . source*: here M.W. reveals her allegiance to the empirical psychology of Locke and Hartley as adapted by Richard Price and Rousseau; cf. Rousseau's *Confessions* (Pléiade edn.), p. 174.

Page 1. (1) *Mary*: M.W. also gave her own name to the heroine of her adaptation of C. G. Salzmann's *Elements of Morality, for the Use of Children* (1790).

(2) *Edward . . . Eliza*: based on M.W.'s father Edward John Wollstonecraft. Eliza: based on Lady Kingsborough and M.W.'s mother Elizabeth, although the type appeared in much of the moral literature M.W. was reading at this time; see her *Female Reader* (1789).

(3) *negative good-nature*: from La Rochefoucauld, *Maxims*, no. 237.

(4) *attendants*: M.W. felt that the flattering attentions of servants interfered with a child's education by creating unnatural ideas of self-importance; cf. *Thoughts on the Education of Daughters* (1787), pp. 14–15.

(5) *accomplishments*: used pejoratively by liberal writers on education; cf. *Thoughts on the Education of Daughters*, ch. iii; *Original Stories* (1788), p. 160; and Elizabeth Inchbald's *A Simple Story* (1791), ed. J. M. S. Tompkins (Oxford English Novels), pp. 4–5.

(6) *in duty bound*: cf. *Rights of Woman*, chs. x and xi, for M.W.'s fully developed views on filial duty.

Page 2. (1) *delicacy*: 'weakness of constitution' (Johnson). In *Rights of Woman* (p. 33) M.W. condemned this supposed attribute of women; cf. p. 39 n., and Essay iv of Catharine Talbot's *Essays on Various Subjects* (1772), which M.W. read.

(2) *Week's Preparation*: 'the action of preparing for Holy Communion' by certain prayers (*OED*). The best known book on this subject which M.W. read was Catharine Talbot's *Reflections on the Seven Days of the Week* (1770).

(3) *her's*: an accepted eighteenth-century usage; see Sterling A. Leonard, *The Doctrine of Correctness in English Usage 1700–1800* (1929), p. 197. Most of M.W.'s apparent solecisms were common usage of the day.

(4) *The Platonic Marriage*: by Mrs. H. Cartwright, 2 vols. (1787); *Eliza Warwick*: *The History of Eliza Warwick* (anon.), 2 vols. (1777).

Page 3. (1) *The picture . . . lover's face*: incidents in *The Platonic Marriage*. *Mary* is in effect a criticism of this novel.

(2) *dogs*: M.W. thought Lady Kingsborough was more fond of her dogs than of her children (Flexner, p. 77). The point was given a more general application in *Rights of Woman*, p. 172.

(3) *attendrissement*: M.W. is mocking the fashionable *penchant* for French phrases in place of simple English ones.

(4) *the world*: i.e. the fashionable world; cf. *Rights of Woman*, pp. 106–7; and see C. S. Lewis, *Studies in Words* (2nd edn. 1967), p. 263. The idea here is drawn from La Rochefoucauld, maxim 205.

(5) *novels*: cf. M.W.'s condemnation of dissatisfaction engendered by reading sentimental novels, in *Thoughts on the Education of Daughters* (1787), pp. 50–1, and *Rights of Woman*, p. 33.

Page 4. (1) *in their infancy*: owing to the 'delicacy' (see p. 2 n. 1) of their mother. M.W., even more than most other female writers at this time, strongly recommended regular exercise for women as well as men; see *Rights of Woman*, ch. iii, where she opposes Rousseau on this subject.

(2) *send the awkward thing away*: M.W. felt she had been neglected by her own mother (Flexner, p. 36).

(3) *school*: all efforts are expended in educating boys, but girls are left to be educated as they can; on the other hand, boarding-schools are regarded as pernicious in *Thoughts on the Education of Daughters*, ch. viii. M.W. recommended day-schools in *Rights of Woman*.

Page 5. (1) *native wood notes wild*: Milton's *L'Allegro*, line 134, referring to Shakespeare, but the phrase was in common use.

(2) *death*: while still an adolescent M.W. had frequently to protect her mother against the drunken brutality of her father (*Memoirs*, p. 11).

(3) *sublime ideas*: the novel shows numerous proofs of M.W.'s familiarity with the literature on the sublime; see below, pp. 10 n.1, 13 n.2.

(4) *goodness*: like Rousseau's noble savage, Mary develops her religious ideas through a personal and emotional relationship with Nature, a process described in most of the works on education consulted by M.W. for her own *Thoughts on the Education of Daughters* (1787), including Sarah Trimmer's *An Easy Introduction to the Knowledge of Nature, And Reading the Holy Scriptures* (1780) and *Fabulous Histories* (1786), and Mrs Barbauld's *Lessons for Children* (1779 and 1788) and *Hymns in Prose for Children* (1781). All were published by Joseph Johnson.

(5) *sensibility*: 'And what is sensibility? "Quickness of sensation; quickness of perception; delicacy." Thus is it defined by Dr. Johnson; and the definition gives me no other idea than of the most exquisitely polished instinct' (*Rights of Woman*, p. 63). Cf. her attack on Burke's sensibility in *Rights of Men*, p. 5.

Page 7. (1) *Her* ... *compassion*: M.W. is describing the 'necessary' development of Mary's characteristically feminine excess of sensibility; cf. *Rights of Woman*, ch. ii. The heroine of *The Wrongs of Woman* is also a 'creature of impulse'.

Page 8. (1) *Ann*: based partly on Jane Arden, mostly on Fanny Blood; see Flexner, p. 26.

Page 9. (1) *Near* ... *castle*: The scene is Laugharne in Carmarthenshire, where the Wollstonecrafts had lived in 1776–7 when M.W. was seventeen. M.W.'s father and his second wife, as well as her brother Charles, were again living there by 1787.

Page 10. (1) *Thomson's Season's, Young's Night-Thoughts, and Paradise Lost*: respectively, examples of the descriptive, the pathetic, and the epic sublime in poetry; see Hugh Blair, *Lectures on Rhetoric and Belles Lettres* (2nd edn., corr. 1785), iii. 157, 160, 288. On 12 February 1787 she wrote to her sister Everina, 'I lately met with Blairs lectures on genius taste &c &c—and found them an intellectual feast' (Abinger collection).

(2) *denied* ... *inhabitants*: cf. *Original Stories* (1788), ch. xxiv, for the relationship between economy and benevolence, a common theme in the female moral writers M.W. had read.

(3) *superfice*: 'outside; surface' (Johnson).

(4) *enthusiastic*: *Mary* was published at the height of the return to fashion and favour of the word 'enthusiasm'; see Susie Tucker, *Protean Shape* (1967), pp. 232–8.

Page 11. (1) *conversing*: rational religion's term for praying; cf. Hester Chapone, *Letters on the Improvement of the Mind* (1773), ii. 23. M.W. shows Mary coming at the truths of religion not by revelation or the intercession of priests, but by the 'exercise' of her own heart and mind. Her approach is that of Prévost's heroes, Rousseau's Savoyard Vicar in *Émile*, and Richard Price in his sermons and *Review of Morals*. See also M.W.'s letter of 16 April 1787 to Henry Gabell, in *Shelley and His Circle*, ed. K. N. Cameron, iv. 857–8.

(2) *genius*: 'nature; disposition' (Johnson).

(3) *through a glass darkly*: I Corinthians 13:12. M.W. follows Paul's argument that there are mysteries which man's reason is not meant to unveil; see also p. 40. She used the quotation in her letter to Henry Gabell on 16 April 1787 (*Shelley and His Circle*, iv. 857), and she could have taken both the quotation and the argument from one of Jeremiah Seed's sermons which she had read, or from Richard Price's sermon *The Vanity, Misery, and Infamy, of Knowledge without suitable Practice* (1770), pp.

15–16. Her reference to the limitations of this 'probationary' life on earth is certainly informed by Price's account of human existence and a future state, in both his *Review of Morals* and his sermons.

Page 12. (1) *heiress*: Richard Price, and later the English Jacobins, especially opposed male primogeniture; cf. M.W.'s *Rights of Men*, pp. 45 ff., and Godwin's *Political Justice* (3rd edn., 1798), ii. 95.

(2) *dance*: so she can enter the marriage market.

(3) *Chancery suit*: the Court of Chancery was an example of the degeneration of English law from spirit to letter. Originally established to provide remedies not available in common-law courts, it became increasingly bound by rules and procedures so that litigation took years and cost great sums of money. By the late eighteenth century it dealt principally with claims for damages or the possession of property, as in contested inheritances. See also *The Wrongs of Woman*, p. 201.

Page 13. (1) *this ill-fated love*: Fanny Blood's love for Hugh Skeys.

(2) *In every . . . speculations*: Mary's preference for the sublime is contrasted with Ann's for the beautiful. The contrast was a commonplace after Burke's *Philosophical Enquiry into the Origin of our Ideas of the Sublime and Beautiful* (1757). M.W.'s familiarity with the vocabulary and basic issues would indicate some knowledge of the subject, if not of Burke's treatise itself, which was firmly in the tradition of the psychology of Locke and Hartley; and she certainly knew James Usher's *Clio: or, A Discourse on Taste* (1767). By the time she came to write her next novel she had moved closer to the romantic attitude to nature and the sublime; cf. *The Wrongs of Woman*, p. 163.

Page 15. (1) *sense . . . brain*: M.W. is using the language of Locke and Hartley to describe Mary's 'mental phenomena' in a 'scientific' way.

(2) *statue of Despair*: *OED* cites Godwin's *Caleb Williams* (1794); cf. 'statue of grief' in Gessner's *Death of Abel*, bk. iv (Mary Collyer's translation).

(3) *Her husband . . . same day*: possibly based on the story of Polydore and Emilia in Lord Lyttelton's *Letters from a Persian in England* (letter xxxiv). The rest of the novel could be a kind of feminist revision of most of Lyttelton's tale.

(4) *maiden aunt . . . or cousin*: ironic reference to the common fate of poorer, unwed female relatives; cf. *Rights of Woman*, p. 11 and note.

Page 16. (1) *black bile*: a momentary descent into an older psychological tradition, that of the four 'humours', after the Lockean jargon of the first part of the chapter. Black bile was supposed to cause melancholy, to which the English were thought to be particularly susceptible.

Page 17. (1) *physic*: M.W. particularly recommended the study of elementary medicine for women in *Thoughts on the Education of Daughters*,

p. 104. Here she recognizes that such study is not without its drawbacks, as Rousseau pointed out in *Émile* (Pléiade edn.), p. 270.

Page 18. (1) *physical tribe*: doctors. Rousseau was especially violent in his condemnation of the profession; see *Émile* (Pléiade edn.), pp. 269–70.

Page 19. (1) *transient likings*: M.W.'s passing interest in several men, all clergymen, in the 1780s.

(2) *philosophic turn*: both the revulsion against sex and the preference for older men were characteristic of M.W. herself; see Flexner, pp. 134, 138, and cf. Rousseau's '*maman*', Mme de Warens.

Page 20. (1) *romantic*: M.W.'s use of the word retains the original associations with romance (Susie Tucker, *Protean Shape*, p. 148), but varies between approval and disapproval; e.g. her application of the word to Burke's argument in his *Reflections*, with the meaning of 'false, or rather artificial feelings' (*Rights of Men*, p. 61).

Page 21. (1) *unnumbered worlds*: the idea of a plurality of worlds was first popularized by Fontenelle in 1686, and aroused a debate on the degree of God's involvement in mundane and individual affairs; the phrase is probably remembered from Young's *The Complaint: or, Night-Thoughts*, Night the Fourth, line 710.

Page 22. (1) *german-flute*: one of a number of names for the normal, side-blown flute.

(2) *violin*: like Rousseau, Henry can express himself on that most romantic of instruments. In *Thoughts on the Education of Daughters* M.W. wrote, 'In music I prefer expression to execution' (p. 43).

(3) *lines of genius*: reference to yet another psychological theory, which tried to relate psychology to physiognomy. The classic work, *Essays on Physiognomy*, was by Fuseli's friend J. K. Lavater, and M.W. tried her hand at translating it in 1788, but was forestalled by publication of Thomas Holcroft's translation in 1789. M.W. later met Lavater's son, through Fuseli (cf. Flexner, p. 168). Flexner argues that Henry is drawn after Henry Gabell, whom M.W. met in 1786 on her way to Ireland (*Shelley and His Circle*, ed. K. N. Cameron, iv. 854–5); but a letter from Fanny Blood in Lisbon (30 March 1785; Abinger Collection) to M.W.'s sisters Eliza and Everina described a young and romantic but ugly physician there, and concluded, 'I have given a description of him to Mary; and she is, I hope, already prepared to love him.' Henry was possibly named after M.W.'s neglected brother; see *Notes and Queries*, ccxx (Jan. 1975).

Page 23. (1) *Butler's Analogy*: Joseph Butler (1692–1752), bishop of Durham. His *Analogy of Religion, Natural and Revealed, to the Constitution and Course of Nature* (1736) was one of the most influential theological works of the century. It had a strong influence, for example, on M.W.'s own philosophical mentor, Richard Price.

(2) *some reason on their side*: M.W.'s views on 'sectaries' would seem to be influenced by Richard Price's *Sermons on the Christian Doctrine as Received by the Different Denominations of Christians* . . . (1787), where he argued for toleration and the universality of essential religious beliefs.

Page 24. (1) *rank*: the society at Lisbon is drawn after that encountered by M.W. in Dublin and Bristol while in the employ of the Kingsboroughs. From Dublin she wrote to her sister Everina (24 March 1787), 'Lords are not the sort of being who afford me amusement —'; and three months later she wrote to Eliza from Bristol (27 June), 'I thank Heaven that I was not so unfortunate as to be born a Lady of quality' (both letters in Abinger Collection). By 1792 one of the basic premisses of *Rights of Woman* is a violent condemnation of rank (p. 13).

(2) *gusto*: taste. The passage as a whole is a satire on the education of girls for mere fashionable 'accomplishments', as well as an epitome of the basic argument of *Rights of Woman*.

Page 26. (1) *And came stealing on the senses like the sweet south*: adapted from Twelfth Night, I.i. 8–10, as emended by Pope (the standard eighteenth-century text of Shakespeare), and quoted by John Aikin in *The Calendar of Nature* (2nd edn., 1785, p. 22), one of the books M.W. knew.

Page 27. (1) *dress*: according to *Rights of Woman* (pp. 186–7) fondness for dress is a sign of an uncultivated mind; cf. *Thoughts on the Education of Daughters*, ch. v.

Page 28. (1) *the earthquake*: of 1755, devasted Lisbon and killed 10,000 to 20,000 people, and thus became a major point in the debate on God's beneficence. See Rousseau's *Lettre à Voltaire* (written 1756, published 1759) in reply to Voltaire's *Poème sur le désastre de Lisbonne* (1756).

(2) *portraits*: according to eighteenth-century theory, painting of historical subjects was superior to portraiture because it stimulated greater thoughts. See Joshua Reynolds, Fourth Discourse (1771); John Stedman, *Laelius and Hortensia* (1782), letter xxvi; and especially Johnson, *The Idler*, no. 45.

Page 29. (1) *She saw . . . the heart*: cf. *Émile* (Pléiade edn.), p. 127, where the Savoyard Vicar expresses an identical view.

(2) *good*: like Richard Price, M.W. is preaching a religion of works as well as faith; cf. p. 58n. Her opposition to solitude was shared by Rousseau in his *Lettre à d'Alembert*; and the psychological, social, ethical, and religious thought of Richard Price, as embodied in his *Review of Morals*, and his numerous sermons, informs most of the philosophical passages in *Mary*.

(3) *The exercise . . . genius*: cf. the novel's epigraph, and *Rights of Woman* (p. 21): 'the most perfect education, in my opinion, is such an exercise of the understanding as is best calculated to strengthen the body and form the heart. Or, in other words, to enable the individual to attain such habits of virtue as will render it independent.' The argument was also the basis of Price's *Review of Morals*.

Page 30. (1) *They have the least mind*: either a reference to Johnson's assertion that 'mind' comprises both imagination and judgment, in Boswell, *Journal of a Tour to the Hebrides*, 1785 ('August 15'), or to Johnson's citation from Raleigh in the *Dictionary*. See also below, p. 41 n. M.W. also used her experience of Portugal for her review of Arthur Costigan's *Sketches of Society and Manners in Portugal*, in the *Analytical Review* (Aug. 1788), i. 451-7.

Page 31. (1) *pity*: on 21 July 1784 M.W. wrote to Fanny Blood's brother George, 'pity is one of my prevailing passions' (Abinger Collection).

(2) *That . . . evaporates*: the point may be traced to Locke's *Essay Concerning Human Understanding*, book ii, ch. xi, section 2. Cf. 'Hints' for a continuation of *Rights of Woman* in *Posthumous Works*, iv. 185.

Page 32. (1) *slow, sudden-death*: Edward Young, *The Complaint: or, Night-Thoughts*, Night the First, line 388.

(2) *The body . . . night*: according to Godwin, M.W.'s aversion to the 'superstition' of the Portuguese was increased by the fact that Fanny had to be buried at night because she was a Protestant (*Memoirs*, p. 36).

Page 36. (1) *My child . . . ideas*: cf. p. 19 n. 1. The passage that follows is based on the theory of 'association of ideas' derived from Locke through Hartley; see especially Hartley's *Observations on Man* (1749) ch. iii, section 5, and Locke's *Essay Concerning Human Understanding*, book ii, ch. i, section 17.

(2) *vulgar*: 'plebeian; suiting to the common people' (Johnson). Not used pejoratively here; cf. *Rights of Woman*, p. 172.

Page 37. (1) *tempest*: M.W. is consistent (and scrupulous by late eighteenth-century standards) in her use of pathetic fallacy.

Page 39. (1) *delicacy*: 'refined sense of what is becoming, modest or proper' (*OED*); cf. p. 2 n. 1.

Page 40. (1) *That . . . ascend*: adapted from *Paradise Lost*, viii. 591-2. M.W. also quoted Milton to her purpose in *Rights of Woman* (p. 20). M.W.'s argument for sensibility in this paragraph would seem to draw from Price's *Review of Morals* and Adam Smith's *Theory of Moral Sentiments*.

(2) *modifications of it*: Mary rejects the materialist account of nature and the existence of the soul which some philosophers had derived from Locke and empirical psychology. M.W.'s source here was probably *A Free*

Discussion of the Doctrines of Materialism, and Philosophical Necessity, In a Correspondence Between Dr. Price and Dr. Priestley (1778).

(3) *am of subtler essence than the trodden clod*: Edward Young, *The Complaint: or, Night-Thoughts*, Night the First, line 100. This argument for life after death on the evidence of human intelligence is drawn from Price's *Review of Morals* and *Sermons*, and was re-echoed by most of the moral writers in Joseph Johnson's circle.

(4) *prudence*: Mary also rejects the principles of prudence, worldliness, and self-interest which had been opposed to sensibility and benevolence by Mandeville and Lord Chesterfield. M.W. perhaps derived some of her ideas on prudence from Adam Smith's *Theory of Moral Sentiments* (1759), Introduction, section ii, ch. ii (she referred to Smith's work in *Rights of Woman*, pp. 58–9), or Essay xi of Catharine Talbot's *Essays on Various Subjects* (1772).

Page 41. (1) *when ... consists*: Mary's text is again I Cor. 13:12; see below p. 55 n. 1. M.W.'s preference for the mystic and his imagination over the philosopher and his reason was in tune with late eighteenth-century aesthetic theory (see above pp. 10 n. 1, 13 n. 2, and 'Advertisement'), and was expressed more strongly in her 'Hints' for a continuation of *Rights of Woman* (*Posthumous Works*, iv. 187–9), and in a letter to Godwin (17 August 1796, *Godwin and Mary*, p. 18); Godwin acknowledged the difference in their sensibilities in his *Memoirs* of her (pp. 124–5).

Page 44. (1) *darkness visible*: *Paradise Lost*, i. 63; but the phrase was in common use.

(2) *to-morrow, and to-morrow*: an echo from Macbeth's soliloquy on world-weariness (V.v. 19), which M.W. printed in *The Female Reader* (1789), p. 208.

Page 45. (1) *distress*: the following incident occurred during M.W.'s return from Portugal at the end of 1785; see Flexner, p. 55.

Page 46. (1) *when she gazed ... the people*: cf. the association of the tempest and the sublime, in James Usher's *Clio: or, A Discourse on Taste* (3rd edn., 1772), pp. 111–12, and Hugh Blair's *Lectures on Rhetoric and Belles Lettres* (2nd edn., 1785) i. 61, both of which M.W. read.

(2) *The Lord ... and ever*: misquoted from the Hallelujah chorus of Handel's oratorio *The Messiah*. M.W. had attended a two-day commemoration of Handel's music in Dublin early in 1787 (Flexner, p. 75), and she paid high tribute to its sublimity in *Thoughts on the Education of Daughters*, p. 43.

(3) *when all ... fade away*: a favourite theme in the letters of M.W. and her sisters. In the passage that follows the sublimity of the Last Day anticipates the revolutionary apocalypse, and reveals the religious

enthusiast as a potential revolutionary (cf. E. P. Thompson, *The Making of the English Working Class*, ch. xi, pt. ii, 'The Chiliasm of Despair').

Page 48. (1) *her soul . . . sight*: M.W.'s own experience on her return from Portugal (Flexner, pp. 55–6). The contrast between nature and the man-made world that follows was made commonplace by Rousseau, through his Savoyard Vicar (*Émile*, Pléiade edn. p. 588), although M.W. disagreed with him on the evil effects of civilization, in *Rights of Woman* (pp. 13–14).

Page 50. (1) *mansion-house . . . luxury*: an appropriate symbol for 'a world in ruins' (p. 48), the ruined mansion also appears in *Original Stories*, ch. x.

Page 52. (1) *imagination . . . woe*: cf. M.W.'s condemnation of novelists for encouraging excesses of imagination, in *Rights of Woman*, p. 183, and see above, p. 3 n. 5.

(2) *it visits not my haunts forlorn*: a misquotation from Charlotte Smith's *Elegiac Sonnets* (3rd edn., 1786, p. 7; 'To Hope'), a work which she used for *The Female Reader*.

Page 53. (1) *spring*: the Wollstonecraft girls seem each to have had a special season. M.W.'s favourite sister, Everina, expected spring would always right the world, a belief often bitterly commented on by her other sister Eliza, who preferred autumn (letters, Abinger Collection). See also *Émile* (Pléiade edn.), p. 418.

(2) *rhapsody on sensibility*: cf. a passage in *The Cave of Fancy*, an unfinished philosophic tale written 1787, in *Posthumous Works*, iv. 135–6. M.W.'s source for both is obviously Rousseau, although the passage in *The Cave of Fancy* is more marked by Hartleyan psychological theory.

Page 55. (1) *Apostle*: Paul. The text is adapted from I Cor. 2:9; cf. p. 41 n. 1. Hester Chapone especially recommended study of Paul's epistles for young ladies, in *Letters on the Improvement of the Mind* (1773), i. 94.

(2) *can only*: the sense is clearer in this and the preceding sentence if these two words are transposed.

Page 58. (1) *Heaven . . . inclinations*: an echo of Richard Price and an anticipation of the English Jacobin's doctrine that social utility is the highest duty; cf. *Thoughts on the Education of Daughters*, p. 91.

Page 59. (1) *village*: probably Henley, where M.W. visited her sister Everina in September 1787 (Flexner, p. 89).

Page 60. (1) *this accident*: the boating excursion and its unfortunate consequences are possibly combined from Rousseau's *La Nouvelle Héloïse*, part iv, letter 17, and part vi, letter 9.

Page 71. (1) *friend*: George Dyson, one of Godwin's 'four principal oral instructors' (C. Kegan Paul, *William Godwin*, i. 47–9), he contributed greatly to Godwin's revision of the arguments of *Political Justice*. The complete text of the letter (May, 1797) is in *Shelley and His Circle*, ed. K. N. Cameron, iv. 887–8.

(2) *the Sorcerer*: a novel by Veit Weber: the translation of 1795, published by M.W.'s publisher Johnson, is tentatively ascribed to R. Huish in the British Library catalogue.

Page 72. (1) *In revising . . . press*: judging from Godwin's journal and his and M.W.'s letters, he read or edited the MS in July–September, 1796; 26 January, 27–30 April, and, after M.W.'s death, 17–19, 26, 28 September (in conjunction with writing a 'Life' of M.W.), 7–9, 11 October, 1797; 29 January, 2 February, 1798. It was, according to the journal, published 29 January, 1798.

Page 73. (1) *The . . . embodied*: i.e. she has embodied personal feelings in the form of characters and a story.

(2) *friend*: see p. 71 n. 1.

Page 74. (1) *delicacy*: 'tenderness, scrupulousness' (Johnson); cf. *Mary* p. 39 n. 1.

(2) *What . . . novels*: cf. the preface to *Memoirs of Emma Courtney* (1796), by Mary Hays, which was known to both Godwin and M.W. in MS and which was heavily influenced by the former; cf. also the preface to Godwin's *Fleetwood* (1805). One of the 'best novels' M.W. may have in mind here was Elizabeth Inchbald's *A Simple Story* (1791). The novel was greatly appreciated by both Holcroft and Godwin, and M.W. knew Mrs. Inchbald well.

Page 75. (1) *such stuff as dreams are made of*: cf. *The Tempest* IV.i.156–8: 'We are such stuff As dreams are made on; and our little life Is rounded with a sleep.' This was a favourite sentiment of M.W. (cf. p. 81 n. 2). M.W. could have heard these lines in Kemble's adaptation at Drury Lane in February–March 1797.

Page 76. (1) *huge pile of buildings*: M.W. probably intended the building to symbolize British political history, thereby turning Burke's well-known symbol of the constitution to her own purposes.

Page 79. (1) *curiosity*: the key to freedom, but not to be used lightly, as Godwin had attempted to show in the character of Caleb Williams, who was also from the lower class, and was impelled by curiosity to find out his master's secrets. M.W. had borrowed *Caleb Williams* from Godwin in September 1796 and again in February 1797 (*Godwin and Mary*, pp. 39, 69). On the latter occasion she wanted volume ii, probably for Godwin's descriptions of prison.

(2) *sophisticated*: 'altered from, deprived of, primitive simplicity or naturalness' (*OED*).

Page 80. (1) *Jemima*: the first of Job's three daughters after his restoration to prosperity (Job 42: 13–15): 'And in all the land there were no women so fair as Job's daughters, and their father gave them inheritance among their brothers.' There is also a character named Jemima in Mary Robinson's *Walsingham* (published December 1797); Godwin saw a good deal of Mrs Robinson in 1796–7. Caleb Williams's Christian name had also come from the Bible, and Godwin could have told M.W. that Jemima meant 'dove', a not inappropriate name for a messenger of peace and deliverance.

(2) *only a claim to a Christian name*: i.e. she could not claim her father's surname because she was a bastard. M.W. is attacking both the law, for arbitrarily distinguishing between legitimate and illegitimate children to the exclusive benefit of the former, and Christian religion, for accepting this discrimination. Cf. *Rights of Woman*, chs. x and xi, and *Rights of Men*, p. 45, where she blames the system of property for debasing family relationships.

(3) *the woman*: M.W. equates the essence of female character with compassion, although she realized that such an equation could be used to oppress women; cf. *Rights of Woman*, ch. ii.

(4) *A sense ... reason*: the premise that reason, rightly exercised, necessarily distinguishes right from wrong and presides over the feelings which alone can induce action, was derived by M.W. from Richard Price, and was clarified in Godwin's mind partly through his discussions with M.W., to be definitively expressed in the third (1798) edition of *Political Justice*.

(5) *The wages ... independence*: the equation of moral and financial independence underlay M.W.'s whole assault on the system of property, dominated by men, in *Rights of Woman* and this novel, and was one of her major contributions to the feminist debate. See G. R. Stirling Taylor, *Mary Wollstonecraft, A Study in Economics and Romance* (1911).

Page 81. (1) *grateful*: 'pleasing; acceptable; delicious' (Johnson).

(2) *the ills ... heir to*: cf. *Hamlet* III.i. 62–3: 'The heart-ache, and the thousand natural shocks That flesh is heir to'.

Page 83. (1) *a sublime concentration of thought*: Maria's reflection on the sublimity of madness resembles that in part two of Burke's *A Philosophical Enquiry into the Origin of our Ideas of the Sublime and Beautiful*. Godwin's Journal shows that he, M.W., and Joseph Johnson visited Bedlam Hospital for the insane on 6 February 1797.

Page 85. (1) *to sleep to dream no more*: misquoted from Hamlet's well-known soliloquy (III.i. 60–1). M.W. uses allusions to Shakespeare on the whole better than Godwin, but the presence of the echo here suggests his influence.

(2) *Dryden's Fables, Milton's Paradise Lost*: for Milton, see *Mary* p. 10

n. 1; Dryden's *Fables Ancient and Modern* from Homer, Ovid, Boccaccio, and Chaucer was amongst Godwin's favourite reading.

Page 86. (1) *Dryden's Guiscard and Sigismunda*: Maria prefers to see the powers of mind and heart displayed in a narrative, rather than abstracted in a treatise; cf. M.W.'s Preface to *Original Stories* (1788). 'Sigismonda and Guiscardo, from Boccace', was one of Dryden's *Fables*, and contains a daughter's spirited defiance of her father as well as an ardent vindication of the rights of woman. Godwin had read it at least twice by the time he met M.W. in 1796. The 'book on the powers of the human mind' may have been Dugald Stewart's *Elements of the Philosophy of the Human Mind* (vol. i, 1792), or one of its sources, Thomas Reid's *Essays on the Intellectual Powers of Man* (1785).

Page 87. (1) *no active duties or pursuits*: cf. *Rights of Woman*, ch. xiii, section 2.

Page 88. (1) *the pathetic ballad of old Robin Gray*: Lady Anne Lindsay's 'Auld Robin Gray' (published 1776) tells of Jenny's love for Jamie, who goes to sea to make his fortune; but when her parents fall on evil days she agrees to marry 'auld Robin Gray'; after she does so Jamie returns, to take a final farewell (*The Oxford Book of Eighteenth-Century Verse*, pp. 541–2). There is a gap in the original text between *Rob* and *with*, but the full title is in the French translation (1798) as well as the American edition (Philadelphia, 1799).

(2) *lost her senses*: the story of the fair maniac is a melodramatic version of the brief married life of M.W.'s sister Eliza. Married in October 1782 to Meridith Bishop, Eliza had a child, and then suffered 'an acute post partum breakdown' (Flexner, p. 40). M.W. persuaded Eliza to run away from her husband and she never returned. M.W. had quoted the description of a fair maniac from Fanny Burney's *Camilla* (bk. iv, ch. vi) in her review for the *Analytical Review* (xxiv, Aug. 1796, 142–8).

(3) *the only one worth inhabiting*: a similar point is made in Mary Hays, *Memoirs of Emma Courtney* (1796), i. 41.

Page 89. (1) *thrilled*: 'pierced, penetrated' (*OED*), the original sense of the word.

(2) *conjectures*: see Godwin's note, p. 97.

(3) *Saint Preux*: the hero of *La Nouvelle Héloïse*; Mary Hays also identifies her hero, Augustus Harley, with St. Preux (*Memoirs of Emma Courtney*, i. 113). On the danger of such fantasies, see *Mary*, p. 52 n. 1.

(4) *Prometheus*: the god who defied his ruler to bring fire to man greatly interested the Romantics: the sub-title of *Frankenstein*, by M.W.'s daughter and Shelley's wife, was 'The Modern Prometheus'; but Rousseau himself would not have liked M.W.'s comparison (cf. *Discourse on the Arts and Sciences*, trans. G. D. H. Cole, rev. edn. 1973, p. 14).

Page 90. (1) *their former meeting*: see Godwin's note to p. 175.

(2) *to wish . . . respect and love*: an obvious reference to M.W.'s feelings towards Imlay, in the early part of 1796 at least; see her letter of 26 January 1796 to Archibald Hamilton Rowan (C. Kegan Paul, *William Godwin*, i. 229–30).

Page 91. (1) *seclusion*: *Wrongs of Woman* develops the detailed observation of the psychological effects of solitude, begun in *Mary*. In France, and in the aftermath of her affair with Imlay, M.W. confirmed her earlier identification with Rousseau; cf. Introduction and her reference to becoming a Solitary Walker in her letter to Godwin of 17 August 1796 (*Godwin and Mary*, p. 15).

(2) *Henry Darnford*: M.W. has taken the simple 'Henry' of *Mary* and romanticized it by the addition of the name of Darnford. M.W. may be introducing the same kind of historical allusion by which Godwin attempted to enrich *Caleb Williams* (see G. Kelly, *The English Jacobin Novel*, Oxford, 1976): Darnford is a variation on Henry Lord Darnley, just as Maria is a variation on Mary, Queen of Scots, and one of history's most notable 'prisoners of sex'. Both Maria and the Scottish Queen have 'romantic dispositions, both are willing to risk all for love, both are imprisoned because of the property they 'own', both have their child taken from them because of the child's inheritance. M.W.'s favourite Mrs Siddons played the title role in John St John's *Mary Queen of Scots* at Drury Lane, on 2 January 1797, and as recently as November 1795 Godwin had read Hume's Chapters on Elizabeth I in his *History of England*, which contained a full account of the adventures of Mary Stuart; but M.W. herself had included a 'character' of Mary Queen of Scots from William Robertson in *The Female Reader*.

(3) *former obligation*: i.e. her marriage; M.W. chooses the euphemism carefully here, to bring out what she believes to be the real character of marriage.

Page 92. (1) *their very selves*: M.W. shares the rationalist assumption of Richard Price that the essence of self is the reasoning faculty. The view expressed here, that when reason is weak, the passions are uncontrolled, was applied to Burke in *Rights of Men*, and to the unfair treatment of women in *Rights of Woman*, but was considerably strengthened by the influence of Godwin in 1796–7.

Page 93. (1) *Accustomed . . . opposition*: M.W. explicitly attributes the difference in male and female behaviour to education in the widest sense, or social 'conditioning'; see *Rights of Woman*, ch. vi, 'The Effect which an Early Association of Ideas has upon the Character'.

(2) *The copy . . . state*: all notes at the foot of a page are by Godwin, and usually signed 'Editor'.

Page 95. (1) *prisoner*: Darnford's early career perfectly resembles that of Banastre Tarleton, who broke off a long liaison with Godwin's and M.W.'s friend Mary Robinson in 1796. Godwin and M.W. saw a good deal of 'Perdita' that year and the next, and Godwin saw Tarleton at Debrett's in company with other Whigs and rake-hells, on 31 December 1796.

(2) *impetuosity*: cf. *Mary*, p. 7 n.; this characteristic of the hero of sensibility from Prévost to Scott is given a contemporary relevance by the English Jacobin novelists, and especially by Godwin in *Caleb Williams*: impetuosity, or the over-zealous haste of revolutionaries in France and reformers in England, only led to war, dictatorship, and repression. See Godwin's *Considerations . . .* (1795) for an attack on the impetuosity of the English Jacobins, and the preface to *The Enquirer*, p. ix (dated 4 February 1797).

(3) *travelled*: Darnford's travels are probably based on those of M.W.'s youngest brother Charles, who went to America in November 1792, though no doubt she had also heard a great deal from Imlay. Robert R. Hare argues that M.W. was the real author of *The Emigrants*, a novel set in America and published in 1794 as Imlay's (*The Emigrants*, Gainsville, Florida, 1964, Introduction), but cf. P. M. Pénigault-Duhet, 'Du nouveau sur Mary Woolstonecraft: l'œuvre littéraire de George [*sic*] Imlay', *Études anglaises*, xxiv (1971), 298–303.

(4) *commercial speculations*: both Godwin and M.W. believed that commerce blunted the finer sensibilities. (See Godwin's *The Enquirer*, Part ii, essay v, which M.W. probably read in MS some time late in 1796.) M.W.'s brother Charles, Imlay, and her friend Joel Barlow had all engaged in land speculation. M.W. had also witnessed Imlay's gradual but complete absorption in commerce, while she was living with him; see her letter to him in *Posthumous Works*, iii. 107 ff. Richard Price had anticipated this development in the American character in his *Observations on the Importance of the American Revolution* (1784).

Page 96. (1) *track*: commonly confused with tract (*OED*).

Page 98. (1) *never ending, still beginning*: probably adapted from *Paradise Lost*, iii. 729.

(2) *only born to feel*: cf. *Mary*, p. 7 n.

(3) *almost voluptuous figure*: apparently, like M.W.'s own. A friend once told Amelia Alderson that he considered M.W. 'voluptuous', a fact which Miss Alderson did not dispute, but wondered how he could say it (Amelia Alderson to M.W., 28 August 1796, Abinger Collection).

Page 99. (1) *Pygmalion*: M.W.'s thoughtful re-direction of the well-known myth illustrates the novel's theme of the dangers of imagination. Dryden adapted the story in his *Fables*, which M.W. was certainly familiar with, but Rousseau too had an interest in the myth, and he wrote a one-act '*scène lyrique*' entitled *Pygmalion*, which would have been available to

M.W. in his collected works. She may also have had Pygmalion in mind when remarking on the delusions of love in *Rights of Woman*, p. 111.

Pages 99–100. (1) *the fear . . . love*: cf. M.W.'s restraint in the early period of her relationship with Godwin, after the ardent impetuosity of her passion for Imlay, and Godwin's reply (*Godwin and Mary*, pp. 14–17), especially his remarks on her 'delicacy'.

Page 101. (1) *Armida's garden*: in Tasso's *Jerusalem Delivered*, Armida lures a number of the Christian knights into her delightful garden, where they are overcome by indolence.

(2) *lapt them in Elysium*: from *Comus*, l. 257. Milton's masque had been used by Godwin in his early novel *Imogen* (1784), and by Holcroft in *Anna St. Ives* (1792).

(3) *an account of herself*: Jemima's narrative, with its resemblance to the popular eighteenth-century criminal biography, may, like that of Caleb Williams, owe something to the *Newgate Calendar* and Defoe (see *Caleb Williams*, ed. David McCracken, p. 340).

Page 102. (1) *ruined*: M.W. opposed the double standard of sexual morality with special vehemence in *Rights of Woman*, ch. viii. Her friend Thomas Holcroft had refuted the convention of 'ruin' in his novel *Anna St. Ives* (1792), and Mary Hays also opposed the morality of *Clarissa* in 'On Novel-Writing' (*Monthly Magazine*, iv, September 1797, p. 180).

Page 103. (1) *to manage his passion*: because of their subordinate condition, women must use cunning, if not criminal means to gain an equality with men; thus prudence opposes love (*Rights of Woman*, pp. 19–20).

Page 104. (1) *liquorish*: properly, lickerish: 'fond of delicious fare' (*OED*), i.e. having a sweet tooth. M.W. took charge of a little girl named Ann in the early 1790s, and in February 1792 she complained to Everina that she had caught the girl stealing sugar (Wardle, *Mary Wollstonecraft*, p. 178).

Page 105. (1) *slop-shop*: a shop selling cheap ready-made clothing, for seamen; *Wapping*: borough in the docks area of London.

Page 106. (1) *period*: end, termination.

(2) *a mother's affection*: cf. *Mary*, p. 4 n. 2.

(3) *methodist meeting*: sexual licence was a standard theme in anti-methodist satire; see Albert M. Lyles, *Methodism Mocked* (1960), p. 53. Perhaps M.W. was remembering the account of Rev. Wheatley in *The Newgate Calendar*; he was a Methodist minister of Norwich taken in adultery 'with aggravated circumstances'. The account may also have interested M.W. because of its history of punishments for adultery, especially when committed by women. M.W. shared the antipathy to

fanatical religion of Richard Price and other philosophers of Joseph Johnson's circle; see *Rights of Men*, p. 86.

Page 107. (1) *designed*: i.e. to make her abort; cf. a similar incident in Mary Hays's *Memoirs of Emma Courtney* (1796), ii. 210.

Page 108. (1) *utterly destitute*: M.W. declared (twice) in *Rights of Woman* that men should be compelled by law to support the women they seduced (pp. 71, 139); cf. below, p. 116.

(2) *parish-officer*: responsible for providing (usually a minimum) for bastards, and the destitute. In 1787 Fanny Blood's sister Caroline had been taken up by the parish officers 'in a dreadful situation', and M.W. had undertaken the cost of her maintenance for a time, as the parish officers seemed to insist on it (Flexner, p. 108).

Page 109. (1) *vice*: M.W. was violently opposed to prostitution; in September 1792 she reviewed a book entitled *The Evils of Adultery and Prostitution* for the *Analytical Review* (xiii. 100–2).

Page 110. (1) *watchmen*: the equivalent of policemen at that time. The corrupt practices described below led to calls for reform, and M.W. is echoing a point made in ch. ix of Patrick Colquhoun's *Treatise on the Police of the Metropolis* (pub. first half of 1796).

(2) *a gentleman*: this episode in Jemima's career resembles the life of Jane Butterfield, recounted in *The Newgate Calendar*.

Page 111. (1) *With such . . . sensuality*: cf. M.W.'s letter to Eliza from Bristol, 27 June 1787: 'I am sorry to hear a man of sensibility and cleverness *talking* of sentiment sink into sensuality—such will ever I fear be the case with the inconsistent human heart when there are no principles to restrain and direct the wayward impulses of it' (Abinger Collection).

Page 112. (1) *The aim . . . wisdom*: The philosopher of feeling with a weakness for women resembles both Rousseau and his ardent disciple Fuseli. At the time of her infatuation with Fuseli, before 1792, M.W. did not consciously recognize his powerful erotic imagination (Flexner, p. 137), even though she suggested a (probably platonic) *ménage-à-trois* with Fuseli and his wife. Her recognition of Fuseli's sensual side may be surfacing here, discreetly transposed in fiction.

(2) *such a creature as she supposed me to be*: cf. *Rights of Woman*, pp. 131–2 and above, p. 102 n. 1. M.W. may be describing the reaction of Fuseli's wife to the proposal mentioned in the preceding note.

Page 113. (1) *ready-made linen shops*: shops making and selling linen, i.e. garments of linen such as shirts and underclothes.

Page 114. (1) *How writers . . . imagine*: M.W. is probably referring to the controversy surrounding Pitt's attempt to reform the Poor Law in 1796–7.

See J.L. and Barbara Hammond, *The Village Labourer* (1911; 1966), p. 145 ff.

Page 115. (1) *things are very well as they are*: a case argued by, amongst others, William Paley in *Reasons for Contentment Addressed to the Labouring Part of the British Public* (1793).

(2) *kindly turn them over to another*: the grand argument of Hannah More's *Cheap Repository Tracts* (1795-6), and also found in Burke's *Reflections*; see *Rights of Men*, p. 143.

(3) *improvement*: contemporaries would probably have related Darnford's sentiments to the debate on Samuel Whitbread's bill to introduce a minimum wage. Pitt had opposed the bill on the grounds that the hardships of the poor were exaggerated, and that there was in any case a great deal of voluntary charity that could cope with the problem. The debate took place in February 1796 and arose out of the famine of 1795 (J.L. and Barbara Hammond, *The Village Labourer*, pp. 137-8).

(4) *to wash . . . a day*: Jemima's account of the hours, wages, and working conditions of washerwomen is meticulously accurate (see M. Dorothy George, *London Life in the Eighteenth Century*, 1966, p. 207). Godwin's former friend John Thelwall had turned attention to the actual conditions of the poor in *The Tribune* (1795), and Godwin had corresponded on the subject with Tom Wedgwood in late 1795.

Page 117. (1) *hospital*: on abuses in the eighteenth-century hospitals, including fees and security-money, see M. Dorothy George, *London Life in the Eighteenth Century*, pp. 61-2.

(2) *passed me*: by the Settlement Laws those who were or might become dependent on poor relief were to be passed to the parish where they last legally settled, a measure threatened against Caroline Blood (see above, p. 108 n. 2). The weight of these laws fell on single women and unmarried mothers (J. R. Poynter, *Society and Pauperism*, 1969, p. 7). In 1795 Pitt had changes made which somewhat ameliorated the hardships of this law (J.L. and Barbara Hammond, *The Village Labourer*, pp. 108-9, 149).

Page 118. (1) *a thief from principle*: cf. the speech of the captain of thieves, Mr. Raymond, in Godwin's *Caleb Williams* (ed. McCracken), p. 220.

(2) *paid enough . . . charity*: those who owned property exceeding a certain value had to pay a 'poor rate' to support the poor in the parish; hence the refusal to give more in 'charity' (J. R. Poynter, *Society and Pauperism*, p. 3).

(3) *these wretched asylums*: there was also widespread demand for reform of workhouses; see J.L. and Barbara Hammond, *The Village Labourer*, pp. 143-4, and J. R. Poynter, *Society and Pauperism*, pp. 14-16.

Page 119. (1) *farmed the poor*: i.e. hired them out locally as labourers and pocketed a part of the wages paid, as provided for in Acts of 1722, 1782, and 1788 (J.L. and Barbara Hammond, *The Village Labourer*, p. 145 and n. 1).

Page 124. (1) *The tenderness . . . all her kind*: M.W. is probably thinking of John Gregory's *A Father's Legacy to His Daughters* (1774), which he treated with some severity in *Rights of Woman*, ch. v, section iii. The moral purpose of Maria's memoir may also reflect that of the memoirs of Marie Roland, and anticipates the tone of the memoirs of M.W.'s friend Mary Robinson.

(2) *exercise*: on the particular importance of this word is M.W.'s works see *Mary*, p. 29 n. 3.

(3) *Death . . . reasoning*: cf. Gregory's *Legacy*, Introduction.

(4) *the owl of the goddess*: the owl was the symbol of Athena, goddess of wisdom.

Page 125. (1) *My father . . . borough interest*: M.W.'s brother James found he could not obtain promotion in the navy without money or connections (Flexner, p. 129).

(2) *His orders were not to be disputed*: Maria's tyrannical father is patterned after Mary's and M.W.'s own (cf. *Mary*, p. 5 n. 2).

(3) *My eldest brother*: patterned after M.W.'s brother Edward (see Flexner, pp. 23, 29).

Page 126. (1) *a neighbouring heath*: probably that outside Beverley in Yorkshire (see Flexner, p. 22).

(2) *The brother of my father*: Maria's uncle may be based on a relative of M.W.'s named Edward Bland Wollstonecraft (Flexner, p. 268).

Page 128. (1) *romantic*: cf. Mary's romantic character (*Mary*, p. 20 n. 1).

(2) *articled to a neighbouring attorney*: M.W.'s brother Edward was apprenticed around 1774, and began to practise as a solicitor in 1779 (Flexner, pp. 25, 29).

Page 129. (1) *Had my home . . . affections*: on the relation between narrow education and experience and the tendency to errors of sensibility, see *Rights of Woman*, pp. 116 ff. Maria's romance with George Venables is based on M.W.'s love-affair with Gilbert Imlay, although W. Clark Durant suggests that Venables is a portrait of Meridith Bishop, friend of Fanny Blood's suitor Hugh Skeys, and married to M.W.'s sister Eliza (*Memoirs*, p. 155).

Page 130. (1) *Peggy*: this story may have been conceived as a counter to the picture of the poor presented in Hannah More's *Cheap Repository Tracts* (1795–6). *Nature and Art* (published early 1796) by Godwin's and M.W.'s friend Elizabeth Inchbald was an attempt of a similar kind. See also the story of Peggy in Charlotte Smith's *Marchmont* (1796), iv. 297–8, and in Elizabeth de Charrière's *Mistress Henley* (1784).

(2) *a green-stall*: see p. 132.

(3) *alls*: 'belongings, goods and chattels', a northern dialect word (Joseph Wright, *English Dialect Dictionary*).

Page 131. (1) *pressed*: reformers particularly opposed enforced enlistment in the army and especially the navy (see M.W.'s *Rights of Men*, p. 25). The practice was defended however as a necessity during the long war with France, since conditions in the armed services were such that only the most destitute would volunteer. Mutinies in the fleet at Spithead in April–May 1797, and The Nore in May–June, had caused considerable stir. Over half these sailors had been pressed into the service (James Dugan, *The Great Mutiny*, 1965, ch. iii).

(2) *to send them to her husband's parish*: cf. p. 117 n. 2.

Page 132. (1) *It was pleasant to work for her children*: in September 1796 M.W. wrote to Archibald Hamilton Rowan, whom she had known in Paris, regarding her desertion by Imlay, and said of her own daughter Fanny, 'she is a motive, as well as a reward, for exertion' (*Memoirs*, pp. 302–3).

(2) *borough interest*: i.e. the owner of the property was entitled to vote for the borough officers and the borough's M.P., a fact which often made the property much more valuable, since control of the property meant control of the voting, which in turn could be sold to the highest bidder (see G. S. Veitch, *The Genesis of Parliamentary Reform*, 1913, pp. 3–4). M.W. would have had her attention drawn to abuses in the electoral system by the general election of 1796.

Page 134. (1) *than the distress of an old one*: cf. M.W.'s sarcastic dismissal of Burke's sympathy for Marie-Antoinette, in *Rights of Men*, pp. 63–4, and the violent attack on attorneys (especially the interview of the heroine Althea with Mohun, vol. iv, ch. 12) in Charlotte Smith's *Marchmont*, which Godwin read at the end of 1796.

(2) *to work*: i.e. to do needlework.

Page 135. (1) *My fancy . . . they germinate*: a fundamental principle of Richard Price's *Review of Morals*.

(2) *attending a dying parent*: the strain of attending her mother in her last illness eventually forced M.W. to leave home (see Flexner, pp. 36–7).

(3) *the first-born, the son*: see *Mary*, p. 12 n. 1.

Page 136. (1) *an artful kind of upper servant*: possibly the second Mrs Wollstonecraft; see Flexner, pp. 38–9.

(2) *a mother to them*: M.W. did in fact take over much of the direction of her sisters' lives, and on 7 November 1787 she wrote to Everina 'I wish to be a mother to you both' (Flexner, p. 91).

(3) *the ruined state of my father's circumstances*: M.W.'s father ran through a small fortune by the time his wife died, and in the 1790s he was

living in virtual indigence (Flexner, pp. 21, 131).

Page 137. (1) *By allowing . . . intellect*: cf. *Rights of Woman*, pp. 193–4.

Page 138. (1) *on each of my sisters*: M.W. led Eliza and Everina to believe that Imlay was about to make a fortune in trade and would ensure their financial independence (letter from M.W. to Eliza, 29 April 1795, in Flexner, pp. 207–8; a similar letter in the Abinger Collection was written to Everina, 27 April).

Page 143. (1) *a home at which I could receive them*: between 1788 and 1792 M.W. often had one or more of her brothers and sisters with her, but she outraged her sister Eliza by telling her that she and Imlay would not be able to offer her a home on their return to London in 1795 (Flexner, p. 208). Here, M.W. blames Imlay for this.

Page 144. (1) *very opportunely*: cf. the 'deranged' affairs of Mary Robinson's husband, as well as his character, as recounted in her *Memoirs* (1803).

(2) *Mrs. Siddons . . . Calista*: Sarah (Kemble) Siddons (1755–1830), the greatest tragic actress of her day, and friend of both M.W. and Godwin. On 6 August 1796 M.W. had supper with her (*Godwin and Mary*, p. 13). Calista: the heroine of Nicholas Rowe's popular 'she-tragedy' *The Fair Penitent*, who is seduced by the original Lothario. Mrs Siddons acted the part on 22 and 23 November 1796.

(3) *Hearts . . . match'd*: *The Fair Penitent* (ed. Malcolm Goldstein, 1969), II.i. 99–100; Calista tells Altamont, to whom she has been betrothed by her father, 'Such hearts as ours were never paired above; Ill suited to each other; joined not matched.' Mary Robinson, who had herself acted Calista, and with whom Godwin and M.W. were acquainted at this time, also quoted from these lines in her partly autobiographical novel *Vancenza* (1793, i. 132–3).

Page 146. (1) *of the grossest kind*: Imlay had had affairs before he met M.W. (see below, p. 160 n.1), and when he left M.W. in 1795 he took up with a woman whom Godwin described as 'a young actress' (*Memoirs*, p. 81); nevertheless, M.W. is probably exaggerating his promiscuity here. She may be thinking of Mary Robinson's husband.

Page 147. (1) *I now see him*: the graphic description that follows is reminiscent of the second plate of Hogarth's *Marriage à la Mode*. Plate three may depict a gentleman procuring pills to induce an abortion in his mistress (see above, p. 107 n. 1); and the series as a whole is an interesting comparison with M.W.'s picture of marriage. Her friend Fuseli thought Hogarth's engravings 'exquisite' (Peter Tomory, *The Life and Art of Henry Fuseli*, 1972, p. 69).

(2) *powdering gown*: 'a garment worn over the ordinary clothes to protect them while the hair was being powdered' (*OED*); Maria's husband is only wearing it as a casual outer garment.

Page 148. (1) *set it aside*: M.W.'s brother Edward apparently tried to keep some of her rightful inheritance from her (Flexner, p. 74).

(2) *governesses*: both Eliza and Everina eventually became school-mistresses and governesses, as did M.W. herself before she adventured into a writing career.

(3) *to a very old man*: M.W.'s younger and favourite sister Everina was indeed in ill health judging by the letters of her sister Eliza, but she did not die until 1843. George Blood, who was somewhat older, if not exactly 'a very old man', had offered to marry her in 1791 (Flexner, p. 130), but M.W. had declined the offer on her behalf.

Page 149. (1) *the mistress of your own actions*: M.W.'s only child in 1796 was her daughter by Imlay. Fanny grew up with a mild and passive character, but killed herself with an overdose of laudanum in 1816, two years after her younger half-sister had eloped with Shelley (Flexner, p. 259).

Page 150. (1) *parish-nurse*: again, M.W.'s facts, including the nurse's wages, are accurate; see M. Dorothy George, *London Life in the Eighteenth Century*, p. 215.

Page 151. (1) *my native village*: although M.W.'s father was living in actual distress at Laugharne, she is here referring to her return to Beverley in Yorkshire while on her way to Scandinavia in May 1795; in fact she found the reality 'very much below the picture in her imagination' (*Memoirs*, p. 15).

Page 153. (1) *When novelists or moralists ... disgusted*: M.W. is probably referring to the advice given in Dr Gregory's *A Father's Legacy to His Daughters*; cf. *Rights of Woman*, p. 32.

(2) *finely fashioned nerves*: not identified.

Page 154. (1) *youth, and genial years were flown*: not identified.

Page 155. (1) *bastilled*: imprisoned; used as a verb in 1742, but *OED* records this as the next use.

Page 156. (1) *out-laws*: the novel fulfills the promise in the Advertisement to *Rights of Woman* of a full-scale treatment of the legal position of women.

(2) *My more than father*: cf. *Mary*, p. 36.

Page 157. (1) *their reputation in the world*: cf. *Rights of Woman*, ch. viii.

Page 158. (1) *his ass*: cf. Exodus 20:17.

(2) *what the law considers as his*: M.W.'s account of the laws of property in marriage is an accurate one; see William Blackstone, *Commentary on the Laws of England*, book i, ch. xiv, section 3, and book ii, ch. xxix, section 6. For Maria's relations with her husband M.W. probably had in mind the deposition of Anne Collet against her husband's suit for adultery

in *Trials for Adultery* (1779–80), vol. iii, a work certainly known to Godwin.

Page 159. (1) *être suprême*: the cult of the Supreme Being was established by Robespierre in May–June 1794, drawing from the religious ideas of Rousseau, and abolishing the Cult of Reason established in November 1793. M.W. was in France at this time.

Page 160. (1) *Mr. S*———: before he became involved with M.W., Imlay had possibly had an affair with Helen Maria Williams (Ralph M. Wardle, *Mary Wollstonecraft*, p. 187), who was living in Paris with John Stone. Here M.W. may be exacting revenge by a fictional reversal of roles; cf. above, p. 146 n.

(2) *accommodation bills*: 'bills not representing or originating in an actual commercial transaction, but for the purpose of raising money on credit' (*OED*).

Page 163. (1) *he had never struck me*: the only grounds for legal separation were cruelty and adultery, and in 1790 the courts had defined what would be admitted as cruelty in Evans *v.* Evans: 'What merely wounds the mental feelings is in few cases to be admitted, where not accompanied with bodily injury, either actual or menaced' (in Julia O'Faolain and Lauro Martines, eds., *Not in God's Image*, 1973, p. 324).

(2) *ought to adopt*: M.W.'s equating liberty with the power to perceive one's duty is based on Price's *Review of Morals* (1787 edn., ch. viii), and reinforced by Godwin.

Page 165. (1) *the warm precincts of the cheerful day*: Gray's *Elegy*, l. 87.

Page 166. (1) *Roxana*: one of the heroines of Nathaniel Lee's *The Rival Queens, or the Death of Alexander the Great*; the title suggests the relevance of Venables's reference, for both Maria and M.W. An adaptation of the play was performed at intervals from November 1795 to January 1796, and again on 12 April 1796, with Mrs Siddons in the role of Roxana.

Page 167. (1) *Of the black rod*: the gentleman usher of the black rod, an original officer of the Order of the Garter, was by a statute of Henry VIII to keep the doors where any council was held and thus became a virtual officer of the House of Lords whose most notable duty was to summon the Commons to attend the monarch in the upper house; he also summoned defendants before the bar of the House for any trial there, a fact which would have been brought to M.W.'s attention by reading trials for adultery or bigamy, in which the defendants were almost always women. Maria's witticism thus combines an attack on the system of chivalry and privilege with a reference to the way that system legally oppresses women.

Page 170. (1) *a distant part of the town*: M.W. is describing her escape with Eliza from Eliza's husband Meridith Bishop, in 1784; see Flexner, pp. 41 ff.

(2) *grizzled*: possibly, fretted or rendered grey-haired; probably a verb derived from Grizzle, a form of the name of patient Griselda, known through Chaucer's Clerk's Tale as a model of wifely submissiveness.

Page 171. (1) *Russian breed of wives*: proverbial for their submissiveness to brutal husbands.

Page 174. (1) *Come ... train*: song from Handel's *Judas Maccabaeus*, which M.W. could have heard sung at Covent Garden during 'A Grand Selection of Sacred Music from the Works of Handel' on 24 February 1796 or 30 April 1797.

Page 176. (1) *I was ever ... to exercise*: a favourite theme in M.W.'s letters, and expressive of her view, derived from Adam Smith's *Moral Sentiments* and Richard Price's *Review of Morals*, that sympathy was the basic social tie.

Page 177. (1) *how she had been used in the world*: the tale of Maria's second landlady illustrated the property laws relating to married women; see Julia O'Faolain and Lauro Martines, eds., *Not in God's Image*, p. 229. The tale is probably based on that of Martha Robinson in *Trials for Adultery* (1779–80), vol. iv.

(2) *an execution*: a married woman's property was virtually at her husband's disposal (see J. O'Faolain and L. Martines, eds., *Not in God's Image*, p. 329).

Page 178. (1) *hunted*: cf. *Caleb Williams*, vol. iii, chs. 8–10.

Page 179. (1) *the heart-enlarging virtues of antiquity*: Rousseau (*Confessions*, Pléiade edn., p. 9), Godwin (C. Kegan Paul, *William Godwin*, i. 12), and especially Madam Roland (*The Private Memoirs of Madam Roland*, ed. E. G. Johnson, p 64) had been inspired by reading Plutarch or Rollin

Page 181. (1) *the killing frost*: cf. *Henry VIII*, III.ii. 355. This play too was performed in November 1795 and January 1796, with Mrs Siddons as Queen Katharine, and could be seen by M.W. as bearing on her own situation.

(2) *that weakness   despotism*: the argument, basic to *Rights of Woman*, and developed in the first part of its second chapter

Page 182. (1) *I sent a supply .. situations*: M.W. tried to obtain situations for Eliza, Everina, and Charles, and, along with her brothers and sisters, gave what assistance she could to her father (Flexner, ch. xi).

(2) *claim the child*: 'Before the passing of Serjent Talfourd's Act (1839) cases constantly occurred where, by a tyrannical use of the paternal power, the mother was excluded not only from the custody of her children,

but also from access to them. Thus the apprehensions of the mother paralyzed the wife, who, dreading the father's power, was obliged to submit to the husband's misconduct.' John F. Macqueen, *A Practical Treatise on the Law of Marriage* . . . (1860), p. 154 (cited in J. O'Faolain and L. Martines, *Not in God's Image*, p. 327).

Page 183. (1) *did I set out for Dover*: M.W. is probably describing her feelings when she set out for France in June 1792 in company with Fuseli and his wife; like Maria, she did not complete her journey. Eventually she left alone in December (Flexner, pp. 171–2). In the depths of despair in 1795–6, she again thought of leaving England as a solution to her problems (Flexner, p. 223); even when Godwin's courtship of her was at its crisis she wrote to him, 'Could a wish have transported me to France or Italy, last night, I should have caught up my Fanny and been off in a twinkle, though convinced that it is my mind, not the place, which requires changing' (*Godwin and Mary*, p. 15).

Page 185. (1) *buried alive*: Maria's fictional imprisonment in a mad-house, for in effect daring to challenge the power of men, anticipates the experiences of Elizabeth Packard recounted in Phyllis Chesler, *Women and Madness* (1972; London, 1974, pp. 9–10).

Page 187. (1) *Ties . . consequence*: in the first edition of the *Memoirs*, Godwin tentatively agreed with this principle; but in the second edition (also published 1798), after the reviews had held his picture of M.W. up to obloquy, he admitted that he had come to feel it was wiser to conform with the 'customs and institutions' of society (*Memoirs*, p. 101 n. 9).

(2) *esteem seemed to have rivalled love*: apparently, the character of the early courtship of M.W. and Godwin; see the early letters in *Godwin and Mary* and Godwin's own account in *Memoirs*: 'It was friendship melting into love' (p. 100).

Page 190. (1) *the Adelphi*: a development of several terraces of houses built 1768–72 by Robert and James Adam between Fleet Street and the Thames.

Page 191. (1) *planned his confinement*: a similar situation involves the hero of Charlotte Smith's *Marchmont* (1796), but M.W.'s source was probably *Belcher's Address to Humanity: . . . A Receipt to Make a Lunatic, and Seize the Estate* (1796), reviewed, possibly by M.W., in the *Analytical Review* (xxiii, Feb 1796, 217–18).

Page 192. (1) *seduction and adultery*: the first stage of suing for adultery was an action by the husband in a civil court for damages against the alleged seducer (J. O'Faolain and L. Martines, eds., *Not in God's Image*, p. 321).

(2) *was refused admittance*: M.W.'s acquaintance was dropped by several

people when her marriage to Godwin (29 March 1797) made it obvious
she had not been married to Imlay (Wardle, *Mary Wollstonecraft*, p. 288).

(3) *an honourable woman*: cf. M.W.'s vehement attack on the importance
attached to reputation, in *Rights of Woman*, ch. viii.

Page 193. (1) *painfully*: 'painful' in the original text.

(2) *the happy valley*: the reference to *Rasselas* here suggests a development away from M.W.'s earlier acceptance of Johnson's pious stoicism,
evident in *Mary*, towards the Romantics' optimistic attitude to aspiring
imagination. Johnson's novel was one of M.W.'s favourite books, since
Godwin read it along with others from her library shortly after her death.
In this sentence 'dose' should perhaps be 'doze', and 'wilds' was 'wiles'
in the original text.

Page 194. (1) *very different motives*: M.W. may have had in mind the
celebrated trial of the Duchess of Kingston for bigamy, recounted in *The
Newgate Calendar*. The duchess died at the end of August 1796, when
M.W. was beginning her novel and her liaison with Godwin. Both
Godwin and M.W. were at pains to justify a marriage which seemed against
all their principles (Flexner, pp. 238–9).

(2) *upon herself*: M.W.'s information on trials for adultery and damages
probably came from *Trials for Adultery* (1779–80), published by Bladon.

Page 197. (1) *a false morality . . . injuries*: cf. *Rights of Woman*, p. 33,
where M.W. attacks both Dr Gregory and Rousseau on this subject.

Page 198. (1) *in the present state of society*: M.W. desired marriage with
Godwin because she felt she could no longer bear to support the role of
solitary rebellion against the institutions and conventions of society
(*Memoirs*, p. 103).

(2) *the justice and humanity of the jury*: Maria's appeal was not altogether
misguided; juries frequently acquitted where they felt a punishment
enjoined by law was more severe than natural justice would allow, and
they especially did so during the 1790s (E. P. Thompson, *The Making of
the English Working Class*, p. 509).

(3) *definite rules can never apply to indefinite circumstances*: the distinction between law and justice in Godwin's *Political Justice* is based upon
this maxim.

Page 199. (1) *French principles*: 'innovation' and 'French principles' were
used, successfully, to stigmatize and stifle any attempt at reform or
alteration in the laws, whether they related to 'public or private life' (see
P. A. Brown, *The French Revolution in English History*, pp. 165–6).

(2) *separation from bed and board*: Godwin inserted the qualifying phrase
because such decisions were given in an ecclesiastical court rather than
the civil court which decided damages for adultery; a woman could not
obtain a divorce except on grounds of bigamy or incest (there were only

four divorces granted to women in two hundred years), and divorce could in any case only be tried in parliament (J. O'Faolain and L. Martines, eds., *Not in God's Image*, pp. 319, 320, 324).

Page 201. (1) *delays*: M.W. evidently drew on her separation from Imlay in 1794–5; probably she originally conceived Darnford as another version of Imlay throughout the novel, but altered the character to resemble Godwin when experience changed her views.

(2) *chancery*: see *Mary*, p. 12 n. 3. Charlotte Smith's *Marchmont*, which Godwin read at the end of 1796, contained a bitter attack on the Chancery Court (iv. 41–4).

Page 202. (1) *Expectation—Discovery—Interview—Consequence*: this version of the novel's ending is based on M.W.'s return from France in 1795, and her discovery of Imlay's infidelity, followed by her first suicide attempt (Flexner, pp. 200–1).

(2) *the laudanum*: M.W.'s first attempt at suicide is probably described here; Imlay intervened. Her second and more serious attempt, jumping from Putney Bridge, occurred after her return from Scandinavia, in November 1795 (*Memoirs*, pp. 83, 87). Since M.W. did decide to live for her child Fanny, the scene that follows, perhaps drawn from life, may not be mere tear-jerking.

THE WORLD'S CLASSICS

A Select List

Life's Handicap
Edited by A. O. J. Cockshut

The Man Who Would be King and Other Stories
Edited by Louis L. Cornell

Plain Tales From the Hills
Edited by Andrew Rutherford

Stalky & Co.
Edited by Isobel Quigly